# Troubadours and Troublemakers
## (Ireland Now: A Culture Reclaimed)

## Joe Jackson

**BLACKWATER PRESS**

*Editor*
Ríona MacNamara

*Design & Layout*
Paula Byrne

*ISBN*
0 86121 669 5

© 1996 Joe Jackson

Produced and printed in Ireland by
Blackwater Press,
7/8 Broomhill Business Park,
Tallaght, Dublin 24.

*British Library Cataloguing-in-Publication Data*
*A catalogue record is available from the British Library.*

This book is dedicated to my mother and father, Phyllis and Joe Jackson Snr. May they both live forever through the pages of this book. Particularly my Dad who died believing he had 'no name' but now breathes again each time 'Joe Jackson' is signed to anything written by his son. That single gesture is the 'tombstone' I never could bring myself to place on his grave.

# ACKNOWLEDGEMENTS

There are so many people I should thank that I apologise in advance for any omissions. Fortunately, the list is limited by the fact that this book covers mostly a ten-year period in my life, but it would be remiss of me not to name-check seminal figures from my past, such as Frieda, Stephanie, Susan, Paul, Jack, Gregg and Clare. More recently, Francine, and two women who must remain nameless, became what Scott Walker would describe as 'Angels of Ashes'. You know who you are. Thanks also to Yasmina, Louise, M.E., Anne, Cathy, Hilary, Sunnive, Virginia, Karla and the gang. Plus male friends like Pat Cassidy, who gave me the perfect final line for this book, and his brother, Frank, who came up with the fabulous title.

I am also deeply indebted to that handful of 'stars' who became friends, of varying degrees, such as Tori Amos, Richard Harris and Dory Previn in particular, who took the time to read my adolescent poetry nearly twenty years ago and wrote and assured me, when I desperately needed such an injection of inspiration, that I 'definitely have the talent necessary' to make it as a writer. Love to you, and Joby.

Of course, my break as a writer did finally come courtesy of Niall Stokes, founder and editor of *Hot Press* – a man of vision, obviously! But seriously, I will stand over my previously published assertion that he is one of the most innovative and committed editors this country has ever known. And a man blessed to have the backing of his wife and partner-in-vision, Mairin Sheehy, his family, a sub-editor like Liam Mackey and other pivotal figures in a magazine that is too rarely given full credit for its role in changing the cultural landscape in Ireland for nearly twenty years. That should be evident from the fact that so much of the work in this book originally appeared, in one form or another, in *Hot Press*. Niall also pushed me down paths I wouldn't otherwise have even considered, such as undertaking the bulk of the magazine's political interviews during that time.

Thanks also to Paddy Woodworth, of *The Irish Times*, who was the original architect of the *Sound and Vision* slot which has appeared in the newspaper every Friday since 1992 and has since become what one Irish musician described as 'a monolith' in relation to music coverage in this country. Again, he's lucky to have on his side colleagues such as Conor

Brady, Gerry Smyth, Caroline Walsh, Patsy Murphy, Victoria White, Katie Donovan, Arminta Wallace and the numberless other workers who are the backbone of *The Irish Times*. Likewise, Mike Murphy and producers such as Ann Walsh and Bernadette Comerford, have seen to it that popular culture is given serious attention on RTE's *The Arts Show*.

I also, of course, must thank not only the countless publicists and record company people who helped me set up many of these interviews but also the interviewees themselves. Particularly those who are included in this book. I hope you all agree with, at least, my attempt to serve some greater good and to pass on to people 'some useful information', to quote Leonard Cohen.

Finally, thank you to Ríona MacNamara, who first approached me with the idea of publishing a book, John O'Connor, of Blackwater Press, who took this particular concept on board, and Anna O'Donovan who exhausted herself helping me to prepare a 'no-more-revisions-please-Joe' set of proofs. And to my previous literary agent, Lisa Eveleigh, formerly of AP Watt, London and to my new agent Carole Blake, of Blake, Friedman. Plus, on a more personal level, Fionnula Sherry and Nuala O'Faolain, both of whom made me scrap my original preface to this book and try to be as honest as they both are, in terms of the shadows in their lives. Thank you.

Joe Jackson was born in the Dublin suburb of Glasthule and began writing journals, poetry, short stories and articles in his teens. He also has worked as a labourer, sheet metalworker, bank clerk, photographer and was Ireland's first Writer-in-Residence in a Vocational School, in Lucan, Co. Dublin. Jackson also co-hosted RTE's *The Arts Show*, in 1995. His interviews and articles have been published world-wide in magazines and newspapers such as *Hibernia, Theatre Review, Musician, Vox, Prinz, La Vangardia, Dimanche Matin* and *El Pais*.
Joe Jackson is single and lives in Dublin.

'Thank you for the most penetrating interview I've done since, at least, the Dick Cavett show in the 1960s.'

*(Richard Harris, actor, 1988)*

'That article you wrote (on Sinatra) tells me more about art and makers of art in the twentieth century than ninety-five per cent of the essays I read in literary journals.'

*(Paul Durcan, poet, 1988)*

'*Hot Press* is noted for its probing interviews conducted by Joe Jackson.'

*(Deaglan De Bradún, political correspondent, The Irish Times, 1988)*

'I decided that if I was going to talk to just one journalist about something as sensitive as my position on the IRA it should be you.'

*(Christy Moore, singer, 1991)*

'Every "celebrity" in the world should be interviewed by you, because you ask questions that make the interviewee ask profound questions of themselves.'

*(Gabriel Byrne, actor, 1992)*

'I will tell this story once and only once and only to you, because I trust you, feel you are a medium I can tell my story through and neither it, nor I will be violated.'

*(Tori Amos, 1994)*

'Once a week in *The Irish Times* you are marking the Irish psyche with those interviews, which is how it should be.'

*(Shay Healy, broadcaster, writer, 1994)*

'Joe Jackson is not a "rock critic", he's a writer. There is a difference.'

*(Van Morrison, singer, 1995)*

'There is no one in Ireland doing what you do, in terms of those in-depth *Hot Press* interviews on politics and the arts. These are important social documents.'

*(Ciaran Benson, Professor of Psychology UCD and Chairperson of the Arts Council, 1995)*

# CONTENTS

# 1

# IRISH? IRISH? IRISH?

'A lot of the time we ask the question "Irish? Irish? Irish?" and it's a mantra, to me, of lack of self possession and lack of self-centredness. We're always trying to find out who we are, we're always trying to find out our identity, because somewhere, maybe deep down, we feel we don't have one.'

Thus spake director Jim Sheridan during the 1995 documentary on Irish cinema, *Ourselves Alone*. Happily, I wasn't exposed to this homily until nearly a year later, which meant that while compiling *Troubadours and Troublemakers* I was spared the sense that the characteristically impish Mr Sheridan was sitting on my shoulder laughing, like that demented leprechaun played by Jimmy O'Dea in *Darby O'Gill and the Little People*. And why would he be laughing? Because this book was provisionally entitled *Irish in Identity* and probably does revolve around that one question, 'Irish? Irish? Irish?' which, I admit, is hardly startlingly new. Okay, it may even be so old that it has already slipped from the lips of at least all quizzical people since Mesolithic hunter-gatherers first landed on these shores. Yes, long before the English. Or the Vikings or Celts, for that matter.

But then, if Mr Sheridan were to mock me, the laugh would be on both of us. Because, even more recently, Jim disclosed that he himself is decidedly lacking when it comes to a sense of 'self-centredness' he can access 'deep down'. Racially, emotionally, psychologically, artistically and in a religious sense. Indeed, Jim Sheridan's impulse towards self expression probably stems from his need to locate himself in these areas and thus redefine what he perceives as this otherwise potentially maddening plurality of selves. Plus, as such, his sense of personal and national identity.

Likewise, in relation to the majority of people I interview in this book, including Gabriel Byrne, Henry Mountcharles, Finbar Furey, Frank McGuinness, Kenneth Branagh, Christy Moore and Edna O'Brien. In this setting even so-called 'mortal enemies' such as Gerry Adams and Ian Paisley Jnr can be seen as soul-brothers, searching for their own variation of the holy grail. And, more importantly, as equally potent signifiers of the dreams and aspirations that pulse through the hearts of people on all sides of the numberless divides in Northern Ireland. Particularly those who recognise the multicultural nature of Irish identity in a postmodern era and the multidimensional nature of national identity, in general – concepts which, too often, are reduced to notions of 'nationalism' that belong back where they originated, in the Europe of the eighteenth century.

A similar belief in the universality of the particular also dictated which voices I should include in *Troubadours and Troublemakers*. That certainly was the premise applied, say, when it came to editing the John Bruton interview from several thousand to six hundred words or adding material that was previously unpublished, as was the case in relation to at least half of the Richard Harris interview. My primary objective, at all times, was to choose subjects, not because of who they are, but what their reflected views tell us about who we are. Or were. Specifically in a post-Civil War scenario. And also to choose those texts that reflect cultural changes in Ireland during the years 1985–1995, a decade which I suspect will prove to be pivotal in Irish history.

Wishful thinking? I think not. After all, this decade began with tales of moving statues in Ballinspittle, County Cork; the tragedy of the Kerry babies; the signing of the Anglo-Irish Agreement and the resignation of Senator Mary Robinson from the Labour Party because of her objections to that Agreement. It ended with the moving of a metaphorical religious 'statue' named Bishop Eamon Casey to another country after it was revealed that he had fathered, and abandoned, a child – a scandal that was the first of many which have since undermined the previously unassailable power of the Church in 'Catholic Ireland' and possibly Christian mythology itself, which first slapped its vice-grip on this country fifteen hundred years ago. There also was the similarly historic referenda that led to the introduction of the right to access of information on abortion and the introduction of divorce. Plus, relative peace in Northern Ireland after the cessation of violence by republican and loyalist paramilitaries.

However, to bring it all back home, on an even more personal level, this book also is the record of a journey of rediscovery for a 'Paddy' whose surname has its origins in Ulster and who was the son of a pretty powerful man who pretty much dictated, 'You should be ashamed of everything that is Irish, particularly Catholicism.' And who, as part of this process of psychic amputation, declared, for example, that we should tune into the BBC rather than RTE. Read British rather than Irish newspapers. Never wear green. And who simply said, 'Don't be so fucking stupid, go out and play!' when I came home from the Christian Brothers School one day and suggested I might become a priest. And one who hauled me out of the FCA in 1970 coldly stating, 'There's going to be war up North, who'd want to die for this God-forsaken country?'

But then again, symptomatic of the endlessly conflicting signals sent out by my father, Joe Jackson 'Senior', was the fact that he also rated Irish writers as 'some of the best in the world – apart from Shakespeare,' an opinion he'd held ever since he 'began to devour literature' during his 'stay' at Glencree Remand Centre, in his early teens. 'Joyce, Shaw, Behan and O'Casey!' he'd proudly boast, clearly having absorbed into his blood cells the ideology of James Joyce, in particular, before attempting to inject it into mine.

Not that I'm complaining. At a time when I maybe should have been more interested in *Tales of Brave Ulysses*, by Cream, my Dad was delighting me with tales of how he once had to brave the great-divide from Glasthule into the library of Trinity College in order to read, 'one of the great books, if not banned, then somehow strangely unavailable in this ridiculous country': Joyce's *Ulysses*. Later, however, he did get his own hardback copy which religiously replaced the Bible on our family bookshelf – even though its cover was green. Likewise, my Dad bought, during one of his lengthy visits to Britain, the copy of *Stephen Hero* which was 'actually banned' and he insisted I read 'after *Dubliners* but before going anywhere near *Portrait of the Artist as a Young Man.*'

Extending this relatively liberal education my father also introduced me to authors such as Edna O'Brien and Tennessee Williams, telling me in particular, about the time a production of Tennessee's *The Rose Tattoo* was 'stopped in the middle of the show' at the Gas Company Theatre, in

Dun Laoghaire. Apparently, because at one point in the play a condom fell onto the stage floor, nearly killing a local parish priest in the process and forcing him to call for the banning of this 'filthy play'. No doubt that priest would have reacted in a similarly hysterical manner had he known that my father also later moved against every known tenet in Catholicism by categorically stating that 'a woman's orgasm is more important than a man's', as well as suggesting I read Wilhelm Reich's *The Function of the Orgasm* plus nearly every issue of *Playboy* for, he said, the 'epic' interviews with 'free thinking individuals' such as Sinatra, Martin Luther King, 'radical organiser' Saul Alinsky, and 'convicted publisher of Eros and other erotica' Ralph Ginsburg, among others. And, he probably accurately pointed out that the magazine was banned in Ireland at the time 'not so much because of the pin-ups but because of its outspoken views on sex and religion'.

Though, needless to say, I had my own adolescent reasons for sneaking many a peek at the pin-ups in such magazines. And God knows what that priest would have done if he'd known that I myself once smuggled a Christmas issue of *Playboy* across the border from Northern Ireland for my father. And, worse still, had it hidden down the front of my pants which, I'm sure, had a long-term effect on my sexuality. As did my Dad insisting that I watch 'foreign films' such as those by Bergman, De Sica and Kurosawa, though his love of David Lean, Chaplin, and Orson Welles – 'the man who scared the shit out of America, with his radio version of *The War of The Worlds*' – also inspired in me a life-long fascination with the work of British and American directors and with cinema itself. Similarly, as a form of counterpoint to the rock and blues music I loved, he introduced me to classical music and some of the most sublime pop singers of our time, particularly Sinatra, who shared that space in my father's blood with Joyce, and, subsequently slid into mine. As an artist of supreme merit with 'total respect for the word, above all else', a symbol of that sybaritic Playboy lifestyle my father also espoused and a 'Twentieth Century Romantic,' to cull the title from the Arnold Shaw biography Dad also insisted I read, when I was seventeen. And a title which probably perfectly summarises Sinatra's appeal to this particular father and son, both of whom were blessed, and cursed, with similar inclinations.

However, as a young man who came of age, intellectually, in the early 1970s, I obviously had my own brace of cultural reference points, from 'Beat' writers, Black poets and British 'kitchensink' novelists to playwrights such as Chekhov and Ibsen and movie directors like Scorcese, Kazan and Bertolucci. Plus, of course, that school of introspective singer-songwriters dominating rock at the time, which included Dory Previn, Leonard Cohen, Rod McKuen, Jim Webb/ Richard Harris, Kris Kristofferson, Tony Joe White, Dion, and, above all else, Scott Walker, who led me even deeper into Bergman territory and introduced me to his own other, decidedly European influences such as Brel, Aznavour, Camus and Sartre.

As for the preceding decade, well, these influences can be summed up in just two words: Elvis Presley. In fact, the first lines I ever had published in *Hot Press* were quite prescient, in relation to the theme of *Troubadours and Troublemakers*. Responding to Presley's death I proclaimed: 'Let's get one thing straight before I start. For eleven years of my life I had no identity other than that of being... an Elvis fan.' An exaggeration? Not in the slightest. However, having spent nearly a further two decades studying this phenomenon and writing a still-unfinished book about the experience, I can, perhaps, elaborate by explaining that I was wrong. Rather than leave me with 'no identity' Elvis Presley virtually redefined my identity, at a core level, when he fired in me the faith to believe that, 'as long as man has the strength to dream/ He can redeem his soul and fly.' And, yes, I now realise that this vision, as articulated in Presley's song, 'If I Can Dream', is a crystallisation of the craving that inspired Joyce's *Stephen Hero*, or rather, the more-appropriately named Stephen Daedalus in *Portrait of the Artist...* Indeed, the mythical Daedalus may have been the first man to fly, but it was the very-real Sun-King of Memphis who first sent my soul soaring. And body, with a glorious, guilt-free perception of sexuality which ensured, of course, that James Joyce never could quite seep into my system in as central a sense as applied to my father.

But why do I bother to list all these influences and therefore risk moving myself centre-stage, even momentarily, after a decade of despising journalists who assume themselves to be more important than the people they write about, and who endlessly, make love to little more than their own egos *through* other people? To balance the book, I guess, define the kind of Irish-ness that sits at the soul of this particular postmodern 'Paddy' and highlight my earlier assertion that national identity is determined more by the mass of multicultural forces we absorb, on an everyday level, rather than by the colour of the political flag we walk behind. And to explain, at least, the aspirational tilt in the admittedly idiosyncratic interviews that follow, which also were heavily influenced by my Dad introducing me to the work of Erich Fromm and my own, more recent, reading of similar work by the likes of cultural analysts such as Ernst Fischer, Antonio Gramsci, Roland Barthes and Raymond Williams. Plus countless other 'teachers' along the way, including many of the people I interview.

However, in the beginning, that list of seminal influences also obviously was a 'fuck Ireland' list and, as such, a denial of my own basic roots. Particularly in terms of my mother, who couldn't have been more proud to be Irish, in terms of either her family name, Kelly, or the fact that her aunt Maggie 'used to carry food and IRA guns in the bottom of a pram' for her brother 'Mickey' who was Michael Collins's aide-de-camp up in the Wicklow Mountains, went on one of the first hunger strikes in this country and was best man when his sister married a British naval officer – even though, at the same time, he also was a 'most wanted' man! And who finally had to escape to America, paying his own passage because the IRA wouldn't help him out after they'd been outlawed by the State. At least, according to childhood tales told round the fireside in my grandmother's and aunt Olive's houses but never even mentioned in our home, which explains why they remained unknown to me until I began work on the introduction to this book.

However, my father's reasons for rarely discussing such matters weren't rooted purely in Joyce's rejection of Irish politics. Nor were they even purely political. They also stemmed from the fact that my grandparents never really accepted Dad, deeming him to be 'not good enough' for their youngest daughter, Phyllis – a value judgement which is particularly invidious when applied by the Irish working class to one of their own.

And yet if, while growing up, I did almost totally reject my 'Irish-ness' it wasn't simply because I agreed with Dad's detestation of all things green. As primarily a product of pop culture I also saw little to admire in Ireland, at the time. Or, to which I could identify. Especially in relation to movies and popular music, those two art forms I most adored and which have almost double-handedly redefined the cultural realm this century. Even if, in a shamefully belated sense, when it comes to this 'God-forsaken' isle of saints and scholars. Or, rather, troubadours and troublemakers.

Unlike Luka Bloom, Dolores O'Riordan and Ger Whelan, however, I did not rediscover a pride in my own cultural legacy courtesy of U2. On the contrary, for over a decade, I thought that Bono and his buddies were over-deified dickheads – an opinion that wasn't revised, in part, until as late as 1993, when I did the Bono interview featured near the end of this book. But I definitely did tap into the culture of confidence U2 helped inspire in this country. They, and their peers in the world of popular music, sport, cinema, journalism, television and theatre. All of whom, thankfully, also have finally liberated Ireland from its tedious tendency to genuflect only in the direction of literary 'gods' such as 'Joyce, Shaw, Behan and O'Casey' (sorry, Dad!) – a gesture which kept us locked inside the first half of this century for far too long, in terms of both our cultural identity and State recognition of, or subsidised support for, the so-called popular arts.

In saying this I do not, of course, mean to belittle the magnificent achievements of contemporary literary heavyweights such as Seamus Heaney, Eavan Boland, John Banville, Jennifer Johnston or John McGahern. Not at all. It's just that I believe that too many books on Irish identity over-rate the importance of literature in relation to the common experience. Particularly the common experience of the 'common man' during an audio-visual age when we clearly are socially constructed, to a greater degree, by the 'texts' we read via television, videos, movies, fashion, rock music and all the attendant paraphernalia of pop culture, in general. Let's face it, when it comes to the question of self-definition, the lines sung by Bono, over nearly the past twenty years, have insinuated their way into the minds of more people in an intrinsic sense than Joyce could ever have dreamed of reaching when he declared, at the end of *Portrait of the Artist...* 'I go to encounter for the millionth time the reality of experience, and to forge in the smithy of my soul the uncreated conscience of my race.' Likewise, in terms of the global perception of Dublin and, in a broader sense, Ireland itself.

And yet, to get back to the layer of self-exploration that sits at the soul of *Troubadours and Troublemakers* I should explain that the question of identity is one which has obsessed me all my life. At least, since that night when I was eleven, or so, and cried as my Dad told me about the pain he felt, at roughly the same age, after he'd been called 'a dirt bird's droppings' and had to run from a football field to ask his parents what that phrase meant. Or rather ask the couple who, until that point, he thought were his parents. Though, their failings in this capacity soon became apparent when Dad became the only one of a group of boys sent to Glencree for three years after they were caught at the back of

Findlaters in Dun Laoghaire, frying bacon they'd earlier stolen from that store. Yes, you read that right. In the clearly enlightened Ireland of the 1940s, he got three years for stealing a few rashers. 'The other lads got off because their parents went and talked to the Gardaí, but your father had no one to plead his case, so he was put away' my mother later remarked, also recalling how often Dad would refer to 'being badly beaten by the Christian Brothers who ran that place.'

Not surprisingly, my own sense of psychic pain, and rage, in relation to this subject, was further compounded on the evening of April 4th 1978 when I found my father at the foot of the stairs in our home, where he'd fallen and died at the age of only forty-nine – never knowing for sure who he was or who his 'real' parents were. 'Tripped by a bastard god/who used a similar trick/To kick him into life,' I wrote in a poem at the time, similarly kicking the concept of a 'Christian' deity, and, indeed any form of patriarchal power figure, into the abyss beside my father's body. Partly because the 'God' I once believed in had also seen fit to kill my father just one week after he and I spoke together for the first time in four years, a reconciliation which gave him back, he said, on the morning of the day he died, his 'appetite for life.'

I also saw the rather savage irony in the fact that my father's fall – all the way from an 'illegitimate' womb into the soil beneath an unmarked grave – was partly caused by alcohol. Drink was something he rarely 'touched' for at least forty-five years of his life and even despised because it was 'so typical of the Irish to indulge.' In fact, only once did I see Dad drunk. And at that point, when I was about fifteen, as I held him in my arms at the bottom of those same stairs at which he later would die, his far-from-characteristic cries of 'but, don't you love your Daddy, Joseph?' totally shattered his part-Sinatra-part-Brando-like persona, in my eyes, turning me off drink until I was at least twenty-two. As did his death, when I was roughly the same age, which had a similar influence on my attitude to drugs. During his final years Dad also became addicted to 'uppers and downers', like Elvis, my other boyhood hero, who died in similar circumstances, around the same time.

Of course, at the time of my father's death, these circumstances were seen as something shameful. As with the circumstances of his birth. And as is probably still the norm in an Ireland where most of us were told we should only disclose such 'sins' in the safety of a confession box. Bullshit. 'Only silence is shame,' to quote Scott Walker. Indeed, I remember one Saturday afternoon I was playing Scott's song, 'Old Folks' and as he sang, 'always leavin' his spoon in his coffee,' my father suddenly looked at the spoon in his cup and blushed. Moments later, however, when Walker added, 'you needn't be ashamed of him' Dad immediately regained his composure, smiled and said, quite slyly, 'Did you hear that Mr Smart-arse?' I did. I do. And I still see that smile and must say there isn't anything about my father of which I am ashamed or which lessens my love for the man. Despite the fact that there were so many times when I did want to kill him.

Should I be ashamed simply because, later in life, my father leaned more towards alcohol than strong tea, a trait that is, as he noted, not exactly alien to the Irish? Or because, near the end, he substituted amphetamines for the sense of transcendence he used to find in Sinatra's music and stupidly took-to-heart the claim supposedly made by Ol' Blue Eyes in that much-quoted *Playboy* interview: 'I'm for anything that gets you through the night, be it prayer, tranquillisers or a bottle of Jack Daniel's' – a statement which, it now transpires, didn't even emanate from Sinatra, but instead was written by his press agent for an 'interview' that never actually took place? Likewise, should I feel ashamed because my father may also have finally foolishly tried to substitute both drink and drugs for the son he forced to leave home and, later, the wife and daughter who followed because of his clearly uncontrollable, self-eroding tendency towards physical and psychological violence? Namely, that tendency that left him to die alone at the foot of those stairs, beneath a framed portrait of Frank Sinatra with a drink in his hand and a caption which read, 'Hope I die before I get old.' And a portrait on top of which Dad had pasted these lines: 'Sometimes in turning he falls down/And hardly anybody picks him up'. Not fucking likely. Particularly given the fact that my father's life-long fall has also left me with a relentless craving to ask the question 'Why?' which has since propelled me through life and will probably echo as I am lowered into my own grave.

My father also obviously added to this process by so often repeating, when I was a boy, this charmingly paradoxical epigram: 'Truth lies at the bottom of a bottomless well.' He was right. Nevertheless, now and again, tentative truths do surface. As with Jim Sheridan recently reminding me that it was Carl Jung who described alcoholism as a 'low-level spiritual experience,' an analysis with which Jim agrees. Likewise, perhaps, Christy Moore, who once joked, 'I lost God and found Guinness!' which is probably a more accurate snapshot of the Irish psyche than I realised at the time. It also is a rationale I believe can be applied to my father's 'substance-abuse.' Particularly, given the fact that he once was the kind of 'devoted Catholic' who participated in pilgrimages to 'holy' sites such as Lough Derg. At least, before such blind devotion gave way to anti-clericalism, after he read Joyce and, around the same time, encountered a priest who refused to help him trace his parents, even though that particular gentleman had access to the necessary information. Indeed, the first time I ever saw my father cry was as he walked back to our car, having been turned away from that church in Ballybrack. 'He asked what I do for a living and, as soon as I told him, said he couldn't help me,' Dad later explained. At that point, what Dad was doing 'for a living' was driving the tower crane being used to build Dublin's Kish Lighthouse, which probably turned out to be more welcoming to lost Irish souls than that priest seemed to be. Especially, perhaps, 'people who do manual work', as Dad also bitterly remarked, 'and who can't afford to give him the necessary backhander.'

Nevertheless, apart from his other seemingly socially embarrassing 'manual' jobs – such as labourer, truck driver, welder and, eventually, self-employed metalworker – my Dad also secretly wrote poetry and dreamed of one day being accepted as a 'literary creator.' However, the first time he used that phrase in my presence he also described that dream as, 'one I know, now, will never be realised.' And effectively sealed my fate moments later by not repeating his wonderful comment, 'Don't be so fucking stupid, go out and play!' when I suggested I do have that 'indefinable something: drive, inspiration, whatever' which he claimed is 'absolutely essential' for anyone wanting to 'make it' as a writer. He simply laughed at my uncharacteristic burst of self-confidence and said, 'good for you!' Then, added the line that turned my life around, 'I'd like to see you go into journalism, if, y'know, that is your thing.'

But whether he himself was a manual worker, poet, or both, my father also, as I indicated earlier, must have been consumed by a spiritual need to reconnect with far more than just his own family. As in, perhaps, the soul of a people torn apart by centuries of colonisation. Despite his patently subservient and ludicrous claims to the contrary, in relation to how 'Great' Britain is. Or was. My father also could be said to have epitomised the postmodern condition, in relation to religion – that challenge of dealing with the 'God-is-Dead' dilemma, which also is a fundamental question we Irish have yet to fully address, being blocked on that particular path by the national obsession with colonialism. But as we slouch towards the next millennium, such questions must be addressed. Particularly given the fact that Britain and Rome both now seem to be loosening their stranglehold on the Irish psyche and will one day, no doubt, leave us with no one 'out there' to blame, curse or keep us from turning the spotlight on ourselves. My one hope for *Troubadours and Troublemakers* is that it will add to this debate. Though, yes, I accept that the parenthetical title of this book, *Ireland Now: A Culture Reclaimed*, is mostly a tease, a taste of the time when we will finally reach that state of independence. And maybe, just maybe, we now are nearer that goal than at any other point in our history.

That said, I also admit I am better at asking questions than providing answers. Partly because I believe that inspiring interviewees, or readers, to ask questions of themselves is more empowering a process than adopting a pose of god-like omniscience, in a post-religious age, and pretending to have answers that are set in Mount Sinai stone when, in fact, the only certainty is change. Besides, even as I complete this introduction to *Troubadours and Troublemakers* I still am asking seemingly unceasing questions about subjects such as Irish identity to people such as Gerry Adams, Brian Kennedy and Barry McGuigan. Obviously, still wondering *'Why?'*, still listening as the voice of my father calls from the bottom of that bottomless well. And, yes, I guess I had better finally admit it – still unsure of who-the-hell I am or where I belong.

But then again, maybe the real fun comes from endlessly seeking, never finding out for sure. Perhaps, in the end, we should simply accept the 'God-like' wisdom of my colleague, John Waters, who once suggested that we Irish really do need to learn to see the concept of 'home' as a journey rather than a fixed destination, a flux of ever-shifting continuities, which liberate rather than enslave us. And as I invariably leave the last word to my interviewees, let's leave these final phrases to the perfectly named – in this context – Mr Waters. He was addressing Bono's suggestion that 'real liberation' comes from 'living with uncertainties', which was the leitmotif running through the U2 album, *Zooropa*. No doubt Jim Sheridan would agree with the following comment. As, perhaps, would many Irish people. Particularly those who are descendants of Mesolithic sea-farers, which probably means all of us.

'We are liberated by our history in that sense but many Irish people seem to have a problem with this concept of Irish identity as fluid rather than a fixture. But, yes, I definitely do believe that identity is a fluid, like a river. And the journey is not so much one of moving towards a point wherein you can fix this notion, as it is towards accepting this flux, which is, I think, what Bono means in relation to *Zooropa*. And I know what he's saying. I live with those uncertainties all the time, in that I feed off them and they feed of me. But, to me, *that's* the black hole inside.'

*Joe Jackson*
*Dublin*
*November 1996*

# 2    SOUND BITES
## 1985-1987

'There is a natural appetite for conversation. It was Yeats or his father who said something about poetry being the social act of the solitary man. Men have been talking to each other the way we are now, for a long time. It says in the Bible, 'It is not good that man should be alone.' We are meant to talk to one another, and one of the conversations is the conversation that takes place in the pages of a book. It's different, very private.'

*(Leonard Cohen, 1985)*

'I believe we are among the most devious of races in the world,' Bunny Carr answered in reply to a question about his fellow countrymen. When asked if this was an objective value judgement on Irish men and women, he unhesitatingly replied, 'I'm Irish.'

*(Opening to interview with broadcaster Bunny Carr, 1986)*

'Mary O'Malley got it right; once a Catholic, always a Catholic. But what really did me in with regards to Catholicism is the total abject sense of inferiority, the feeling that compared to God you are an insect. That's what I hate about it. It never left my mother, never left me. No wonder it was such a strong force, no wonder the working class were kept down, because you really do feel you are of no consequence. One of the reasons I write is because I am good at writing and it is my way of fighting back, saying, "Hang on a minute, this is something I can do".'

*(Alan Bleasdale, 1986)*

'Definitely. It's unbelievable, as if they think we're living in the last century. But then maybe as a people we're partly to blame. Typical, to me, is this woman I know who, when her daughter got pregnant, said, "Isn't it great? At least it means that she wasn't using contraceptives." It's like it's okay to die of AIDS as long as you didn't commit a mortal sin by wearing a condom.'

*(Singer Lesley Dowdall, when asked if the Irish government yielded to pressure from the Church and down played the importance of use of condoms in the battle against AIDS, 1987)*

*Goodnight Sisters*, by Nell McCafferty. I've never known a book to make me so depressed yet at the same time be so funny. The article where Nell tears apart the so-called joys of the virgin birth, with them surrounded by animal shit and with the stale stench of cow's breath for comfort, is just fantastic. And it's not really that much of an exaggeration! It's simply another angle on the romantic schmaltz we're continually fed and continually accept as gospel.'

*(Broadcaster Bibi Baskin on her favourite book of 1987)*

# 3

# RODDY DOYLE
# AND
# PAUL MERCIER
# 1987

As I begin this column Michael Ignatief, on the BBC's *Thinking Aloud*, is introducing Ariel Dorfman as 'the author of that highly acclaimed essay on "Donald Duck comics" as a form of cultural imperialism.' But before you burst a gut laughing at the thought of poor old Donald being slapped under some form of semiological/sociological/structuralist microscope, do remember that Dorfman is just one of a rapidly growing group of cultural analysts (in particular feminists) who no longer accept popular cultural texts such as comics or TV sitcoms as politically innocent or as innocuous as they might at first appear. According to such commentators there is no such thing as an 'innocent text'.

Dorfman therefore would not agree with Roddy Doyle (author of the novel *The Commitments* and of the play being staged at the Olympia, *Brownbread*) who usually describes his work as 'just a bit of fun'. Nor do I. That is why, despite my support for the Passion Machine/SFX philosophy of 'bringing theatre to people who don't usually come to theatre', I now find it difficult to attend, much less recommend, such plays. What was brave and innovative in Paul Mercier's *Drowning* and, to a lesser extent *Studs*, has now degenerated into a rigid adherence to a formula which can best be described as the theatrical equivalent of the British Carry On films.

And, yes, despite the fact that such productions still can be 'great craic', too often the humour is at the expense of working-class characters which the authors persistently present in a way that is both patronising and fundamentally ignorant.

Let's face it, Doyle and Mercier may be masters at capturing surface motions of working-class life but they continually miss the essences by a mile. This may or may not be as a result of the fact that neither author is the product of the background in which these plays are set. Either way, the net result is that Northside working-class kids usually are seen as little more than cartoon characters interested only in pop-stars, drinkin', ridin' and 'the craic'. In Doyle's book *The Commitments*, adults don't fare much better. Perhaps that is why at least one Finglas mother in my own creative writing class was visibly upset at one point while reading aloud what Doyle might describe as a 'funny' representation of her 'kind of people'.

It's just not good enough for the authors to protest that these plays are not meant to be true to life. Tell that to the students who believe that all Eastenders are as depicted in the TV series of the same name. And it's not just young students who fall prey to the confusion caused by the inability to separate signified reality – as produced in plays, books, songs – from reality itself. It was, after all, at the end of a Mercier play that one well-heeled gentleman was heard to say: 'Are they all that thick or is it just footballers?'

This is precisely why, despite disclaimers from both Doyle and Mercier, these plays are potentially politically divisive, in a way that is equally true of all art and/or forms of cultural expression. Each member of the audience responds according to their own political allegiances and how they have been socially constructed, often by texts such as songs, plays, movies and novels. On entering a theatre we do not leave our politics at the door. And although we may say that we're here only to enjoy ourselves, it is at that specific moment – as Pierre Bordieu has suggested – that we are at our most vulnerable in terms of swallowing wholesale the values and ideologies contained in all cultural texts. Therefore pandering (knowingly or unknowingly) to possible prejudices in the traditional, predominantly middle-class audiences who frequent Passion Machine productions is just as damaging as giving back to newer working-class audiences a simplistic and clearly limiting view of themselves.

Furthermore, as one Northside school principal said to me, 'There also is the question involved in the process of Doyle and Mercier, as teachers, virtually plundering the lives of their students. Perhaps it wouldn't be so bad if they gave back something more positive in return.' Amen to that.

And perhaps all this wouldn't be 'so bad' if the condescending Doyle/ Mercier perspective wasn't continually compounded in other areas of the media and the arts. The notion that the lower classes are simply good for a laugh has been the pattern in literature since the time of Chaucer, even Shakespeare. And it is back to Plato we must go to get the first clue of how such processes can be used as an element of social control in a hegemonic sense.

In a *Hot Press* interview earlier this year, Roddy Doyle asked: 'What the fuck do they want us to write? Agit-prop? That's trash!' Depends on your definition of trash, I guess. But, no, politically pointed agit-prop is not what I am expecting; merely that more respect be shown to the people about whom these authors are writing – and maybe theatrical evidence of their acceptance of the fact that working-class people, can, after all, play more than one note in life. It remains to be seen whether or not the same can be said about Paul Mercier and Roddy Doyle. One would hate to discover that in the final analysis, the only note which ever really concerned Passion Machine was the ringing of the cash register.

# 4 REDEFINING THE ARTS

## 1987

'Music lacks an excitement present in other forms,' said Robert O'Byrne, director of Music Network. But surely he isn't speaking of Irish music today? He is. And the fact that such a comment can be made in the immediate shade of *The Joshua Tree* indicates not only that the speaker may be out of touch with contemporary popular culture but also that neither rock, pop nor traditional music was deemed worthy of discussion in the National Gallery's Conference on the State of the Arts in Ireland in 1987.

The morning session consisted of six talks on career opportunities in the arts, with Jennifer Johnston warning would-be authors about the agonies of being a creative writer, Noel Shereton detailing the difficulties of the transition between art college and finding a job, and Joe Dowling echoing Coward's advice to Mrs Worthington: 'Don't put your daughter on the stage.' Joan Denise Moriarty sketched a similarly bleak scenario in terms of ballet, while the aforementioned Mr Byrne bemoaned diminishing audiences (at least among the young) and opportunities, in classical and jazz music. Ironically enough, the only note of hope was struck by a speaker from that art form some still might see as the new kid on the block, that one-time-penny-entertainment-for-the-plebs: film. Indeed, Muiris Mac Conghail referred to the film industry as 'the most extensive area' and as 'a burgeoning industry in terms of job opportunities for the young'.

But is that really the whole picture with regards to career opportunities in/or the state of the arts in Ireland in 1987? What about our neglected buddies, rock/pop/traditional music? Or television? Who draws the lines? Who dictates what is art and what is simply 'entertainment' or 'pop'? If, as one punter suggested, the word 'art' really does alienate seven-eighths of the population (in the sense that art still is seen as the plaything of the so-called elite), perhaps the word itself should be banned. Maybe we also should knock off their pedestals the more pretentious artists and label them as simply 'people employed in the field of cultural activity'? At least, this reading of the word 'culture' clearly is contemporary, loosely defined as 'the level at which social groups develop distinctive patterns of life and give form to those experiences' – continually redefining themselves, which is surely something that is central to the Irish in particular, right now.

Besides, surely the greatest cultural benefit is to be gained not by yielding to the ever-shifting and clearly anachronistic separation of 'high' and 'low' art but by focusing instead on those points at which these meet and can best inform and energise each other, which is, after all, the defining feature of art and culture this century. Likewise, no longer can it be simply a case of saying, 'If the arts are paid for by everyone then they must be accessible to all'; true democratisation now means spreading of the net to include all forms of cultural expression. For it really was quite ludicrous to realise that while Adrian Munnely spoke glowingly of 'the cultural diplomacy effected by groups like the Druid Theatre Company touring Europe and America', no mention was made of that other small touring ensemble, U2, during a week when *The Irish Times* reported how a U2 'devotee' in Phoenix enthused: 'They're so polite, they don't smoke and they don't drink, they're so cute.' What is that, if not cultural diplomacy in action?

But then perhaps it was also an act of cultural, and political diplomacy on behalf of Mr Munnelly not to mention U2. He was, after all, speaking during the afternoon session: 'The Business of the Arts.' And perhaps after hearing his colleague Richard Stokes (from the Department of the Taoiseach) speak of how pleased the government was with the return on their investment in *Eat the Peach*, he didn't want to suggest that it would take 100 movies as 'successful' as ETP to generate for the government of Ireland a profit margin equal to the amount U2 will gross on their current tour. And although U2 are, of course, the exception rather than the rule, they are representative of the economic potential of rock and popular culture – particularly in terms of the potential for jobs in a time of lamentably high unemployment figures.

As such, it is not just 'good business' to invest in rock; the government also has a moral obligation to do so. And when the government says that money from the National Lottery is already earmarked for art and sports, must we ask: whose art? whose sport? Does it really all come down to whether you play upright bass in a rockabilly band or cello in the RTE Light Orchestra? Should being part of the relatively privileged few who participate in the latter – and similar criteria in all the arts – really be the decisive factor in terms of who gets government funding? If the State of the Arts in Ireland conference really was – as has been suggested – set up primarily to discuss 'problematic areas in terms of the funding of the arts', who finally decides that the dole queue-tied rock trio trying to start a band doesn't constitute a 'problematic area in the arts'? Who will speak on their behalf at the next conference such as this? Maybe even more importantly: when will Ireland finally move into the second half of the twentieth century?

# 5 **RICHARD HARRIS**
## 1987

'If you get Richard Harris pinned down, you'll capture the essence of a whole generation of Irish men, at a very particular point in our history.'

*(Brian Lenihan)*

'Here I am/a tramp shining/a brand new clown'

('A Tramp Shining', by Jim Web)

**Joe Jackson:**

On TV, Russell Harty once introduced you as 'the one time rat-catcher from Limerick'. Yet wasn't that misleading, in that it implies you were just another worker on the factory floor whereas, in fact your father owned the flour mill?

**Richard Harris:**

It is not misleading. I remember great wealth and opulence when I was small but I also remember it disappearing. My mother, who once had servants coming out of her ears, was, in the end, down on her knees scrubbing floors. That's how I knew it was going. There is no misconception about that. And later, during my period of convalescence after TB, my father put me to work in a part of the factory where I guess I wouldn't be a nuisance, chasing out rats and mice.

J: Yet you also usually place yourself alongside the likes of Albert Finney and Peter O'Toole who are perceived, largely, as working-class icons from the 1960s.

**H:** I've said the English labelled us that. The British consider the Irish as working class, whatever status we have, or part of society we come from. We're all peasants to them.

**J:** Linking many of the poems in your book on *I, In The Membership of that Day* is that song, 'The Old House' with its lyric 'Lonely I wandered/Through scenes of my childhood/They call back to memory/Those happy days gone by'. Is loneliness or longing the predominant feeling evoked when you think of your childhood?

**H:** No; Warmth. And yet there is a tremendous psychological danger involved in being part of families that are absolutely united. It's as dangerous to be closeted with too much love as it is to be without it; the aim should be to strike an even balance. So I was lucky, being situated in the no-man's-land in my family. As I wrote in another poem, I had my brother's hand-me-downs; I never remember getting a new suit, bike or anything new at all. But being in that no-man's-land was good. The two sisters got much of the attention and Ivan was the favourite. So I was lost in the middle of the Harris brigade. But this makes you fight for the affection of your parents, fight for attention. You don't get it free. You got it from the age of one day to maybe two years but then you had to fight for it.

**J:** So, to paraphrase Dory Previn's poem about her relationship with her family, and father in particular, you had to tap dance from an early age?

**H:** Exactly, yes. You had to put up the flag and say, 'Hey, I'm here too, don't miss me.' And you were missed. There's no question, you were passed over.

**J:** But you had the essential security during the earliest formative years?

**H:** Yes. The over-arching feeling was one of warmth, of being part of a large family – but, on the other hand, I can't remember the parental stroke. I can't remember the touch from the mother or the affection from the father. And you're right to class it as a tap dance for attention. I remember being very rebellious, running away from home and such.

**J:** As in the poem where, after you return, you realise they hadn't even noticed you'd gone?

**H:** Yes. 'Father still practising golf/Mother still knitting.'

**J:** In another poem you write of how you one day knelt beside the corpse of your father and said a final prayer for acceptance. Didn't you ever feel you were singled out for the ultimate 'stroke of affection' from your father?

**H:** I don't think so. Even though as soon as I heard my mother was ill I went back to Limerick and stayed with her for months before she died. Then when I was doing *Mutiny on the Bounty* my father called and said, 'When are you coming back to see me? Come on now, the next one might take me.' And I said to my brother, 'What does that mean?' And he told me, 'He's had a couple of heart attacks since you left.' So I planned with Elizabeth to go back, but then got the call to say he'd died. But though one tries to resist the sort of reply you are looking for, yes, I do think that answer is there in the poem 'On the One Day Dead Face of My Father'.

**J:** As in where you say: 'Guide me/now/in your silence/ cough up one silent prayer/ and stare/at me again/ and see the woven fabric/of your doing/bend his knee/ and plea in the tired optic of your stare/a prayer/ of acceptance'?

**H:** Yes. And I think he probably died without that recognition.

**J:** Did that realisation cause grief?

**H:** There is another side to it. Dermot, my poor brother who's also dead now, summed it up when he said, 'It's the greatest tragedy ever that they died before you were successful. I know it would have meant so much to you to take care of them, get someone to look after them.' But that didn't happen, I'm afraid.

**J:** But surely the fact that you had gone away to become an actor itself had a great deal to do with your parents?

**H:** Yes. But I didn't set out, as Olivier did at the age of six, to be a great actor. I didn't realise I wanted to be an actor until I had TB in my late teens. There had been a sense of desperation before then, like 'What the hell am I going to be, or do?' I think, yes, much of it had to do with establishing an identity, saying, 'I may be just number five in the family but I must assert an identity above and beyond all that.' You also asked me earlier about an identity crisis. If there was one, that was it. I wanted my parents to recognise who I was. That probably gave me my energy, my drive.

**J:** Apart from the poem about the death of your father, one of the other most moving poems in your collection is the one about the death of your sister, 'Before the Hired Spade'.

**H:** I'm glad you see it as that because I've always found that poem particularly moving. I read it at the Poetry Centre in New York and got choked up reading it. I had to walk off the stage, get away from it, for five minutes. But even when I came back I didn't finish it, had to do another one. And I know if I took your copy of the book and started reading it now it probably would affect me the same way.

**J:** Writing can be a way of distancing oneself from the real force of the pain at the loss of a loved one. Is that how you deal with something as cataclysmic as death?

**H:** There are many ways of dealing with death. Number one, there are those who would just use the occasion to write something dreadful or monumental, right? Number two, it can be a case of having to express yourself in some way, and number three, it is the closing of the door, saying goodbye, having one last enormous convulsive cry and saying, 'I've done it, vomited it up, now I can move on to the next thing.' For me it is a blend of all three.

**J:** But for those who do write that way and are, in effect, erecting a form of tombstone on paper, shouldn't the poem, novel, song, magazine article, be more than mere vomit or relief for the self? Shouldn't it become something transcendent, to which others can relate, and through which, hopefully, they too will receive release, redemption, whatever?

**H:** I couldn't agree with you more. I can't add to that, except to say that is, and should be, the motivating force behind everything we do as artists.

**J:** On the other hand, can you sympathise with Seamus Heaney's idea of the subject of the poem coming back to pillory the poet for daring to use his/her death as a platform for poetry? Might your sister feel that way, or do you think she would be pleased?

**H:** I think she would be pleased. But, my God, this is a highly relevant question and not one that many creative, and even non-creative people, ever ask themselves. You now have me even questioning the memorial I'm doing for Dermot, the Dermot Harris Foundation, in Scranton University. I didn't say to him before he died, 'Would you like to be remembered forever?' He probably would have said no. But I think he should be, so one way of ensuring that is by creating a scholarship in his name. But maybe, in truth, we're just doing something for ourselves rather than the person who died. Maybe the father and the sister weren't important. Maybe it was just important for me that I wrote those poems, too.

**J:** But if the poem/memorial also was inspired by love, not just self-love, perhaps you can't simply draw a line and say it was solely a selfish act, just ego gratification?

**H:** No you can't. And I think we have to tap whatever talent we have. How am I distinct from Jack Donnelley downstairs? Distinct from – not you, you too are a writer. But how are we, as writers, different from those who don't have this forum, or outlet? We have the ability to translate pain into, hopefully, poetry. My feelings for the death of my sister may be no more profound than the taxi driver felt when he lost his sister, but we can express it a little more eloquently, in poetry or in acting. Are we therefore using their deaths? Are we diminishing those people, diminishing those relationships? Am I, if twenty years later I recall the death of my sister so I can draw on that emotion in a movie? I don't know. You tell me, Joe. You've thought about all this before, I haven't. It is an extremely delicate subject.

**J:** I think it all depends, finally, on what one creates, what one leaves as that 'tombstone'. If, in your poem you grieve more for your own loss than for the fact that life was snatched from the loved one, then maybe you deserve to be pilloried. But if your aim for Dermot, your father, sister, whoever, is to celebrate their lives, even deaths, and thus put a tongue to someone else's silence – to paraphrase Heaney – then that is not questionable or morally suspect. Surely, as you say, that is what all artists are meant to do?

**H:** I understand. And although I may have said I never really questioned my motives, listening to you, I would have to say that if those are the criteria one should apply, then my intentions always were honourable.

**J:** Nevertheless, there is yet another side to all this, as in the question of writing about people who still are alive. Paul Durcan's book *The Berlin Wall Café* is very similar to your album *My Boy*, because both contain hymns to a broken marriage. Yet his book raises the question of whether he has any right to present the pain of his wife, and family, in public. Is it enough to say that art will gain or that it will be of benefit to the greater good? Couldn't one also say that Durcan is violating his wife's privacy and, in a sense, the sanctity of their marriage? Doesn't that make of him, and similar writers, a form of cannibal?

**H:** But we are cannibals. Someone once asked me what you have to be to be a successful actor. I replied, 'Masochistic and sadistic' and, yes, cannibalistic. You have to be able to inflict pain on yourself, walk into a relationship, saying, 'I'm going to be hurt – I hope, I'm going to get something I can use.' And you have to be sadistic, step over the closest of people to get that.

**J:** You've also said that comfort or prolonged emotional involvement is anathema to the creative artist. Why would, for example, a sustained marriage chip away at the possibility of reaching similar artistic goals?

**H:** As an actor the range of experiences is bound to be limited for me if I stay, say, in one staid stable relationship all my life. And as the personal cry in my poetry is joyless, could best be described as a collection of sores, lasting companionship cancels out the poetry because it could bring joy. As I begin a love affair I begin looking to the end of it, the tragedy, the walking on the beach, lost, bleeding, writing poems, singing songs. I thrive on all that.

**J:** Doesn't that make people shy away from you?

**H:** Maybe nobody has thought enough to be aware of that beforehand. Or is interested enough to look into it. I'll tell you, I met a girl this week who I'd known years ago. She's now married to a very successful businessman here in Ireland. And I'd been in love with her very seriously, wondering should I propose to her. But I looked at her the other night and said to myself, God, wasn't she lucky? I must have loved her more than my other two wives as I didn't ask her to marry me.

**J:** In 'The Name of My Sorrow' you sing a laundry list of all the women who have brought you sorrow. But do you think that many of your ex-lovers would bless or curse the fact that they may have loved you?

**H:** I would have to think that there was something good in our relationships, don't you think? That I gave something positive and constructive and rather beautiful, if only for a fleeting moment.

**J:** Have you done a MORI poll?

**H:** *[laughs]* No. But I'm very friendly with Elizabeth, and my second wife, Ann. But it was to Elizabeth I once said, 'What was I really like to be married to?' She said, 'It was absolute magic, a magic carpet ride, but then one day you'd get that look in your eyes, one drink too many, and in the end I couldn't take it. The good moments weren't balancing out the bad.'

**J:** Outside marriage, on a personal level, would you say you've brought more joy into people's lives than sorrow?

**H:** Well, I have no friends, right? I used to have a friend in Wales, but he let me down badly, so he's not a friend any more. I'm talking about real friendships. My brother Dermot had legions of friends, legions turned up for his funeral. They came from London, Scotland, America, Spain, and I watched and in a strange moment said, 'These are genuine people here, all weeping. But not when I'm gone. You won't have that.' You may have one or two debt collectors, or ex-wives, making sure I'm gone so the alimony will be paid. *[laughs]*

**J:** Do you seriously believe that?

**H:** I do, yes. I never had the capacity for – well, let's say I have a great capacity for flashing into a room and being what many see as 'friendly' and making you believe that, eh – *[Harris is suddenly self-conscious, as if anticipating my response]* eh, well, whatever.

**J:** Like you are doing right now?

**H:** Probably. Then, on the other hand, when the door closes, it's gone. I'm off somewhere else again. Probably doing the same thing. And being sincere each time. But picking up a bank of experiences, not gathering a throng of friends. I do not function well with people on a permanent basis.

**J:** You see friends as excess baggage?

**H:** Probably. I live in the Bahamas by myself, function best by myself.

**J:** Who then is your ideal companion, apart from yourself?

**H:** There isn't one.

**J:** Doesn't that bother you?

**H:** No, not at all. We can be loved without suffering the burden of friendship.

**J:** Surely, if everyone felt like that then all we'd have is a world of isolated, insulated, self-obsessed creatures, dead to the soul?

**H:** Less pain, less pain. If that is what was accepted, if we don't expect anything from anybody, then there would be less unhappiness. A lot of the pain we feel is caused not so much by what other people do as by our own expectations of them. Saying this, however, I don't mean we should be self-obsessed or rude or not giving. People who know me will tell you I'm a giving person. But in my own way. And I'm not gregarious.

**J:** And you're never besieged by hunger for companionship in the middle of any night in the Bahamas?

**H:** That doesn't exist for me, no. But that is what it's all about for many people. 'I'm afraid to grow old by myself,' they say. 'I must get someone as I can't bear to be, not just by, but with myself alone.' That's treacherous, the wrong reason for having a relationship. Especially marriage. Marriage can exist for me only if I can say to my lady – I know that sounds feudal, but leave it for the moment – if I can say I'm ready for a week of fun, let's break the boundaries. Then after the week we say, 'It's time for you to go now, for a week, maybe months, whichever. Go do your own thing.' And she has to be happy with that and say, 'Thanks be to God, now I can be by myself.'

**J:** Can the 'lady' impose that decision on her man?

**H:** Of course. You must agree beforehand.

**J:** So then if you say 'I'm ready for a week of fun' and she says, 'Tough shit, I'd rather be by myself this week, my lord,' that's okay?

**H:** Yes, once we both agree that those are the rules.

**J:** In a marriage situation, however, there also can be children involved. Your own song, 'Cries from Broken Children', is a mercilessly accurate depiction of the effect a marriage break-up can have on children. Would you agree that children can be similarly damaged, if not more so, when parents stay in a relationship which is loveless and thus poisonous?

**H:** Yes they can. And I based that song on my relationship with Elizabeth and Damien. And I do think it is healthier if a poisonous relationship ends and a healthier one is created through distance, than have children subjected to two people eternally at war with one another. In fact, Elizabeth and I would have been divorced three or four years previous to the time we had been if I'd conceded to her demands for custody of the children. I said no, I wanted joint custody. I don't want to have to ask to see what is mine.

**J:** You finally got joint custody.

**H:** Luckily for me Elizabeth wanted to marry Rex Harrison, so she finally said, 'This is the only way I'll get my divorce, so I'll have to concede to that.' And she now says, 'Thanks be to God you fought for it, because that's what the children needed.' You couldn't get a stronger family than me and my divorced wife. We aren't married, we didn't live together, but by Christ, we are a family.

**J:** What about that recent article which suggested that part of one of your son's much-publicised drug problems may have been rooted in the famous, or absent, father syndrome?

**H:** Joe, when I said at the beginning of this interview that I can't talk about this, I can't. There is a court case going on. And it can be painful for your children to think that their father is out there talking to the press about them. But as to your suggestion I don't believe it to be true. As you can hear from the kind of honesty in our conversation, I would say that we caused it, if I believed it to be true. But I don't. Because we're unlike most divorced families in that we were never torn apart by the law. You'd think Elizabeth and I still were married. If she called me now and said 'I'm ...' whatever, then I'd be on a plane. If she said 'I need something' she's got it. Someone upsets her, death to them.

**J:** So was it fair, earlier, to say that your ex-wives would be interested in just the alimony? Or say that at your graveside there'd be no friends?

**H:** No, sorry, they'd be there. I didn't mean to exclude them. I meant outside the family circle. But, yes, I have great friends within my family, with my three children, we're fantastically close. Another thing is that I am responsible for them and I can never relinquish that responsibility. I would never want to. I'm not responsible for my wife's life, she came before me, but I am responsible to her.

**H:** But surely it could be said that you relinquished that responsibility to Elizabeth's pain, and perspective, when you recorded the *My Boy* marriage break-up album. The wife's pain is the one dimension which is missing. You focus on just your pain and the pain of the children.

**H:** *[pauses]* You know, you're right. I never thought of that.

**J:** Could you really have written a song in which you go over to the woman's side, empathise fully with her pain and capture her disillusionment at the end of the marriage?

**H:** Yes I could have.

**J:** Why didn't you?

**H:** You are right. It was wrong not to.

**J:** You spoke earlier of the 'war between the sexes' and a fundamental incompatibility between men and women. Indeed, you referred to the 'cesspool' inside us burning with hate and revenge. How do you feel when that war manifests itself physically, within a loving situation? Wife-beating/husband-beating is on the increase.

**H:** As I said, I am a great romantic, the flowers, the tragedy, the songs et cetera. And I would love to fall in love again but the realities of love now are almost prohibitive. They almost force oneself to deny one the ultimate pleasure which is the giving over of oneself to somebody else. What has love become? As you say, violence in love, and in marriage, is on the increase. Is this an accident, part of the game, or is it what love expects and calls forth from the two participants? You must have read Freud; think of the chapters on the different forms of expression: excretion, urination, anal sex. Yet this, we are told in Judeo-Christian terms, is total debasement. While, on the other hand some brilliant theorists and sexologists suggest that we become more secure when we can really draw out of each other all that we are capable of sharing.

**J:** So what are you saying, that love be all-embracing? Even to the extent of giving vent to the darkness through physical violence, saying it's okay to talk with our fists when our tongues, hearts or brains are tangled? That this, ultimately, is the human-bestial condition?

**H:** Isn't it horrendous? But so often the case. Yet I also know women who want to be beaten, women who want to beat. Men who want to humiliate or be humiliated. All in the guise of love. Supposing, to satisfy our partners, at their request we share what we call an 'acceptable' level of bashing of each other, is that okay? I know people like that. And if we do, should we then say to the law, 'It's none of your business, this is an expression of love'?

**J:** It's love-making?

**H:** Or hate-making. And hate-making, both the same thing, as you suggested earlier. But is an acceptable level of bashing each other okay, whereas the bruised eye or broken jaw is not? Where do you draw the line?

**J:** Where did you draw the line in your marriage to Elizabeth, for example? When you were drinking heavily, was violence part of that scenario?

**H:** Elizabeth writes about it in her book. I think she says I beat her once or twice. I probably fucking did give her a smack across the face. I remember once I did. But that had nothing to do with love. This was unjustified. It was horrendous. Yet, on the other hand, with my father and mother it was an arranged marriage. My mother was a working-class lady with a lot of money, my father had no money. It was arranged by relatives that they should marry. They had eight children and loved each other. They had the odd row, now and then, but no more than that, tiffs. My aunt and uncle, arranged marriage, same situation. But what is happening today? There are no arranged marriages because it's not 'civilised', it's 'dehumanising', it's 'feudal'. Instead, people now are free to fall in love and beat the fuck out of each other, damage children then get divorced. Give me the answer, Joe. What is happening to love these days?

**J:** Perhaps it has something to do with the higher the dream, the longer the fall, the greater the force with which we strike out when we reach the ground.

**H:** Why is the dream any higher?

**J:** The selling of facile images of 'romance' and chocolate box notions of love, as propagated in contemporary songs, books, television, movies. Then we meet someone who sometimes needs to slap out and say 'I hate the very air you breathe.' Maybe we go, 'Whoa, wait a minute, that wasn't in the songs or the poem, so you must be to blame, not me.' Or maybe, as you suggest, in this Judeo-Christian society we are taught not to accept the dark or the bestial, or that hate can be a part of love.

**H:** I think you are dead right. My ex-wife, Ann Turkel, married King Arthur. I then discovered a cuttings book she'd had since she was fourteen. She'd been in love with that celluloid image of me from *Camelot*, seen the movie twenty-eight times, so she married Arthur. Then she wakes up one morning, thinks this isn't Arthur at all, and punishes you for not living up to her expectations.

**J:** With regards to a more public form of violence, the run of Camelot in London in 1982 was adversely effected by rumours of your support for the IRA. How much truth was there to those rumours? Those rumours stemmed mostly from you arriving at a Noraid function in the early 1970s. How much truth was there to them?

**H:** Well, yes, I was a tremendous supporter of Noraid. I raised a fortune for them in America in the belief that it was for both Catholics and Protestants and for rehousing wives and children of people who were in jail. But I'm a republican through and through. I believe in a United Ireland. I believe that violence was forced upon the Irish. Go back to the history of the old Provisional IRA and you'll see they were the result of British tyranny, British violence. Whether they do or don't want a United Ireland, I want it. And those who don't want it will have to accept it when it comes. This country has to be united.

**J:** Do you condone the use of IRA violence in the name of that aim?

**H:** I can't approve of them blowing up Harrods. I can't agree with them taking the battle into the private sector. There is a war between the IRA and the British army and that's the territory, but taking it beyond that I cannot condone, believe in or support.

**J:** You said earlier that if someone upset Elizabeth, 'death to them'. Could you kill for what you care about most deeply?

**H:** Yes. Anyone who damaged my children or Elizabeth, because she too is family, the mother of my children, I'd be capable of killing.

**J:** 'One has not lived till one conceives of life as a tragedy' said, I think, Joyce. Would you agree?

**H:** Yes, I'm afraid so. But also, I got the cover of *Life* magazine once and the opening line of the article was something like 'He lived with a smile on his face and a sense that the world was mad'. I do absolutely believe that the world is mad. And when you quote Joyce's wonderful line I have to see things that way. I believe that from the moment of conception to the moment we die life is riddled with, and cloaked in, tragedy. Earlier I fought against your application of psycho-analysis, probably because I don't really want to know why I am as I am. I am as I am and that's that. That's what I usually say. But deep down behind it all I have a very strong conviction of the madness of life, that it should never have happened, it was all a great mistake. And that the miracle of life is absolutely *[voice lowered conspiratorially, as if Harris himself doesn't want to hear what he has to say]* – I hate admitting it, it's all a kind of rubbish, a miracle, but a disastrous miracle. And I think the O'Tooles and the Harrises of this world were very aware of this. That's part of the 'craziness' we project.

**J:** Theatre of the Absurd?

**H:** Exactly. But theatre of the absurd which we have to deal with in a nihilistic way. Or rather vice versa. I am very conscious of the vast stupidity of it all and I, for one have no desire to, no intention, of walking around in sackcloth and ashes. So I choose to go the other route, to present it all in a vaudevillian way, almost like those two wonderful tramps in Beckett.

**J:** As in tramps 'shining'?

**H:** *[laughs]* Yes. But don't you agree we must present life as vaudeville? It is a fucking joke, it's a juggling of hats, a pulling of a rabbit out of a hat then losing it in your pocket. All the thousands of years of Christianity and preaching the gospels and spreading of the 'word of God', all this talk of humanity and kindness and yet, at the end of the day, there now are more people than ever before disillusioned and lost in the world. It is a farce, a black comedy.

**J:** You write in one lyric: 'There's a time in your life/when the growing ceases/when thoughts of the end/ night and day increases.' Is part of having to accept the inevitability of tragedy this conscious, unending awareness of impending death?

**H:** It is. And yet, as always, there is another side to it. I think death will be a great relief. I don't want it to happen yet. But I'm not scared of it at all.

**J:** But many people believe that a constant awareness of death which makes for a more voluptuous form of living. And that the immersion into sex, drugs et cetera, which we spoke about earlier, could also be read as a spitting-out in the face of death, like saying 'Fuck it, till then living well is my best revenge', to quote the line you use to close your song 'This Is My Life' which, itself, closes *My Boy*.

**H:** There is an absolute element of truth in what you say. But, again, there is another layer to it. When I got into drugs it had nothing to do with rebellion, nothing to do with escapism. I won't even concede that my drinking had anything to with escapism, never have.

**J:** Even if you take the word 'escapism' beyond its usual context, in which it is often applied to an inability to cope with everyday problems, and see it instead as a manifestation of an inner voice saying 'Okay, if it's a duel for my soul then until I lose it I'll live'?

**H:** Okay, I agree with that. I accept that. And 'Living Well Is My Best Revenge' was the quote we used to end the *My Boy* album. Okay, if that to you is connoted by the word 'escapism', I accept that. Though, to me, it always had connotations of 'inability' and 'defeatism'. But, perhaps I should look at it that way too. But this is not to say I advocate the use of drugs. Look at the young generation and drugs. My generation, we can't understand them at all. They are more pained than we have ever been. I'm in my mid fifties, right. I've anaesthetised myself. I live by my behaviour patterns against what you identified as my sense of impending doom. But take my children's generation. To understand them we've got to get in there and look out through their eyes. They see nothing. Gloom, no future, no hope. They don't get out of bed in the morning full of hope, as I did in the forties. Though I had tuberculosis there was hope, because there was a chance for me out there. I could dream. I could work to secure that dream. But there is no chance for this generation, for young people of eighteen, nineteen. And the more sensitive you are, the worse it is. If you can, at nineteen, wear a suit of armour and say fuck it anyway, okay – but they can't. That is the real tragedy these days.

**J:** To quote the final song on your poetry album, there is 'no solution' and 'no absolution'?

**H:** There isn't. I still believe that. There is no solution because no one is trying to solve anything. Some are, but not enough. And no absolution because there is no one to receive it from. They don't believe in the God-figure or the Church. The whole concept has been atomised in the second half of this century.

**J:** Do you believe?

**H:** I'm clinging to the last hope, a final hope that there might be. I had a friend who lived in the bowels of the Welsh church and he always says, 'There is something out there all right'. I argue that if there is, he's made a great mistake. And he replies, 'It is we who made the mistake.'

**J:** Beckett is out there, he's not really alive and well and living in Paris.

**H:** Yes *[laughs]* Beckett out there? Wonderful idea. That he is, okay!

**J:** And he has a weird, wicked and very Irish sense of humour.

**H:** Definitely. Or as with Beckett he wonders is there any sense to it at all. Or he knows there isn't. That is the problem. Pain is caused by trying to make sense of it all. You, with all these wonderful questions are probably in for a life of supreme misery! But what we all must do is face it, but then get away from it all. Laugh, dance, sing. But don't hurt anybody in your mad dance. Those who want to come with you, say to them 'dance with me', to those who don't, say 'fair enough.'

**J:** Has your dance left you satisfied?

**H:** Very much so.

**J:** Cynics might scoff, it's easy to be satisfied with life when you own *Camelot*, a show which grossed 92 million dollars.

**H:** That was the gross, but there is a world of difference between that and what I personally earned! Though yes, it was a good 'oul penny alright! But that hasn't helped as much as people assume it will, It hasn't changed that much.

**J:** From living cramped with your family in a small flat in London, to now living in Paradise Island in the Bahamas? Are you kidding, or what?

**H:** But I don't indulge at all. I have got a house in the Bahamas, which is quite nice, I suppose. I live in a hotel here and in London. But I don't have a jet! It hasn't spoiled my tastes, look at the clothes, I have here, mostly rugby shirts.

**J:** So you're just another rich Irish peasant.

**H:** *[laughs]* In a strange way, yes.

**J:** And you would argue against those that say great wealth corrupts?

**H:** I do, and will argue against that.

**J:** But £50,000 on a lily pond, Richard?

**H:** That's not true.

**J:** £49,000?

**H:** I don't have a fucking lily pond! What I was going to do was have a pond in front of my house in the Bahamas designed like the map of Ireland until I discovered, unfortunately, that it attracted mosquitoes.

**J:** Why? Because it was in the shape of Ireland? Were they British mosquitoes, on the attack?

**H:** *[laughs]* No! Just because it was still water! So it wouldn't have worked unless I had a waterfall, so I abandoned that idea. I didn't spend that money at all, though it was reported in the papers at the time. As long as I can travel quickly by Concorde and have a decent suite in a hotel, that's all I need.

**J:** Does this all tie in, philosophically, with your idea that 'living well is my best revenge'? Doesn't it depend on how you define 'well'?

**H:** That's exactly it. I don't think that living well only means living in fucking luxury, though many define it along those lines. It's got nothing to do with that, saying 'I've got fifty fur coats, three Rolls-Royces and a private jet'. Fuck that. 'Living well' is being free, being able to laugh, do the things I believe in, even though, for example, they're not going to be able to pay me for a movie they want me to do here in Ireland. Money gives me the freedom to do that, or to focus on the memorial for Dermot.

**J:** The money you made from *This Sporting Life* you gave to your father so he wouldn't die feeling he'd been a failure.

**H:** That's right. It's very ironic. *This Sporting Life* was made by J. Arthur Rank and it was Ranks Flour in Ireland that had bankrupt my father. So the money I made from that movie my father used to keep Ranks from closing him down.

**J:** Is there anything similar your sons could do, were you in danger of feeling you'd died a failure?

**H:** This is an awful thing for me to say, but I must say it. It isn't possible for me to die a failure. Success or failure has nothing to do with what you make in terms of commercial success or having your name above the title, or your longevity as a movie star. Steve McQueen always believed he was a total failure no matter how successful his films were. Warren Beatty and Jack Nicholson, there's continually conflict between them, though they are the best of friends. It's always 'What has he got? How much did you get for that movie?' Stallone too because he feels he hasn't got enough. I haven't got ten per cent of what Sylvester Stallone has, but I'm one hundred per cent happier. It is attitude that is successful.

**J:** Some gauge 'success' not by the amount of money you make, but the quality of the love you inspire, especially within a family.

**H:** I agree. That probably is one of the reason I feel I have been so successful.

**J:** Would you also find it inspiring to know that many romantic idealists, and otherwise, probably held onto their own particular visions a little tighter after listening to either the middle section of *MacArthur Park* or the final verse of *Camelot*? Is passing on a vision of a better world as important to Richard Harris as it was to the mythical King Arthur? Or do you see a contradiction between this and your own nihilism?

**H:** I think that is extremely important, despite how paradoxical this may seem in the light of all I've said to you today. I'd love to be able to get up and say – okay, out there it is dark, it's black, and that is, as you so wonderfully said, Samuel Beckett up there laughing at us. But 'let's laugh with him'. It is a vicious joke that went astray somewhere. Yet maybe we did misinterpret what it was supposed to be and we began to take it all too seriously. But if we fall into that trap it must strike us as a sick joke, as you also said, as 'theatre of the absurd'.

That is what it is but in the end people must get on with it, try not to take it that seriously.

**J:** King Arthur took it all seriously.

**H:** That's why there was such a sadness to his dream. His message was endless peace and harmony, but it can't be achieved. His was – as written by Alan Jay Lerner – a wonderful forlorn voice suggesting that the round table was the United Nations. But the United Nations has been proved to be a total fucking flop. The EEC hasn't been marvellously successful, has it? It is isolationist, isn't it? Although we've united many countries, it's all against the rest! Nothing is all-embracing. So the myths and dreams he had, though wonderful, were totally impractical. It won't ever be. Though, yes, the paradox is that we must dream.

**J:** But is it not more a question of how we, as individuals, interpret that dream? Many people who saw any of your one thousand performances of *Camelot*, or the movie, may have taken that concept of a better world and time and reapplied it to their own lives, used it to solidify some form of vision. Apparently President John F. Kennedy, often listened to the title song from *Camelot* before he went to bed, treating it almost as if it were a nightly prayer.

**H:** Well yes, it probably does, did, give many people similar hope, a similar belief in a vision. There was a sense that maybe it all could work. 'For one brief shining moment', it could work.

**J:** Before the bullet inevitably hits your head?

**H:** Exactly. For one brief shining moment before that happens something as perfect as *Camelot* can be created. We all can touch it for one moment. That is what I believe.

# 6 PAUL DURCAN
## 1987

'I don't want to be Irish' was the thought still searing through Paul Durcan's mind three days after the massacre at Enniskillen. Phoning him to arrange this interview, I had interrupted his reading of a postcard from a friend in Co. Derry. Its message captured how many of us were feeling at the time. 'After Enniskillen I am silenced, but my whole body is crying how can a people come to this?'

Paul Durcan also was feeling that he wanted to 'disassociate himself from the human race, feel nothing at all'. And yet a pencil line of hope he'd drawn from the previous evening's news report. 'It was an image which will stay with me all my life,' he said, referring to Mr Gordon Wilson' s heartbreaking recollection of the moment he realised that his daughter's screams of pain had given way to death. 'He is the hope for humanity – him, not the Church or governments, they have fellow-travelled all the way with the Provisionals.'

He apologised if he had been ranting and suggested that most people probably would dismiss these 'ramblings' as lunatic. And yet when compared with all the acts of collective madness which have led us to Enniskillen (and beyond), Durcan's 'lunacy' seemed like little more than the anguished cries from an orphaned and disorientated child. But also an articulate and incisive child. For much of his 'rambling' rang disturbingly true. 'I blame our government more than the people who planted that bomb. I know members of all parties, so called "pillars of respectability" in our society, who privately support the IRA while publicly denouncing them.'

In its own way this outpouring of Durcan's pain and revulsion was as moving as the news clip of Gordon Wilson. But the phone conversation took place just seventy-two hours after the bombing. By the time of the actual interview seven days later, would Paul Durcan give credence to the cry of cynics who say that once the high point of pain has passed we all fall back into old and often lethargic patterns of behaviour?

'Yes, there is that danger. We were all so vocal that week, but since last Sunday week I have found myself becoming increasingly inarticulate on the whole nightmare. But yes I do still feel that I don't want to be Irish any more. I live on this island but I do not think of myself as belonging to the Irish nation.'

Does he still want to 'disassociate' himself from the human race?

'Well, I have thought a lot about suicide but I now think that would be the easy way out. But then didn't you and I also discuss the inspiring humanity of Mr Gordon Wilson? It is his kind of courage that I so desperately seek. But even without that courage, overall I am an optimist. And furthermore, as suicide is a negation of not just pain but of all feelings, it would, ultimately, be a betrayal of what my work and my life is all about.'

Lifting from beside his armchair a copy of his new book *Going Home To Russia*, Durcan grips it tightly and says, 'This, and all my books are about having feelings, keeping feelings alive. So this business of numbing oneself through drugs or alcohol or, finally, through suicide is the very opposite of what I am about. You've got to fight every day against this closing of the senses, especially artists. Not to have feelings is, to me, a definition of hell. That too is the true tragedy of ageing, to see people crabbed and closed to the world. The worst part is that these days you see this in even young people.'

Especially those who live in, or near Enniskillen. Does Durcan still believe that the government really must bear as much, if not more blame, than the people who planted the bomb? 'Yes. I saw Eamonn McCann and Robert McCartney on *Question Time* and they said it for me. They said you've got to see what happened in Enniskillen in a wider context. And that the IRA have been setting the agenda for everything in the last fifteen years – Sunningdale, the collapse of Stormont, et cetera. They also pointed out that the IRA are not monsters with twenty-five heads.'

So does Paul Durcan condone the use of violence to bring about change? Does he, in any way, support the IRA?

'Certainly not. I've been against the Provisionals all my life. But I know damn well that they represent a lot of people in Northern Ireland, so I wish they could appear on TV and radio and present their point of view. But in terms of my "condoning" or "supporting" violence, "pacifist" is not sufficient a word to describe me. I hate guns and I hate men who use them. But the IRA are an army like any other army and in ways they are more honest than our politicians as they are doing our dirty work. Didn't we, "the State", get back the twenty-six counties by the same methods?'

Durcan's perception of Irish politicians was, he claims, irreversibly altered soon after the King's Mill massacre. 'What happened at King's Mill was no "blunder".' The IRA were waiting in ambush for ten Protestant workers who were members of nothing other than their families. They mowed them down, like something out of Goya. That is cold-blooded execution of the innocents. Yet it changed nothing. We wept and there were speeches, officially, but I met a man who is, as I said on the phone to you, a pillar of respectability, a right-wing person who is all the things most valued in our society, and I asked him how he felt about King's Mill. He said, "Well, it might teach those Protestants a lesson." I was shocked right through my very being but that was due to my own naïveté. When I thought about it I realised that is the ultimate logic of Cumann na Gael and Fianna Fáil glued together. That's what they really feel, really think, about the Protestants.'

Paul Durcan is similarly disillusioned and aggravated by what he regards as the government's 'cowardice' in the face of the Catholic Church. 'They will not take the Church on. They will not say to them, "You cannot interfere in the political, social and cultural life of Ireland and continue to disturb it as you have done in the past. You cannot continue to cause such psychic damage." No taoiseach has had the guts to do that. If only we had comported ourselves with even the most primitive kind of duty as a state, if we'd gotten rid of articles two and three of the constitution, if we'd brought in civil rights for all people, then we could begin to talk. But we haven't. And yet some still have the astounding arrogance to weep crocodile tears at a tragedy like Enniskillen. The plain people of Ireland, I accept their tears I do not accept the tears of our leaders.'

Does Durcan see any solution?

'John Hewitt – when I asked him if he had any hope for the situation, said no. But insofar as I do, it will have to be some kind of federation of these islands in the distant future. I agree with that.'

Does he hold any hope for the Anglo-Irish Agreement?

'No,' he says. 'One aspect of it alone is that everyone in the north of Ireland, Protestant, Catholic, Nationalist, Loyalist, all are united in that they totally reject it as they were never consulted about it.'

W.H. Auden, a literary paragon to Durcan, apparently felt that his own poetry was invalidated because it had never saved even one Jew from the concentration camps. He also said that 'Poetry makes nothing happen'. So what role, politically, can the poet play?

'Auden is a saint to me but he was wrong when he said that about himself. Look at his effect on Joseph Brodsky, who then went on to win the Nobel prize. The whole point about art is to rescue the feelings of the individual from things like what the Nazi philosophy stood for, which was the obliteration of the individual. So, every time you touch an individual with a poem, a song, even a magazine article like the one you wrote on Sinatra, you are changing the world, that is a political act.'

In reply to those who might suggest that poets and artists could be politically active in a more explicit way, Durcan cites the case of his recent experience touring schools. 'Up to two thousand boys and girls plus many truly radical teachers and principals took part in that project. And myself and three other poets did alter, however slightly, their perspective on life/society/the arts. It is at this level that we all must work. People should not put things like art and education out on the margins, everything is political. But newspaper editors seem totally ignorant of that. No one reported these activities, whereas in a society like the Soviet Union, that kind of radical social activity would receive a lot of coverage.'

Poems that deal directly with his experiences in Russia, however, form only the final section of his latest book. The first two-thirds of the poems deal with his usual themes of fear, lust, love, childhood, Irish politics, loss, betrayal and laughter. But if Durcan's quirky sense of humour still dashes like a wild child with a switchblade through the pages of the book, there has been, he suggests, a shift of focus and a development in terms of attitude. And so, if the humour in poems like 'Cardinal Dies of Heart Attack in Dublin Brothel' or 'Priest Accused of Not Wearing Condom' is still but the tip of a deep detestation of hypocrisy and a lack of real moral commitment in the Church, then in at least one poem ('Six Nuns Die in Convent Inferno') he casts a kinder and more humane light on the lives of some of the women and men who dedicate their lives to Christ.

'Yes, that poem is also a celebration of that life and it shows that I am not as gratuitously anti-clerical as many people assume.' Durcan also has begun to see that satire offers a limited artillery in term of social commentary or of art. 'Even the first two poems you mention are different from those I wrote before. There is a genuine piety at work there, as well as the humour. I do believe deeply in that line by Kavanagh that "Satire is unfruitful prayer/only wild shoots of pity there".'

But if Durcan's work and life are influenced by poets such as Kavanagh, Auden, Eliot, Pound, Pasternak, Baudelaire, he is also very much a child of popular culture. His roots lie nearer cinema (his ultimate artistic heroes still are those poets of the cinema, Pasolini and Tarkovsky), TV, radio and, originally, rock 'n' roll. His first book may have been dedicated to Hart Crane but the writers who first filled him with the joy of 'learning words off by heart' were, he says people like Norman Petty, Leiber and Stoller and, of course, Chuck Berry. 'Music came to us via the wireless, mostly Radio Luxembourg. It didn't matter who wrote the songs, it was the singer we listened to: Buddy Holly, Jerry Lee and of course Elvis. And things like "Rave On", "Great Balls of Fire" and "Heartbreak Hotel" were, and still are, to me a form of pure poetry. Even now I don't see much difference between lyricists like Springsteen, Tom Waits, Lennon and Dylan and those of us for whom the music must remain within the words and on the page.'

Durcan has no time for cultural segregationists. 'Again, if there was any sanity in our society, especially in education, there would be no separation between "low" and "high" culture. Rock songs should be studied in schools as they are in America and Britain. But here the lines are drawn and only a very naive person would not see that these lines too also can be politically divisive.'

But if the street culture of rock 'n' roll brought pride and delight into the life of the young Paul Durcan, he soon encountered attempted oppression. 'A priest said to me: "Elvis Presley is evil incarnate". And that was bound to have a traumatic effect on a boy of twelve whose life revolved round listening to rock 'n' roll and finding a girlfriend. It took me years to deal with that. I went on listening to Elvis but that brought the darkness into it all.'

Pre-darkness, Durcan, born the son of a judge in Dublin in 1944, had spent most of his childhood in Co. Mayo. And although he says of those days that 'It was paradisial, with just the usual demons and disruptions', his life took a decidedly different route as soon as he entered his teens. If the Elvis-fearing priest introduced Durcan to true darkness, another cloak was thrown over his life when, just three days before his thirteenth birthday, he had an accident which almost led to his death. 'I was out of action for a year and had many serious operations. But it wasn't so much my own coming close to death which may have darkened my outlook, it was more being in a hospital ward and seeing so many men die all around me. The first time is still a vivid memory.'

Drawing my attention to his use of the word 'may', Durcan adds: 'I am very dubious about singling out reasons. I have learned how much accident and drift plays a part in human affairs. That has rid me of this dangerous notion of cause and effect. I can't therefore make a definite link between my brush with death and a deepening darkness in my life though yes, it obviously influenced me deeply. And further, 'to hijack those biographers who, when I die, might try to make that a lazy link and say that is where the poetry began, the fact is that I had discovered the joys of writing at least a year before that.'

But although 'paradisial' is the word Durcan chooses to describe his childhood, some critics suggest that the dominant sense one gets from poems recalling his first family is one evoking demons. In 'Poem for My Father', the narrator says: 'My nightmare is my family.' 'Firstly, I must stress that this is my father's voice speaking. But it does reflect a sense I had at the time which was of the family which eats its children. And a sense of possessiveness, of how destructive the family unit can be.'

Did Durcan's family devour its children?

'Every family does,' he replies, tentatively. Durcan's father and mother are still alive, yet he rejects the suggestion that this limits what he can say or will write about them: 'Of my two families I have written quite extensively and, some think, too explicitly.'

Being brought up almost exclusively by women (his aunts in Mayo) helped make of Durcan a highly feminised man, and therefore a man to whom homosexual relationships in his early teens seemed like second nature. 'It was exactly as I've written in poems like "I Was a Twelve-Year-Old Homosexual", a phase.' The path to feminism took a little longer, as did the path to development of his own full potential in terms of his sexuality. 'Well, we were educated to believe that women were, on the one hand, untouchable and pure, and on the other hand, that they were the source of all evil. But because of my own upbringing, my own nature and the nature of the girls I met in my mid teens, I was able to survive all that, break through the darkness and discover the full joys of sex. But there were many boys I knew then who didn't. But, of course the real victims in all this were women. Imagine being eighteen during that period and getting married to a man whose idea of manhood was to drink twenty-six pints of beer on Saturday night having kicked somebody to death on the rugby field that afternoon! And these are the very men who are running our country today.'

Durcan may even have gone to college with those same men, but after just one year at UCD he joined the swelling band of sixties drop-outs. During that Summer of Love, in 1967, he also published his first book *Endsville* and met Nessa O'Neill, the woman who not only became his wife but also finally freed him, for a while, from another route he'd taken to escape that dark world of repression during the 1950s. 'After meeting Nessa and having that book of poetry published, drink ceased to be a form of escape for me. I needed no other reality, I was quite happy where I was,' he admits. But, ten years later, though he couldn't admit it at the time, he realised that even social drinking had left him near addiction. 'For the sake of my sanity and peace I had to stop and finally did.' But though that phase lasted a further five years, all good intentions were undone one day in Rome when, to combat the sweltering heat, he decided to have 'just one beer'.

'It had a lethal effect on me, as if I had been drinking every day of that last five years. That happened in 1982 and since then I've fought a running battle with alcohol. There have been times when I succumbed and nearly paid for it with my life.'

Does he still hear that old demon call out to him every day?

'Well as I speak to you now, November 16th 1987, I can say I'm okay, but there is no guarantee that I won't start drinking in the near future. There is a strong danger of this, especially at Christmas. The loneliness and isolation living on my own at this time of the year.'

Has he taken clinical alternatives to allay depression?

'No. I do suffer from melancholy but I don't think it is a case for clinical treatment. The sadness in me is a consequence of remaining open to the world. But despite, say, the image of me which comes across during my poetry readings, I do have a great capacity for joy and for rejoicing. But yes, I do get the blues quite badly now and then but never so much that I would entrust myself to psychiatrists, in any way. Besides, as Chekhov said, "Suffering brings a human being to perfection". That is what I believe.'

Was the break-up of his marriage part of the price he paid for his addiction to drink?

'No. It didn't help, of course. But that probably was caused more by my addiction to work than drink and by a fundamental failure on my behalf, to love. I was incredibly lucky because my wife is an especially kind, honest and independent woman. I took all that for granted. I wrote about that dimension to the break-up in "Raymond of the Rooftops".'

That poem, along with twenty others in a similar vein, are at the core of Durcan's award-winning collection *The Berlin Wall Café*. For some the poem incisively captures that unceasing conflict between the artist and the non-artist. On the one hand there is the poet/fairytale writer attempting to scale the highest slopes of Mount Olympus, while on the other there is the 'feckless' wife who would be happier if he would even 'stand at the bottom of the stepladder' while she journeys to the roof to fix the damaged slates. 'Have a heart, woman – he bellowed/Can't you see I am up to my eyes and ears in work/breaking my neck to finish "Raymond of the Rooftops"?

'Well, each interpretation of that poem is legitimate,' he says, 'but I do not see the artist as being any different from any other person in society. So, to me it's not so much about the artist pitted against the non-artist as it is about the husband so obsessed with work that he loses sight of all other priorities. In this he becomes an anti-artist, as he therefore is anti-life. I'm sure my work suffered because of that. All our work is good only insofar as it reflects the quality of our life.'

Was the poem worth it?

'I don't think any poem I've written or any book I've published was worth losing my wife and children, no. It would be different if it was only my pain that was involved but there was other people's pain to consider. When people have lived together for a long time, intensely, then sadly must take different roads, it is an exceedingly traumatic experience for all concerned. I rarely see Nessa these days, or my children, unfortunately, as they live in Cork and I live in Dublin.'

How does he respond to those who suggest that he violated Nessa's privacy and the sanctity of their marriage/family by publishing the poems?

'After I had written the book I did have to ask myself if I had the moral right to publish. I considered it at length and quietly and finally decided it would not harm my wife and children. When it was published some people were, yes, angry, and said that I had exploited Nessa and gratuitously used her name in public, but one of the first people to wish me luck with the book was Nessa herself. But as she is a very private person we never discussed the book; we still haven't.'

Is there not a strong contradiction between his describing Nessa as 'a very private person' while at the same time admitting he didn't talk with her about the poems before publishing?

'Perhaps. But this is called having a conscience and acting on it. Perhaps if I had done that more often in my life I wouldn't have ended up in many of the tragic situations I did end up in. You have to take responsibility for your actions and continually lean on the shoulders of women. I had to. I know there are writers, poets, who did exploit their families but in *The Berlin Wall Café* I really don't think that I did. I think of those poems as hymns to Nessa, I have no regrets about it.'

Is the final criteria the fact that from the ashes of their marriage he (and, equally, perhaps, she) did produce a work which might help others to avoid making similar mistakes?

'That is a form of validation, absolutely. As I said to you earlier, I am the kind of poet who believes that the poem is not complete until it reaches and is, in some sense, used by the reader. In this respect I take inspiration from what the son of Balthus said about his father's art: "Balthus aspires instead to the anonymous perfection of the man liberated from the burden of himself. For this purpose he sees both his individuality and his work as a means and not an end." That is how it is for me.'

And yet in 'After the Funeral of the Marriage' Durcan writes: 'My wife and I paced/on either side of the hearse/Our children racing behind it'. Is publication of such poems also part of the process which leaves the children still, in a sense, 'running behind the hearse'?

'Yes. I suppose it is. But that poem also is a celebration of the fact that even in the midst of tragedy, if you are disposed to love you still, in the end, can hold hands walking down that road.'

If Paul Durcan had one hope or prayer for Christmas or for his future, what would it be?

'What I pray for is that I will be good friends with my wife. If I have her friendship I am more than content. It is more than I deserve.'

# 7 GABRIEL BYRNE
# 1988

Inspiring hope is of paramount importance to Gabriel Byrne. Consequentially, when he says, 'I've come a long way from boiling water in a billy-can in a plumber's shed in Dublin,' it is definitely not in those sickly tones of chest-thumping, self-aggrandisement so common among movie stars and other celebrities, particularly in Hollywood. And his feelings are made even more palateable when one realises that the journey he is referring to is more spiritual than physical and has less to do with amassing wealth than with shedding the sense of fear and anonymity which is part of his background, in terms of class, religion and nationality. Furthermore, if self-assertion is now a prime objective of Gabriel Byrne, it is as much the self as a cipher, or a courier of dreams, if you like, as it relates to asserting the self as some form of autonomous entity.

'Ten years ago I was in Dublin totally devoid of hope – now you and I are sitting in Beverly Hills doing this interview. And, that to, me is an indication that dreams, ambitions can be realised. If someone is reading this as I used to read interviews I want them to say, "He did it, so can I." Whatever it is they're reaching for I want to tell them to go for it.'

**Joe Jackson:**

What, to you, are the important differences between being a plumber's mate and being a movie star?

**Gabriel Byrne:**

I always hated the nine-to-five routine, hated the idea of knowing exactly what I was going to be doing in ten years' time, and, as a plumber, I knew I would have been consigned to work for J.M. Baird in Abbey Street for the rest of my life. Being in movies, on the other hand, gives you the chance to travel, meet different people, and that's always appealed to the explorer in me. And, of course, the pay is better! I'd originally trained to be a priest. I used to get the Divine Word at home and I'd read this article when I was twelve and saw these pictures of guys playing billiards, out in the missions – and that was it! Later I found myself with seven other Irish kids setting out from Dun Laoghaire to join a seminary. I was about four and a half years there and, once, there was this uproar when a travelling group of players performed and one girl took off her dress in the play and we saw her slip! And when they were leaving we were all hanging out the window, and I remember thinking, now this is exciting. I discovered women then, and the theatre. So I wasn't too upset when the top guy caught me smoking and said, "I've been looking over your conduct and I don't think you have a vocation." It was a glorious day, I left.

**J:** Apart from fleeting excitement at the sight of that girl in her slip, how did you cope with awakening sexual awareness in those circumstances?

**B:** When you're discovering sexuality and you are deprived of it you have to live the life of the imagination and most of us did that. When the lights went out the beds would become tents immediately! There was homosexuality, though I didn't recognise it as such. Nor, I imagine, did most of the guys who were doing it. But putting all those young guys together at the age of awakening sexual awareness and telling them that women are equated with evil and sin – them exploring sexuality in that way is to be expected.

**J:** Did you partake?

**B:** No. There was 'horseplay'. That's how I'd describe it.

**J:** Did all this leave you nervous of women?

**B:** Yes. Because of this veneration of the blessed Virgin and purity and all that stuff about women being unapproachable and inaccessible and not interested in sex, it took me years to get over all that. One of the great joys of my life was discovering that women love sex as much as men do! But I didn't really go out with my first 'real' girlfriend till I was nineteen. I was very much in awe of, and afraid of, women. I'd have to say that those days in that seminary definitely fucked up my sexuality for a long time.

**J:** A closeted life in a seminary often can lead to a lack of confidence in the outside world in general. Was that also a problem?

**B:** Yes. I do have confidence now, but it is a very delicate confidence. Believe me, it took me quite a long time to gain confidence in my ability as an actor.

**J:** There never was a conscious decision to become an actor. Someone asked if you'd appear in a play and you accepted. Did that leave you feeling you'd entered the profession by default?

**B:** Exactly. I felt I didn't have anything special to offer, wasn't gifted in any way, so I kept saying 'Why the fuck is this happening to me, I don't deserve it?'

**J:** Couldn't that also be seen as part of the legacy of Catholicism?

**B:** Yes. Many Irish people, Catholics in particular do suffer from that sense of 'I'm not entitled to what I have and I should feel guilty about it all and not joyful but miserable'. But I don't think that way now. I know I deserve to be here in Beverly Hills. I've worked for it and I'm entitled to the breaks I get and make. But this sense has come after a long struggle. I was like that when I first moved to London. Isolated, insulated, suffering in silence. It was a really painful period for me. But it made me realise that you must confront pain. Feel it rather than anaesthetise, or avoid it. Avoiding pain is what stunts our growth. I know too many people who spend their lives avoiding pain.

**J:** Did you use drink or drugs to anaesthetise pain?

**B:** Yeah. I went through a period of drinking and doing drugs when, like all people of my generation, I thought that was the answer to everything. Never heavy drugs, never snorted cocaine or tried heroin, but I have smoked marijuana and why I enjoyed it was that it gave me a perception which I thought was real and true. But I now realise you can get to that heightened state of consciousness without drugs. And as for drink, I really had to fight a hard battle against that. I couldn't say I'm in control, but I knew that if I wanted any kind of content in life I'd have to stop drinking. I can't say I'll never drink again, I face it one day at a time, that's the only way I can live.

**J:** Were movies also a form of 'escape' when you were a boy?

**B:** Yeah. They were the one place where you'd be transported from the dreary routine of everyday reality into something magical.

**J:** At the time did you have sexual fantasies about any particular movie star?

**B:** Ann Margret. I saw her in Elvis's *Love in Las Vegas* and I was gone! Funny enough she turned up at a party here two weeks ago and I was thinking, this is too much, that's Ann Margret, it's all come true. I'm still a bit of a stargazer. I still have that impulse to run up to people I meet and say, "Hey, I was always a big fan of yours."

**J:** Is there ever a moment say, when you are holding a woman like Kathleen Turner, and the fantasising boy in you begins to lose control?

**B:** Yeah. Occasionally there are two voices, one saying, "Just do your work," the other saying, "This is unbelievable, me here with" – whoever. And I'm getting paid for this!

**J:** If, as in *Gothic*, you are sitting by a window getting head from one woman while caressing the naked leg of another woman, is that just a job or do you get sexually aroused?

**B:** *[laughs]* It has happened. Not with me, but there are certain scenes in famous films where people actually did fuck on screen, so I hear. But firstly you must remember that when you see people naked on screen, unless they actually get out of the bed, they usually are wearing underclothes. Secondly, for most of us the idea of getting into bed with someone who is virtually a stranger is a weird concept to get hold of. You meet a beautiful actress for the first time, she meets you and you both are thinking, how the hell am I going to do that love scene with this stranger? Not just because it's staged but because there nearly always is a full crew there and a director telling you how to do it. That kills all the spontaneity which is so much a part of sex. And women are so scared when it comes to those scenes.

**J:** Because it is usually their bodies that are being exploited?

**B:** Exactly. And maybe for me that also goes back to my upbringing.

**J:** How would you describe your family, your background?

**B:** Working class from Walkinstown. Six in family, father a labourer, mother worked as a nurse.

**J:** How do the plumbers you once worked with respond when you go home?

**B:** Some are probably thinking, how the fuck did this guy do it? He used to make the tea for us, now he's off there in Hollywood. But one thing that angers me is when people, not plumbers mind you, say, 'You have to try to get rid of that accent.' I've been hearing that since I first went to London. They said if I didn't get rid of my 'thick

Dublin accent' I'd never work. They said people wouldn't understand me. I said as long as they understand what I'm saying on the screen that's what matters, I couldn't give a fuck if they don't understand me after I finish the job. But it is ridiculous, people in Dublin telling me I should lose my accent. Why should I? It's a birthmark, part of my identity. Why should I change it? So many actors do, but that, to me, is amputation, personality suicide. I'm more interested in retaining rather than losing my identity.

**J:** Do you feel rootless, dislocated?

**B:** Quite a lot. I do suffer from that. I often feel I'm a nomad going from oasis to oasis.

**J:** Your break in Ireland came when you appeared on *The Riordans*. As a working-class kid from Walkinstown, how do you feel about what many see as RTE's failure to consistently, some would say, even accurately, represent urban life in TV drama? What do you think of their drama department?

**B:** The drama department doesn't exist. Their entire output for one year consists of a soap opera, *Glenroe*. And that doesn't even accurately capture what's happening in rural areas. All that anger, bitterness and apathy that is now an integral part of Ireland is not reflected in *Glenroe*. But we've got to get away from soap opera, it's safe, it raises no questions. Or if it does, it deals with them in a superficial manner which just washes over people. It doesn't change things.

**J:** Can TV drama, or film, really change things?

**B:** As independent entities, no. But maybe if a network of forms work together changes can come about. But theatre by itself doesn't change things. Who goes to theatre in Dublin? 'Abbey audiences.' I haven't seen anything in the Abbey that is truly exciting over the past five years. Who wants to see *Shadow of a Gunman* again? How relevant is O'Casey's messages to Ireland in 1988? There are no new exciting committed writers producing new work for the Abbey or for Irish television. But it all has to come out of the elitist control within which it is tangled up at the moment. Like the Abbey and the Gate, they are two middle-class theatres. I know people who are afraid to stand in the foyer of the Abbey. That is not how the national theatre should be. It should be theatre for the nation, the people, so that they can come and see plays about issues that concern them. There are also hundreds of young working-class actors who won't get into the Abbey or the Gate so they've nowhere to go but abroad. We were lucky in 1977, those of us who came with the Sheridans. Joe Dowling was the first person who opened up the doors of the Abbey to outsiders, for that I will always respect him. RTE must do the same thing. They've got to get out into the pubs and outside the churches and other meeting places and listen to what really concerns the people of Ireland. We are the poorest country in western Europe, we have a huge level of alcoholism, emigration, abortion, schizophrenia, despair. Television could help people confront those issues and it doesn't. Instead it further weakens people by giving them just escapist crap. RTE has a moral responsibility to reflect Irish society as it is, and not as they or others wish to present it.

**J:** 'Others' being the government? Studies of British cinema in the 1930s have shown that the British government worked very hard to convey through film the lie that 'everybody is content'. Do you think there is this kind of ideology behind film and televisual representations of Ireland? As though it's all just *The Quiet Man* thirty-six years on?

**B:** Exactly. There is that lie, there is that myth. But though most of us do still love the nostalgic and idyllic dimensions to *The Quiet Man*, no one really accepts that crap any more. No one can believe Ireland is as it was thirty-six years ago.

**J:** Does being in the public eye force you to take a stand on public issues which otherwise might not concern you?

**B:** No. I won't talk about things I know nothing about or that I don't care about. And I don't feel I have to say things just because I'm known. But I do feel that if I can say something which will help people identify with me and take hope from that then I should. Ten years ago I was in Dublin devoid of hope – now you and I are sitting here in Beverley Hills doing this interview for *Hot Press*. And that to me is an indication that dreams, ambitions, whatever you want to call them, can be realised. If someone is reading this as I used to read interviews, I want them to say, 'He did it, so can I.' Not necessarily become an actor or live in Hollywood but whatever it is they're reaching for, I want to tell them to go for it. If you and I can talk here today and get that ray of hope across to even one individual, that's what makes this whole exercise worthwhile. If I didn't believe that I wouldn't bother. But I have only realised that recently. I used to do interviews where they'd ask all these mindless tedious questions which left no room for manoeuvre but now I realise that, like here today, we can enter into discussion, debate and hopefully communicate something of worth and importance to somebody out there. I've got the forum, I now feel it's criminal not to use it.

**J:** You were tested for Bond. Many see him as a crass embodiment of British imperialist, sexist and phallic codes. Is that part of why you refused the role?

**B:** Yes. And that character is a carrier of all those codes. That's partly why I wasn't interested. He's a cardboard character so out of date it's a joke. Spouting all that anti-Russian, pro-British crap. He's less offensive and less dangerous that Rambo, but he's cut in the same mould so how could I play that role?

**J:** Nonetheless you do play the 'dark, brooding Byronic hero'. Female stars like Monroe often regard themselves as lumps of meat, processed, packaged and delivered to feed similar, often venial fantasies among their audience. Do you ever feel that way?

**B:** *[laughs loudly]* Well, those venial fantasies were more a consequence of the time when the star system was in operation, when actors and actresses were packaged and sold as gods and goddesses – inaccessible, out of reach. Or if accessible, then accessible only through the realm of fantasy. But Hollywood doesn't work that way any more.

**J:** But on one level, aren't you often packaged, as Monroe was, just to feed sexual fantasies, fill the coffers of the film studio?

**B:** That's probably not as true of me and many of the movies I do as it is of other actors/actresses. I've certainly never thought of myself that way. I know that when the movie goes out there will be certain women who will respond that way but I can't be held responsible for that. I don't feel when I'm being filmed that I'm being used as fantasy fodder but yes, that is all part of the territory.

**J:** How do you respond if you are confronted by a woman obsessed with your film image?

**B:** Well I had a hard time dealing with a few women who came and said, 'You looked lovely in such a movie, I really fell for you.' Okay, it's better than a kick in the bollix but it doesn't mean a thing to me.

**J:** Aren't you tempted to exploit the situation?

**B:** I've never really exploited that. I've gotten blatant invitations from certain women but I've never taken them up on it. Many of these women don't know, or particularly care, who you are, just that you were in a movie. So what's the point? You're being courted for something you're not so how can that be satisfying? I've had one or two experiences where women really made life difficult for me but overall I get a positive, healthy response from women. And I have been involved in a long-term relationship with a woman who gave me tremendous support and gave up her career to go to England with me, and because of my involvement in that relationship I tended not to take advantage of offers made to me on the street or in pubs. That's not to say I haven't been tempted!

**J:** Some feminists would see those women who made life 'difficult' for you as victims of the star-selling process. Many believe that the romantic hero, in particular, is used to reduce women to the role of passive fantasists.

**B:** I agree with that. And that's because most movies are written, produced, directed by and fundamentally aimed at men. And whether one agrees with it, or not, that is the way things are. Women are seen as just satellites in a male universe. That is particularly true in films. Most parts for women are just one-dimensional reflections of the hero's world, and problems. And that won't change until there are more female film directors.

**J:** Do you ever regard yourself as being used in this process of control?

**B:** Yes. But this applies not only to the romantic hero in film, it's been the same in novels since God knows when.

**J:** So if a feminist did a thesis on your films and accused you of allowing yourself to be used in this way, how would you react?

**B:** I'd have to agree. But what am I to do? Give up movies? No. Hang about and hope things will change for the better. But can you see that happening? Look at *Fatal Attraction*, where the female is set up as the embodiment of the AIDS virus.

**J:** Were you attracted to *The Courier* because it confronts the drugs situation in Dublin?

**B:** Partly, yes. And though, as I say, I don't believe films can change things, *The Courier* could help if it is part of a process backed by the government, the Church, teachers, everybody. It will help heighten people's awareness of how things really are.

**J:** However, *The Courier* does not depict Dublin as the government might prefer to have it re-presented, particularly abroad. Mightn't this have a negative effect in terms of getting funding for further projects?

**B:** The government has shown that it doesn't give a fuck about the film industry but, yes, if they change their mind that could be a problem. But if the image they want to sell abroad is of Ireland being a quaint *Finian's Rainbow*-type place, that is fundamentally dishonest. Of course we want to attract visitors but we also must tell the truth about ourselves. If we don't, what happens when the tourists do come here or when they go back home and tell people about how disappointed they were because the reality of the country did not live up to the myth? Maybe as a result of five hundred years of being told we are useless, inferior pigs, we are afraid to reveal truths about ourselves, but confrontation, facing these facts, is the only way. *The Courier* is a contribution towards that.

**J:** You've set up a production company to make movies in Ireland. Eoghan Harris recently said that if we are to create a thriving Irish film industry, we must make action-based, quasi-American movies with none of this European crap of angst-ridden souls sitting in rooms endlessly blabbering to one another.

**B:** If we do then all we'd become is a studio for Hollywood. That action-based escapist crap is not our culture. It's the same thing, movies should reflect what we are not what we think the Americans want. U2 have made music out of Ireland, out of their roots, and made it universal and that's the point.

**J:** They made it because they didn't try to become just another imitation British or American band?

**B:** Exactly. And any film industry must do the same. It must reflect our culture. We are an introspective people, a nation of storytellers and, as Oscar Wilde said, 'a nation of great talkers'. Should we deny that, deny our own nature, just to make a quick buck? Neil Jordan has shown how small a step it is from sitting round a fire telling tales to doing the same thing with a movie camera.

**J:** You once said that in terms of your career there isn't anything you regret having done. Would you say the same of your life?

**B:** I could and should have done certain things differently in my life. Like, instead of beating myself up over things that I really thought were important, I should have given myself an easier time. Maybe it is that Catholic thing of feeling we're put on this earth to suffer, to earn our way into 'heaven'. I don't know. But I really feel I only now am beginning to like myself. I always used to evaluate my worth with the worth of the job I did. That was a dreadful mistake because then if people rejected the job I felt personally devastated. One of the things which really fucked me up during my adolescence, and beyond, was this lack of self-esteem. It doesn't matter how many people say you're great-looking; if you have a weak or negative self-image that message won't get through. That's the way I was. I used to stand in front of the mirror in the morning and say 'You're okay, it's okay, you can do it.' I faked it till I won this self-faith. I acted as if I was confident, acted as if I loved myself until it all became second nature to me.

**J:** If not for a movie role, for what would you like to be remembered?

**B:** Because I succeeded in what I set out to do. And, hopefully, because I improved, however slightly, the quality of the lives of people around me. That's what matters. Being 'famous' is fucking meaningless. I realised that after my father and my sister died. That brought so much into perspective for me. I realised what it was to die because being left behind after the loss of a loved one is a form of death.

**J:** Was that the first time you had to confront a sense of your own mortality?

**B:** Yes. And it made me re-examine my life in a serious and honest way, which I hadn't done before. And it made me begin to value the people around me and my own life so much more. The gift they gave me through their dying was a true sense of the value of life. The experience made me realise that the only thing that matters is to be content and serene within yourself and not full of quilt and fear and envy. I used to look at certain successful actors and really envy them. But I was with one of those guys the other night, he gets three million per movie, and between movies all he does is sits in his Beverly Hills mansion and snorts coke and drinks. If that is success I don't want it. That guy is going to die because of his lifestyle and he knows it but he can't stop. Who would choose a life like that?

**J:** A black romantic like Byron?

**B:** Fuck that black romantic crap. I went through all that sitting over my pint in Nesbitts, thinking that suffering is the only way. But now

I see there is a life beyond all that. But not in wealth or what I used to class as 'success'. I love the business, I love making movies, but if it all was taken away from me tomorrow I really couldn't give a fuck.

**J:** In the end what matters is what you are, irrespective of the job you do?

**B:** Exactly. But only now do I see that. I remember when I was young I had a dream in which I sold my soul to the devil. That idea of selling my soul is still very strong to me. I know that this is a business where it can be sucked out of you really fast but I do not want and I do not intend to ever sell my soul for something as ephemeral as movies.

# 8

# TERESA

# 1988

'If a prostitute brings someone to court, as soon as the word "prostitute" is mentioned she is placed outside whatever justice we can expect from the law,' said Fine Gael TD Monica Barnes in a recent *Hot Press* interview. She was commenting on the violence that is often inflicted on prostitutes. But what does a prostitute do when she discovers what she believes to be proof that the perpetrator of that violence was, himself, in the service of the law? That, claims Teresa, is precisely what happened when a fellow prostitute was recently savagely beaten by a client.

'This guy asked her would she go to his flat,' Teresa claims, 'but when he got her there he punched the head off her. He wanted kinky sex, things we wouldn't do. So, afterwards she went to the police station and they said they'd check it out. They were really into charging him but then later their tune changed. "Well, we didn't really see you marked," they said. So I thought, "Okay, if the guards won't deal with it, we will." We got a few lads, went out and while they were battering your man I ran into the house to get back the money he'd taken on Mary. But as I did, wasn't there a garda uniform in the wardrobe?'

Teresa had suspected that her friends assailant was 'either a guard or a solicitor or a TD ... 'Cause it's the top nobs who are more violent than the lower class. Maybe it's because they are more frustrated. They're too "well bred". To them sex every night is dirty, that's what their mother told them. Or else their women are off getting it somewhere else and their husbands are coming down and taking it out on us.'

Teresa claims that 'lots of girls' she's known have been murdered – 'Like Skinny Melissa from Grange Gorman. She was five minutes late going back and the Legion of Mary people wouldn't let her in. It was a freezing Friday night and she went over to the boiler house to sleep and O'Brien followed her, and when she woke up he was trying it, and she wouldn't let him. When the police found her the next day she had no face, it was completely battered in. She'd been off the town for three years but the solicitor brought all her background up and the papers said, "Ex-prostitute murdered" and that done it. Your man got off.'

Teresa's friends can also die by accident, as happened when a friend ran to avoid being arrested by the Dublin vice squad. 'I saw them taking in a few of the girls so I ran up the canal and shouted, "Josie, get across the bridge, the vice squad is tearing everyone in." So I legged it one way and when I looked back she was gone and I thought, Jaysus, she can move fast for a girl with a bad leg. But the next day I found out she'd fallen into the water. If I'd known that I probably could have gone back and been able to lift her out.'

When Teresa speaks of how she felt about the incident it highlights another, less obvious but still telling form of death which can come to prostitutes: death of sensitivity, death of the senses. 'Well, it wasn't my fault, I didn't push her in,' she says quite matter-of-factly. 'But then working up here you don't be left with any feelings. If mates are murdered we do make a collection but we don't let it bother us. We just get on with our work.'

Does Teresa get any pleasure from sex? Do clients ever consider her need for sexual gratification?

'They don't even try, they'd be wasting their time if they did. Though a lot say, 'Fake it and we'll pay extra, pretend you're enjoying it.' But I got sick the first time. I was pregnant when I first did it for money. Or more so, for somewhere to stay. Because there were so many of us in the house the last one in at night had to sleep on the couch, so I got fed up with that and I decided to get some money and get meself a bed and me own place to stay. I was about fifteen. But I never enjoyed sex. Yet being a prostitute you can't get pleasure off men. Most of them are pathetic, anyway. Especially here, because they come from a religious Irish background.'

Regarding sex with men as 'repulsive', many female prostitutes do turn to their own sex for 'true companionship and maybe sexual pleasure,' claims Teresa, adding that although she herself has been with women, 'the house and my kid are really what I'm into these days.'

However, having children is not an option which is always easily open to prostitutes. 'Years on the pill without a break can cause medical problems,' she says. There also is the problem of AIDS, of course. Teresa claims that 'all the women I know have regular check-ups', but also suggests that working in Dublin's Fitzwilliam Square 'there are five junkies with the antibodies and we know who they are. And we do point them out to the clients. Because the Durex might burst, or anything. And the thing is the junkies don't buy the good ones, the gold packet ones, they use the ones for £2.25 so they can save money for drugs.'

Teresa admits that she has no time for 'the Legion of Mary do-gooders' or 'that God crap', rhetorically asking, 'Where's God if you need a loaf of bread on the table?' However, she herself clearly adopts a high moral tone when asked how she'd react if her young daughter went into prostitution.

'I'd fucking kill her. But I don't think my own daughter would, because I've always told her the bad side of prostitution. She's come up to visit me in the hospital after a client punched me and broke my jaw. And I even get videos that show pimps beating prostitutes and tell her that's happening in Dublin. I also tell her about cases like the pimps in England who make their girlfriends pregnant then beat the baby or lock it away and just show the mother pictures of its bruised face so she will stay on the game.'

Shock tactics such as this are needed to counteract what Teresa regards as the media's tendency to glamorise prostitution, particularly the tabloids. Hearing that I work with teenage students she says, 'I hope you tell young girls the real story, it's so important they should know.' Teresa herself has worked with students and 'definitely agrees' that there is a need for a programme which will bring not just AIDS patients but also junkies and prostitutes to visit Irish schools.

'A nun asked me to talk to young girls and let them ask me questions about the game. As I say, I'm not into religious people but she was genuine. So she asked me to talk with them because the papers do show only the glamorous side. And sure enough this young one says to me, 'But you'se do have loads of money and lovely clothes, I read that in the *Sunday World*.' I said, 'Anything you read in the *Sunday World* you should never believe.' The way that and other papers write about prostitution they may as well be running advertisements for the game. So I make sure to tell my daughter and any young girls about the real facts behind prostitution.'

But does it pay well?

'Like any job you've got to put the hours in if you want it to pay. But the pay doesn't compensate for the risks. Ordinary people go to work and are sure of getting home, we aren't. So, I work just enough to keep me going. But I wouldn't do six nights a week as some do because then I probably would turn to drinking, as many do. Or do speed to keep them awake and to tranquillisers to bring them down. Then they end up doing it six nights a week just to feed the habit and they end up making nothing at all out of it.'

Or, as part of the deal, end up dying if not as junkies then as drunks or because of AIDS? Or murdered?

'Sometimes, yeah, but before that more often the whole game, especially the violence, as I said, kills your feelings and leaves you going around like the walking dead. So, in one way or another it eventually kills us all. Apart, maybe, from those who get out as soon as they cop onto this. If they can get out.'

# 9 DANNY MORRISON

## 1988

It was shortly after 9.30 a.m., Monday, 25 July 1988. In his home in the Markets area of Belfast, Brendan Davison had just finished his breakfast. He heard someone thumping at his front door. Davison, recovering from a shooting last year, cautiously walked into the hallway and shouted, 'Who is it?' A single voice replied: 'It's the Peelers.' Davison leaned close to the door to peer through the spyhole. He saw a blotch of colour which proved the caller was wearing an RUC uniform. He bent down and unlatched the door. A barrage of bullets blasted through his head.

At the same time, in another part of Belfast, Danny Morrison was deciding he had no time for breakfast as he rushed to get ready for the *Hot Press* interview. A short while later as we drove from the Republican Press Centre in the Falls Road to one house from which Morrison could pick up keys to gain access to another 'borrowed house' in which we could talk, he informed me that, as far as he could tell, Davison's attackers were Loyalist assassins disguised as RUC men. 'They put him on the ground and shot him three times last year, but he survived that one,' said Morrison as he forced a smile for a woman who waved as we drove past her.

Before the interview started Morrison, making coffee and toast for the interviewer and interviewee, received a phone call informing him that Davison had died. This was death number 2,667 of the 'current' wave of violence in Northern Ireland. It followed just forty-eight hours after the IRA's killing of the Hanna family in a bombing incident just over the border into the six counties. In the context it was a decidedly muted and depressed Danny Morrison who leaned forward and sat on the edge of his armchair to begin his first *Hot Press* interview.

Danny Morrison describes himself as Publicity Director for Sinn Féin. An IRA person, quoted in *Hot Press* some time ago, described as 'a popular misconception' the claim that Gerry Adams and Danny Morrison also serve on the IRA Army Council.

**Joe Jackson:**

What was the most recent incident which convinced you that what you are doing within the Republican movement is right?

**Danny Morrison:**

Probably just after the grenade went off in Milltown cemetery. There were three families in the Republican plot that day, burying Mairead, Sean and Danny. It was packed so I'd moved out and while I was headed back towards a hearse that grenade went off. Afterwards I went down to the Royal Hospital to find out who'd been injured – I couldn't believe it when the doctor told me three people were dead. Then I learned that a very close friend, Kevin Brady, had been killed, so I went to see his mother and we just put our arms around each other and cried. *[Morrison falters for a moment, obviously moved by the memory]*

**J:** But couldn't that also be seen as a moment where you might have also said, 'Jesus Christ. I've got it all wrong'?

**M:** I moved from being a Republican supporter to being a Republican seventeen years ago and once I made that conversion, though I may have had doubts about tactics or incidents or people's judgements, I have no doubts whatsoever that the nationalist community and the section which became Republicans and those Republicans who became an armed organisation are, ultimately, aiming for social justice – so I've never had that kind of doubt.

**J:** Do you see any contradiction between the Republican view that when an IRA volunteer is killed, as in Gibraltar, it's described as murder yet when a British soldier or RUC man is killed it's 'execution' in the context of 'war'?

**M:** I rarely use the term 'murder' so let me reverse that question. When an IRA volunteer is killed in an unarmed situation, neither the RUC nor the media calls it murder but if the IRA kill armed soldiers it is called murder. So either they are all killed and should be described as such, or they are murdered and should be described as murdered. It's all terminology – but I won't be a hypocrite. If you want to say that the IRA, when they kill British soldiers, the RUC or civilians in the course of an armed struggle, that they are murderers, okay – but let the same term be applied on the other side.

**J:** How do you react when a southern politician says she'd only want to see you interviewed in RTE if the first question were to be 'Who do you plan to kill next?'

**M:** I'd ask her how it feels to bask in freedoms which were paid for by Republicans. How did they get to Leinster House? Why are there no Brits in Ireland? Because young men and young women laid down their lives for the likes of her. But at the same time I can understand ordinary people not being able to empathise with our situation. If I lived in Cork and heard that hundreds of miles away someone had killed eighteen soldiers I'd be horrified. If I hadn't seen a British soldier in sixty years, been harassed or heard of the Emergency Provisions Act or Castlerea, or plastic bullets, if, instead, all I heard on the media was 'another gratuitous killing by the IRA' – then I'd have those kind of reactions.

**J:** Gerry Adams recently suggested that the IRA intends focusing on military targets. Is that how you perceive their plans?

**M:** What Gerry Adams was expressing there was a long-standing desire by the IRA to militarise the war. But in practise that isn't always possible because if you go to South Derry you'll find that the people kicking in doors and trailing people out of cars at checkpoints are the UDR and the RUC. Of course there would be a desire by Republicans to militarise the armed struggle because then its easier to defend, to understand and, seen internationally, it fits into a war of national liberation. Also if the fatality rate of British soldiers rises, then the Troops Out sentiment rises in Britain, and the closer we come to a resolution. The problem is that it is very difficult, if you are an IRA volunteer, to attack these people when they are in full armour or wearing flak jackets or in jeeps or on patrol with fifty of their mates – so the IRA ends up attacking them when they're out of uniform and then of course they're criticised as being 'cowardly'. Which is like saying it's okay to shoot a person dead in the chest but not in the back. It's all propaganda.

**J:** Many would argue that what you've just said is merely propaganda for Sinn Féin and the IRA.

**M:** The people who finally decide if something is just propaganda are the interviewer and readers. Either they say 'That's shit' or 'I don't like what that person is saying but it has the ring of authenticity to it'.

**J:** But people in your position, particularly as Publicity Director of Sinn Féin, usually are less interested in entering into debate than getting across one side of a multi-faceted story.

**M:** I don't see how you can say that about me. I am more inclined towards discussing issues and I have done so in Trinity, UCD Cork and at public meetings up and down the twenty-six counties. If we can't defend our positions we shouldn't hold those positions. This interview is important because I believe that young people are the most important section of society in terms of moving things forward. They did it in the 1960s and 1970s. So I'd like to see young people taking over *An Phoblacht*, standing in the Ard Comhairle, becoming spokespersons. It has happened but not fast or widely enough.

**J:** Some would say Sinn Féin's 1.8 per cent showing in the 1987 elections in the twenty-six counties as an irrefutable barometer of a lack of support for the party – or, perhaps, more specifically, for its support of the armed struggle. Ditto in relation to its relatively weak showing in Northern elections.

**M:** Firstly Sinn Féin is a small organisation in the twenty-six counties. It is competing for support from people who have already got channels through the Workers' Party, Labour and Fianna Fáil. We lack resources. We lack personnel. But I think if Sinn Féin can get its act together, things will improve. It's here I agree totally with what you said earlier about Republicans being unwilling to enter into debate, particularly with people with opposing views. Republicans can be very incestuous, moving about with only their own. But that's no use, it's moving about with the general public we need. We do that more so here – that's why our base in the North is stronger. We must learn to do that in the South.

**J:** But in relation to the IRA's bombing campaign, isn't it possible that the consensus view was captured this morning by my Dublin taxi driver who, on reading about the killing of the Hanna family last Saturday, said 'I'm Irish and them bastards don't represent me'?

**M:** It's possible that is the consensus – and if it is, that's understandable. But then the IRA doesn't claim to be representing the people in the twenty-six counties. Nor does Sinn Féin. The IRA claims to represent the IRA and the oppressed Nationalists who support it. Now some say, 'The IRA declared they were the government in 1916 and still believe it'. I don't think the IRA is the government in Ireland. The IRA don't plant bombs in the name of the people in the twenty-six counties – the IRA plant bombs to bring about a political resolution to the problems of the North. They do not have the arrogance to say, 'We're fighting for the people of Ireland', though it is represented that way.

**J:** What about the view that Gerry Adams's willingness to talk with John Hume is an indication that nearly twenty years of a bombing campaign has, if not failed, then finally yielded far less than you and he and Sinn Féin and the IRA hoped it would?

**M:** No. We talked to the SDLP in 1980. We secretly met them over a period of three months. There is an ongoing dialogue. What we're trying to do is encourage a debate around the question of national self-determination. We're trying to convince the SDLP that their strategy is wrong, that there has to be sovereignty returned to the Irish people. That's the demand we're trying to get the SDLP and the Dublin government to take up.

**J:** To some that may sound less like 'encouraging debate' than attempting to impose your reading of the situation on the SDLP.

**M:** What do you mean 'impose'? 'Impose' has a moral value to it. I haven't got a bucket and spade shovelling views down Seamus Mallon's throat. He is well able to defend himself!

**J:** But 'trying to convince the SDLP that their strategy is wrong' also has a moral value attached to it.

**M:** True. But they're also telling us we're wrong and so the debate continues.

**J:** It's often claimed by Republicans that the IRA bombed the British into abolishing Stormont, et cetera. But what about the counterview that a metaphorical gun placed to the head of the British government, particularly in the person of Margaret Thatcher, merely elongates the process of British involvement?

**M:** If I thought the British government ever had any intention of withdrawing I'd publicly state that, as I would want to see friends' or comrades' lives saved. Surely if they were going, it would be in their interest to tell Republicans, so that they would stop the shooting and maybe trying to kill Mrs Thatcher? But all the evidence now points to the opposite.

**J:** Are you nervous that the Adams-Hume talks could lead to a point where Gerry Adams and a growing number of people within Sinn Féin would be opposed to the armed struggle?

**M:** No. I'm involved in these talks. I know what's going on. Gerry Adams is the most competent and articulate spokesperson Republicans have and I'm totally confident in terms of what's being done, totally supportive. There is a duty on people involved in the struggle to talk. We are open to talking to anyone.

**J:** However Enniskillen, Lisnaskea et cetera all have swelled the tide of political and public protest against the IRA. Even Gerry Adams has publicly said they should 'put their house in order'.

**M:** I'm sure the IRA would agree with what Gerry Adams said. There is a responsibility and a duty on people in armed struggle to ensure that the maximum care is taken. Where that doesn't happen, innocent people die. And bad operations — by that I mean those that are carried out in a way that is hard to understand or subscribe to or support — demoralise the Nationalist community and Republicans and other IRA volunteers. I'm sure a lot of people who are new to the Republican cause, or might be considering coming over to it, are alienated by things like that and that's where we suffer. I don't think our broad base suffers. I think they just feel as I do today, which is deeply depressed at what's happening recently.

**J:** This morning's killing and/or last Saturday's bombing of the Hanna family?

**M:** Billy Davison's killing — that's the ongoing price we pay, but Saturday is even harder to take because they were completely innocent people killed by the IRA. *[Pause]* For a cause that I dearly believe in.

**J:** Gerry Adams recently prefaced comments on the armed struggle with the line: 'If you start off from the basic position that this is morally the right way to do it.' However fewer and fewer people can start off from that position. How can you justify applying the phrase 'morally right' to a campaign which has led to tragedies like Enniskillen, Lisnaskea and last Saturday?

**M:** I would like to know how you quantify this because I am on the ground and I know the feelings and I can assure you that I would not risk my life if people no longer believed in our cause. Besides, Gerry Adams never attempted to justify the killing of innocent civilians. What he's saying in that quote is that the armed struggle itself is morally right.

**J:** But one is the consequence of the other. And my argument isn't that people no longer believe in 'the cause' but that more and more are being alienated by the IRA's methods, methods you support. And my question is: when the armed struggle manifests itself in 'accidents' like the killing of the Hanna family, how can you justify the application of the phrase 'morally right'?

**M:** You're into philosophy now. I accept moral responsibility – I have to – for everything Republicans do. That's from last Saturday, right through to some Republican hitting someone in a bar. I will pay the penalty for that, either in terms of the urge of a Loyalist assassin to kill me, or our struggle losing out either in terms of votes, or somebody closing the door or no longer lending you a car. We pay the price for all those things so, arguably, if you support a cause you have to accept responsibility for all the actions of people within that cause. But then there comes into play a theory of diminished responsibility. For example, a woman in Ballymun who supports us can't be held as responsible for a bad IRA operation as the OC of that area. But we all do suffer in real terms. Personally, as I say, it is deeply depressing.

**J:** In the depths of this depression, say late last Saturday night, wasn't there one moment when you had to stand in front of the mirror and finally question your own reading of what is and what isn't 'morally right'?

**M:** I believe that feeling cannot be predicted. When it hits it hits. And when it does I imagine it would shatter your life and your composure. If, suddenly, it did enter into my conscience that this was no longer morally right, then I would have to change my life, reverse my life completely.

**J:** And you don't feel you've come close to that moment?

**M:** No. But what I do is always entertain questions and doubts in order to strengthen my convictions. Questions like you are asking now. You have to have those or else you are living a delusion.

**J:** As part of your support for the armed struggle, would you agree with the placing of a bomb on that school bus at Lisnaskea? If not, why didn't you publicly condemn it?

**M:** Do I agree with it? No. I think it was a very bad operation.

**J:** Could you define 'bad operation' in this context?

**M:** It wasn't thought out in terms of what would happen if it didn't detonate when the UDR man got on board. It was bad because the children subsequently got on. But I don't publicly condemn the IRA.

**J:** Why?

**M:** I think there are enough people criticising the IRA. And any problem I have with IRA operations I can communicate to Republicans through informal channels.

**J:** You say Republicans 'suffer in real terms' because of tragedies such as occurred to the members of the Hanna family last Saturday, but surely the highest price was paid by the people who died. Someone described the IRA's apologies after such events as like spitting in the faces of the dead and the faces of their remaining relatives.

**M:** That's just a graphic description. In wars these things inevitably happen. Especially in a war waged by a civilian organisation which doesn't have the advantages of Sandhurst or the advantages at the disposal of the enemy. And, again, people who are one-sided in their condemnation shouldn't comment. Or people who are offering no alternative. Or particularly those looking at it all through a telescope. I think more of the criticism of people who have lost loved ones because of the IRA, than I do of what politicians say and I take those criticisms from them and a lot of the time it hurts.

**J:** So you can sympathise if the relatives of the Hanna family say 'Fuck the IRA and their apologies, a lot of good that will do. It won't bring back our loved ones'?

**M:** I can understand them saying that, it probably wouldn't be human if they didn't. But what's the IRA supposed to do? Issue a statement saying 'It was us, so what?' The person who detonated that bomb or pulled the trigger of a rifle aimed at a soldier and the bloody thing ricochets and hits a woman over the street – they have to live with that for the rest of their lives. They're not blasé about it, no matter what image of the IRA the media might like to present. And they are working under great pressure – they too could die at any moment, as many have. The rate of deaths among IRA volunteers is very high. Hundreds of people have laid down their lives; we've been burying people steadily for eighteen years. You must remember that the IRA have no monopoly on killing.

**J:** So would you personally feel responsible for the deaths of many people?

**M:** Of course.

**J:** And you can live with that.

**M:** You have to, otherwise you're a hypocrite. You can't say 'I only support the IRA when they do legitimate military operations' and disassociate yourself from the rest.

**J:** If you pulled the trigger of that rifle which then killed an innocent woman, could you also live with that?

**M:** It's an academic question. My basic position is that you have to accept all that flows from these things. But I also believe that the responsibility does not end with membership of the Republican movement. The people in government are responsible for it and, right down the line, people in the twenty-six counties are responsible for it as well. They can't just walk away from the situation because they too have a responsibility to find peace in Ireland. It's not just as simple as saying 'Fuck the IRA'. We, up here, were ditched in 1921, our people never had jobs, we had poor housing, lots of us had to emigrate and when we tried to change the situation we were batoned into the ground. And when we were trying to get guns to defend ourselves, the British curfewed us and it was only then the IRA started to fight. That's the situation we were left with. I only wish I had been born in Dublin or in Cork and had the luxury of making these judgements from afar, sitting in that chair and saying 'Could you live with it if you pulled the trigger'? And I say this not in an accusatory way. As I said earlier, I understand why such questions are asked. But you can't start judgements from yesterday. You can't walk into this room and say, 'The IRA killed three people last Saturday, defend that', because then you are taking it out of context. You have to say, 'Okay, how did it happen? Where did their grievances come from?' Then you make a judgement in that context.

**J:** Many people would argue that no amount of rationalisation can justify what happened to the Hannas, and that that is a central moral issue.

**M:** If you or anyone wants to set the question 'Is it morally right' you must first ask: 'Is it morally right for the British to be here?' Then you either have a pacifist approach to opposition to the British, which is the only other attitude I sympathise with, or you have an armed approach. And the only pacifist approach I sympathise with is a truly Quaker approach, like a Father Dessie Wilson approach. The Irish government say they are for peace but they might have been responsible for passing on information on the movements of Dan, Mairead and Sean, which led to their execution in Gibraltar. So it is either a dignified pacifist approach or an armed struggle. These are the two options. Sinn Féin supports the armed struggle.

**J:** Could you elaborate on your suggestion that the Irish government might have passed on information which led to the killings in Gibraltar?

**M:** Well, the Southern authorities were able, on the Sunday night, to name the volunteers. Besides they wouldn't deny that under the Hillsborough Treaty they regularly pass on information on the movements of Republicans to the British authorities and to Interpol.

**J:** Some would argue that the southern authorities have a duty to pass on such information in order to save lives.

**M:** It depends on what side they are on. And the point is that they have picked their side and as far as I'm concerned they are not after a resolution of the political conflict in this country. And they are certainly not after a resolution along the lines of their own ideology, established in Fianna Fáil in 1926.

**J:** So you claim that Thatcher and Haughey also have their fingers on the trigger?

**M:** Of course they have. They have far more influence and power than I have. They could sort out the situation much quicker, and instead we're into a painstakingly long, tragic death struggle. Our people are dying and, yes, soldiers are dying and innocent civilians are dying. We're not immune to that. But at the movement our backs are up against the wall. If the IRA were to stop tomorrow the situation for Nationalists would only get worse. The Brits would say, 'Ha, we stuck it out, we screwed them in the end, now we can do what we like.' And the SDLP would lose their negotiating power, which is built on the back of the armed struggle. The equation they work on with the British government is: 'Give us reforms and support drops for Sinn Féin and the IRA.' So they need the IRA. So my point is there is no other alternative. If I thought there was another alternative which would bring justice and peace, then I would jump at it.

J: What about power sharing which, to some, is an option which could bring about 'justice and peace'? What if the majority of Catholics said they wanted to give their allegiance to a northern state, changed through reformation?

M: It's not that simple. There are certain Catholic politicians who have a vested interest in the six counties and in my opinion could live happily as long as the steps to power were open to them. We call them Castle Catholics – as long as they are in their own castles, they don't give a damn about the others. So I would not subscribe to the policies of Catholics who were well off, at the expense of people in West Belfast who are still unemployed and depressed.

J: What if it emerges from Martin Smyth's or even the Hume/Adams position papers that an IRA ceasefire would have to be the first step on the road towards Sinn Féin having any part to play in terms of power sharing – would that be unacceptable to you?

M: Yes, it would be. We're not after a power-sharing assembly in the North. And there's going to be no IRA ceasefire. The only point in the IRA having a ceasefire or a permanent truce is if it is to facilitate British disengagement.

J: So when you say you'd 'jump at' other alternatives which would bring justice and peace, you mean only 'justice and peace' on your terms?

M: There can only be justice and peace if there is a British withdrawal.

J: What is the justification for the IRA's killing of those they describe as 'collaborators', say ordinary workmen involved in building work relating to the security forces?

M: Again, for example, Seamus Woods, an IRA volunteer, was killed in a mortar attack on a barracks two weeks ago. The IRA destroys that barracks and then some guy comes along and says, 'I'll build up the wall to restore the electricity.' You can say that's okay, that's legitimate, they're not operating the thing. So? Is it therefore legitimate to build Belsen? Dachau? Is it? So what the IRA has done is hit the leading contractors. Though it has hit the people who have been doing the shovel work, largely it's the contractors. And it has been effective, it has created headaches for the British army and the RUC.

**J:** If you support a death sentence being passed for a bricklayer who services security forces, could you protest if the British government brings in the death sentence for, say, the people who planted the bomb in Enniskillen?

**M:** Of course I could. And would. Firstly, in any peaceful society I would not support capital punishment, once that society was a democratic society. I don't agree with capital punishment in terms of the government legally killing somebody. There is a completely different set of circumstances, a war situation here. There is a line drawn and people have taken up sides. And in this case, the fact is that from that barracks come gunmen, and probably information which goes to Loyalist paramilitaries, which results in death. Our people are being tortured in those barracks and it's not just Republicans saying this. It's been established by Amnesty International, by the European Committee on Human Rights. So that barracks is an enemy installation. And the people you're talking about may as well be carrying guns and doing the shooting themselves. They're part of the process.

**J:** 'The democratic belief is something I subscribe to,' you said to me earlier. How can you reconcile that claim with the fact that you support a campaign which cancels out the basic democratic right – the right to live?

**M:** Because the British occupation, repression, has thwarted the democratic right of the Irish to determine its own future. And it is aimed at thwarting the democratic expression of the Irish role to determine its own future. Now the Dublin government has not got the will to resolve that on behalf of oppressed Nationalists in the North, so oppressed Nationalists take to force.

**J:** Is that another way of saying, 'If they're fucking around with democratic rights it's okay for us to do it'?

**M:** No. Because what the IRA wants to establish is a democratic Ireland.

**J:** Even if that means subverting democracy to achieve that goal?

**M:** Look, if the people of the twenty-six counties don't want to see a united Ireland they should tell the nationalist people in the North.

**J:** But isn't there a huge contradiction between your claim that the IRA wants to establish 'a democratic Ireland' when it begins firstly, by taking say, from that bricklayer his democratic right to choose the work he wants to do and secondly his right to life?

**M:** But the point is, from the barracks comes a government of oppression. That's like saying hasn't the RUC man got the right to work? His work involves carrying a rifle and shooting people if ordered to. So it becomes ridiculous. The fact is that there is a corrupt system of government in Ireland which isn't of the making of the Irish people. I don't see why the IRA should have a ceasefire. There has to be a cause for it, peace has to be just around the corner. And that's not there at the minute. On the other hand, if it suited the IRA to have a ceasefire, say, even for a weekend, Republicans shouldn't be frightened that that's a sell-out. I do not think armed struggle is written on a holy tablet. I see it as just a tactic which can bring about a desired end.

**J:** What to you would be the ultimate victory?

**M:** Peace for all. To be no longer worried about getting killed. But the worst thing that could happen would be defeat. Because then you pass on to future generations, seeds of despair. And some of those young people will become frustrated and take up guns where the IRA left off. And they'll be in this dreadful cycle again. And worse, the Brits will then have the example of a previous victory for holding out.

**J:** In terms of a political solution, what about those who don't want a united Ireland?

**M:** Tell us. People of the twenty-six counties that don't want the six counties, let us know. If they're telling us to fuck off, telling us they're happy with the state they've got and fuck 1916, then tell us. Because if they don't want us, then I would have to look again at the situation. Because as far as I'm concerned, the struggle is to bring justice and permanent peace and dignity to the Irish nation. And if they think they've got an Irish nation inside the twenty-six counties, they should build a wall and lock us out. But that, to me, would really be falling into the British trap. That would be successful divide and conquer and we would have to accept our lot. Then the people of the twenty-six counties would be forcing us to be British and, though it would be a twist in our soul, if that's how they really feel, then let us know. We need to know.

**J:** But the people of the twenty-six counties wouldn't necessarily be saying 'fuck off' or 'fuck 1916'. What about those who fear that the ultimate victory for Sinn Féin and the IRA would mean overthrowing both states as they now exist?

**M:** Fianna Fáil say they want a united Ireland and if that is true surely that too would mean that the twenty-six-county state as well as the six-county-state would have to be dismantled? They say we're trying to bring down the state but they are threatening to do exactly the same thing!

**J:** Hardly 'exactly'. After all Fianna Fáil would be 'dismantling' the state from an angle which would seem diametrically opposed to that of Sinn Féin.

**M:** Of course they would be, yes.

**J:** And is that then the point at which conflict would resume?

**M:** That's right. And also if they didn't give us the rights that others have: the right to run for elections, the right to be heard on the radio, civil rights everyone deserves. But by 'conflict' I don't mean 'revolution'. But because the others control the media, it usually is seen in those terms as 'posing an armed threat to the twenty-six counties'. But as I say, I believe there is no room for armed struggle in the twenty-six counties. It has to be peaceful, agitational revolution there.

**J:** So would the IRA cease to exist if the British pulled out?

**M:** That's difficult to answer. The Brits could withdraw and leave power in the hands of Loyalists. It would be naïve to hand over all the weapons only to find that in three years you were living again in a repressive regime. There would have to be guarantees that the peace was a permanent one.

**J:** If civil war occurred after the British pull out, would that make the final victory theirs?

**M:** But would there be a civil war after the Brits pull out? The Republicans have no intention of invading Loyalist areas. And the people who continually threaten civil war are Loyalists and they do that just to make the Brits stay. But I think a lot of Loyalists and Unionists, if they were forced into a final acceptance that the party was over, would negotiate. And I believe that if negotiations are handled properly, if the Brits are definitive and if the final resolution rests on an Irish democracy, then the majority of Loyalists will be coaxed over to the point of negotiation and that will remove from the others the will towards civil war. That's why Loyalists now must be given all sorts of assurances. That's why it's up to the twenty-six counties to realise that Ireland must come into the twentieth century.

**J:** What about the fact that the Unionists won't talk to you?

**M:** I've talked to them privately and during elections. But they will talk. We'll all talk eventually. And there will be a resolution in time. I firmly believe that.

**J:** Is it not likely that you and I may have a similar conversation in ten years time, with very little having been resolved?

**M:** I'll be lucky if I'm alive in ten years. I'll either be dead or in jail.

**J:** Do you really expect to be killed within the decade?

**M:** Within the week, maybe. But if so, I've no complaint. I had friends who were shot dead at seventeen, so I've counted every day after that as surplus.

**J:** Do you think there is, on both sides, a rather naïve belief that if you, to quote a politician this week, 'remove the heads of the monster the beast then will die'?

**M:** I disagree with the analogy. I find it contemptuous. The fact is that there is a motion behind the armed struggle in the North based on the injustices of the situation. And the theory that you can just take out a few people was what was behind the shoot-to-kill policy in North Armagh, behind internment. It was the same thing behind Bloody Sunday. 'Open up on civilians and the IRA will come out on the streets and we can wipe them out.' The fact is that next year is the twentieth anniversary of the open deployment of the British army on the streets. And, as the IRA says, it represents twenty years of British military failure.

**J:** But if the theory is invalid, why might the IRA still be intent on killing Thatcher?

**M:** The IRA say she is a target because she has been fundamental to the repression over the last nine years. And so enthusiastic about it that they would consider the killing of her as a major blow against British presence in Ireland.

**J:** What about those religious zealots who might say that you deserve to 'die by the sword'?

**M:** That's okay by me. I'm not going to be a hypocrite.

**J:** But you describe yourself as a Catholic. What kind of Catholic is it that supports an armed struggle which involves the taking of life?

**M:** I'd describe myself as a poor Catholic. *[laughs]* I can only speak from the background and the experience I know. What I am doing I can square up to my conscience. Whether or not it meets the values of other people is quite another thing.

**J:** Do you believe in God as defined within Catholic ideology?

**M:** Yes. And I believe that at the end of the day we all have to stand before a God and be judged for what we did.

**J:** Do you also believe that, in the end, you will be able to square up your beliefs and actions against your conscience and finally face that God?

**M:** Yes. But then to say yes is to be conceited. All I can say is I hope so.

# 10 KEN MAGINNIS 1988

At one point during this interview Ken Maginnis quickly shifted to the edge of the sofa in his living room and locked part of his attention on a red Fiat which had paused briefly before passing by his window. 'Part of his attention' because at the same time he didn't miss even one microbeat of the rhythm of the sentence he was speaking. I asked if such reactions were now totally instinctual. 'Very much so,' he replied, 'Second nature by now, but although I may have appeared to react casually to what I saw, in truth I felt they were too obvious to be terrorists.'

**Joe Jackson:**

Does the thought of losing your life and the pain that then would cause your family ever make you say to yourself, 'I will talk to anyone even Gerry Adams and Danny Morrison – just to avoid that, to find a solution for all this in 1988?

**Ken Maginnis:**

No. Because the pain that I would cause my family if I compromise what I believe in would be a hell of a lot greater. My family understands that. I can't compromise by making a pact with the devil. You can't sell out on what you believe.

**J:** So, to you, is even entering into dialogue with these people 'selling out'?

**M:** Yes. If you treat with the devil you've already sold out irrespective of whether you think you've won or lost at the end of the day. You don't descend to the level of dealing with terrorists.

**J:** So you think that John Hume has sold out?

**M:** I think that John Hume has sold out. I am absolutely convinced that John Hume, who has a tremendous international persona and a great feel for international politics, has totally misjudged it at a parish pump level. John Hume will never have the support of his party to participate in talks with Sinn Féin as he did on this occasion. And the lesson Unionists have again learned from this episode is that you cannot sit down and talk on an equal level with someone who has a gun stuck down his trousers.

**J:** But mightn't John Hume be trying to serve a much larger community than those who would benefit if he focused only on the parish pump politics? Mightn't he believe this is exactly what he is doing by entering into dialogue with Sinn Féin?

**M:** No. You cannot talk with people on the basis that they are principled when you know they are totally unprincipled. I do have a great deal of faith in dialogue but I'm not committed to dialogue where the outcome must inevitably be that I concede or face violence. That's what terrorism is. You either concede to the terrorists or you face the violence of the terrorist. By eschewing that I'm not opposing dialogue.

**J:** How do you account for the fact that Sinn Féin has strong support in your own constituency?

**M:** Sinn Féin has always had strong support here. We're a fifty/fifty community with the majority living in peace with one another. I can't understand why thirty thousand people voted for Owen Carron the first time I fought him, I'm told they voted because of the hunger strike.

**J:** Mightn't they also have voted because they believed in his policies, his politics and his cause?

**M:** Many Catholics have told me it had to do with the hunger strike. But that is something you will not get any Unionist to understand. He can't understand that psyche.

**J:** Is that why any talks are inevitably doomed to failure?

**M:** Talks would be doomed to failure anyway if we were talking about an acceptance of Sinn Féin values.

**J:** But surely their potential is further crippled by you and fellow Unionists admitting that you don't even understand the psyche of the so-called 'average person' in your own constituency who votes for Sinn Féin?

**M:** Yes, but they voted that way when they weren't given an alternative. And at the next election I will find it very hard to understand them if, after Enniskillen, they still want to give their support to Sinn Féin.

**J:** So what is your response to Danny Morrison saying recently that Loyalists and Unionists, if forced into a final acceptance that the party was over, would negotiate?

**M:** I would be foolish to say that a community could not be defeated but I don't see a defeat of a million Unionists. And certainly as far as negotiation is concerned, the answer is no. As for us talking with Morrison, let him forget it. He has not, in terms of what this country needs, anything to offer. Only despair. And if we could take steps to end the violence and had a degree of normality tomorrow it would be proved that Morrison has nothing to offer to the community. I've seen four Sinn Féin councillors on my council for the last four years with not one single word to say. They are four dummies sitting in the council chamber. Three total dummies and one fellow who has nothing to say except roar obscenities.

**J:** Are you suggesting that this is representative of the Sinn Féin approach to politics?

**M:** With the exception of one or two, Corrigan and Adams, yes. But I wouldn't put Morrison in that category. He hasn't even justified his own argument to his own people. He has nothing to offer.

**J:** And if he asked you what have you to offer to Sinn Féin or the people they represent?

**M:** In the terms they seek, nothing. But in terms of a quality of life in Northern Ireland, exactly the same as I have to offer to my own people. It's not just a matter of sharing, it's a matter of dominance. One community wondering whether it can dominate another.

**J:** But surely, as I said earlier, that's always been the case in Northern Ireland, in the form of a Protestant ruling class involved in a systematic process of oppression to maintain that position? One community attempting to, and effectively, dominating another?

**M:** Yes. *[pause]* I don't accept that is the case. Or was. There were inequities, mainly, in terms of housing. But otherwise I don't believe there was any desire to dominate. The greatest problem with the

Nationalists is that they wanted to be left alone. They didn't want to participate.

**J:** And there were also, maybe more often, those areas in terms of employment, education, the civil service, the police force, politics where they simply weren't allowed to participate. Surely it is far from as clearly-defined a line, as you have persistently suggested throughout this interview. And most Unionists still seem unwilling even to concede to their sins in the past.

**M:** Maybe it's not. But I am arguing from the point that too often Unionists appear to be the total aggressors, to have had a jack-boot approach to the Catholic community, and that this pervaded the whole Protestant psyche. That never was the case, though it is convenient for some to present it as though it was.

**J:** What about those who might see your intransigent position, in terms of talks, and even this discussion today, as the last desperate bid of a drowning man and a drowning social order?

**M:** No. There is an underlying desire among Unionists for talk but because they do not have a powerful card to play, a violence card, no one is giving them a forum wherein they can talk.

**J:** But among Unionists, isn't there also the fear that if you enter into talks you will find there is no way you can sustain the old order and that you will then be forced to surrender?

**M:** The 'Old Order', whatever that might be, is gone and is so far dismantled that we've now got to turn around to our government in Westminster and say, 'Now, the Union, which you dismantled on the fifteenth of November 1985, can we now put something else in its place?'

**J:** But where is the area for compromise? What will Unionists concede?

**M:** When two governments implement a commitment to end terrorism and to give the people of this country a chance to live at peace, then the people of this part of the United Kingdom will be obliged to sit around the table and work out how we're going to live at peace. The Anglo-Irish Agreement is not an indication of that form of commitment. And it flounders not because Unionists are suspicious but because it was ambiguous. Article One was where the Irish Government 'for the first time' – I quote them – 'recognised the legitimacy of the Unionist position'. But it doesn't define what the status quo is. So it's more than on empty gesture it is a callous deceit. So we don't even have to go beyond article one to see that the agreement epitomises everything we fear. We've endeavoured to make it much easier for Charlie Haughey in terms of the agreement. We've said to our own government, 'Give us a commitment to an alternative agreement', and our government has not responded to that. That is a reasonable request. In many ways when we initially said that the Agreement must go, we might have appeared to be unreasonable, but now we're more reasonable, saying, 'You've got an agreement, we've lost out on it, it's not acceptable, so negotiate a new one and we'll sit down around a table with you.' But the two governments are unable to give us that commitment. So who's crippling potential talks from even beginning? Is it the Unionists or the two governments? Peace through political progress, I sincerely hope is on the agenda. However, political progress is impossible where around the mythical table there are still men who hold guns to our head. Those people have got to be removed. The guns cannot be part of the scenario.

# 11 CHRIS DE BURGH
## 1988

'You can't fuck with success,' said Chris de Burgh as we wrapped up this interview. 'If there are those who, on seeing my picture on the cover of *Hot Press*, say, "Pass the sick bag", I really couldn't care less. And it's not the old I'm-all-right-Jack syndrome – it's just that I'm thoroughly aware that a man who likes Beethoven may not like Bach. And that doesn't mean Bach is a pile of shit.' De Burgh's subdued but still palpable anger certainly gave validation to his comment after the interview when, laughingly, this 'Mr Nice Guy of Pop' said, 'Perhaps you've spotted the fact that at forty I now am beginning to show my teeth...'

Reacting to the news of last year's bombing in Enniskillen, Chris de Burgh wrote a lyric in which the narrator sings of those who, at the time were feeling 'ashamed of being Irish'. How would he respond to the group of adults in my creative writing class in Finglas, Co. Dublin, who found 'totally offensive' the suggestion that Irish people should feel collective shame and collectively apologise to the world for being Irish?

'The lyric says, "Let them hear the voice of the millions/who said on that day/I am ashamed to be Irish" and I firmly believe a lot of people were ashamed. You have to get out of the country to sense it. I was in England and West Germany soon after and people were asking, "What kind of animals are doing this?" '

But can he understand why, for example, those adults in Finglas might find offensive the central sentiment expressed in the song, particularly as it was written by a person who himself is Argentinian, not Irish?

'Bugger them,' says de Burgh angrily. 'Sorry about their sensibilities. I did what I wanted and I also spoke on behalf of a lot of people. I didn't put myself up as a spokesman. I just felt sure that by performing a tune like that it might bring comfort to the bereaved. The fact that it offended some, I'm sorry about. But let's not forget that eleven people were killed. Do I have to be Irish to comment on that? Now you've just read out the comments of people in Finglas and I find that personally offensive. They've missed the point. If that's how they construe my motives for doing the song, they should look a little harder into their own feelings about what happened that day in Enniskillen. I think that what's gotten up people's noses about me saying "ashamed to be Irish", whether they think I'm Irish or not, is possibly I hit them on a raw nerve. A lot of people are offended by the U2 song, "Sunday Bloody Sunday" – those who take the opposing view. And that's the point: when you talk about politics and especially politics in Northern Ireland you are bound to run into opposing viewpoints very quickly.

'But "Sunday Bloody Sunday" is a powerful song and I personally would agree with those sentiments but political songs are always, by their nature, contentious and it's never been an intention of mine to create contention in music.'

# 12 BEN BRISCOE, LORD MAYOR OF DUBLIN

## 1988

There was no handshake as Lord Mayor Ben Briscoe welcomed me into his office in Dublin's Mansion House. But then 'welcome' is hardly the appropriate word. His greeting was: 'I didn't really, and don't really, want to do this interview.' He elaborated as we sat beside his desk. 'What happened was that this nice person approached me and said she wanted to interview me for *Hot Press* – then when I found that was not to be the case I felt I'd been –' The statement remained unfinished because, at that moment, we were interrupted by a gentleman asking if we'd like some coffee.

Looking at my watch I noted that it was 10.04 a.m. so I asked how much time, exactly, had been allotted for our interview. Mr Briscoe responded, 'I've to be somewhere at 10.40.' I replied: 'My understanding was that we would have a minimum of an hour.' He immediately held up to my face a typed timetable for the day and said, 'See that? I've got to be there by 11 a.m. So to do that I'd rather leave by 10.40.'

It was quite obvious there was no further time for mere chit-chat. Before, or during, the interview.

**Joe Jackson:**

One quote I read about you suggested that your 'political approach seems fashioned by insecurity'. Is it?

**Ben Briscoe:**

No.

**J:** No insecurity in your being?

**B:** No. I'm very much a constituency man. I know how the people feel about me. They know I care about them.

**J:** As Lord Mayor you don't have much political clout or money to spend on projects. What, in real terms, is the most you can do in relation to the problems say of the inner city?

**B:** The beauty of the mayor is that it is non-political. As Lord Mayor of Dublin I represent all the people of Dublin whether they are Fine Gael, Workers' Party, Progressive Democrats, non-party. Whatever they are I represent them. I'm in a position of being first citizen and as such I believe one should behave in such a manner as will reflect credit on one's city. You can do that without being pompous. I'm not a pompous person. But no, there is no money to spend on projects. But what you can do is direct monies that are given for charities to different organisations.

**J:** In relation to those areas into which you might direct money did you, during the Gay Sweatshop controversy, 'publicly voice your dislike of homosexuals', as was reported at the time?

**B:** No. I have no recollection of having done that at all.

**J:** Did you object to Corporation funds being given to the Project Arts Centre because they were staging such a production?

**B:** No, I never specifically stated – people will take the thing up. That does not mean I approve *[pause]* of, necessarily, plays that are put on to shock people or to attract people in by exhibitionism of sorts.

**J:** Do you mean specifically gay plays?

**B:** No. I'm not talking specifically.

**J:** If, in their attempt to rebuild the Hirschfeld Centre, the gay community approached the corporation or the Lord Mayor for funds, would you have any moral objections?

**B:** We're not in the business of financing any community stuff of that sort. That's like saying, would you believe that you should finance any cult of some other sort – whether it's a 'cult' or not is for other people to say. I know you are trying to trap me into attacking the gay community.

**J:** I don't want you to make an attack on the gay community, on the contrary. Why not use the opportunity to reassure those readers who may have thought, judging from newspaper reports, that you are prejudiced against the gay community? If you want to attack that is your choice.

**B:** I'm saying to you that my own view has always been known in relation to those things. These are just issues which are sometimes raised by other people on which I've made no comment at all. It's as simple as that. Next question, as they say.

**J:** So you're not willing to say whether you –

**B:** *[interrupts]* I don't think that money is entitled to be voted –

**J:** *[finishes question, which is ignored]* – are or are not prejudiced against gays?

**B:** *[continues]* for something whether it is a moral or an immoral organisation. That has nothing to do with public funding. I think even the suggestion that people who profess to be homosexual and are quite proud of the fact, and believe that therefore the state or state agencies, through Dublin Corporation or any county council, should build them a centre where they can... I don't understand the logic.

**J:** Where they can 'what'?

**B:** Gather, get together, have their own clubhouse. They're not the scouts, they're not the girl guides, y'know. *[laughs]* I think the question just doesn't arise.

**J:** So you can't reassure readers who might feel you are prejudiced against gays, that in fact you are not?

**B:** If they can interpret any prejudice against them in my saying that public funding should not go toward building clubs for people to gather who profess to be homosexual – well... *[sentence fades]*

**J:** Some may read implications of such prejudices in 'They're not the scouts or the girl guides'.

**B:** I'm talking about youth organisations. For example I have a letter on my desk from a unit of the Order of Malta whose equipment was vandalised when their premises was broken into. Now I think something like that is entitled to a grant from the Corporation because these people are helping people who are handicapped. They are doing something in the community for others, not for themselves. They're serving their fellow human beings. I use that as an example of where public funding should be allocated.

**J:** How would you respond if your son told you he was homosexual?

**B:** *[incredulously]* Say that again.

**J:** How would you respond if Andrew told you he was homosexual?

**B:** *[answers slowly, seethingly]* I have no comment to make about my family whatsoever. This is an interview between you and me. I'm not bringing my family into this. I have no other comment to make, good, bad or indifferent, on homosexuality. On to the next question, if you like.

**J:** In relation to the collision between yourself and Mr Haughey some years ago which now –

**B:** *[interrupts]* I'm not going into that either. I've gone into that *ad infinitum*. That's history, it's past. Our relationship now is excellent.

**J:** But readers might be interested to know how the relationship was repaired or can now be 'excellent' after you publicly likened Mr Haughey's leadership to a 'fascist dictatorship'?

**B:** I didn't.

**J:** Then don't you think it's best such reports should be cleared up?

**B:** I'm just telling you that I never said that.

**J:** How then do you explain an *Irish Times* report of 1983 which claimed you said that one of Mr Haughey's statements at the time 'smacked of dictatorship and an attempt to undermine democracy'?

**B:** I did say – look, we're going back into an era which is gone. It's finished, it's history. I have no comment to make on that. Next question.

**J:** This will leave a huge gap in our interview.

**B:** It can leave as big a gap as you like in the interview. I've no comment. I'm not going over all that ground again. I'm sick and tired of answering questions. People say, 'Well, these things have to be cleared up.' I've answered them again and again. As far as I'm concerned when the decision of the party was made on that motion *[in 1983 Ben Briscoe tabled the motion that Fianna Fáil should request the resignation of Charles Haughey]* that was the end of it. Those allegations that I called him those names are totally untrue.

**J:** So if they are on file as being said, I think, in the Dáil –

**B:** *[interrupts]* They weren't said in the Dáil – besides, which article in *The Irish Times* are you referring to?

**J:** A number of *The Irish Times* reports written in 1983.

**B:** Who wrote them?

**J:** Well, I'm afraid I can't quite recall who *The Irish Times* reporters would have been at the time – those who may have covered events in the Dail. But the reports can be verified.

**B:** *[smirking]* Well, those things weren't said in the Dáil, the debate wasn't in the Dáil.

**J:** Well, wherever it was is not as important as what was said.

**B:** *The Irish Times* wasn't present.

**J:** The fact is that these quotes are on record, so would you now say that they are inaccurate or a lie?

**B:** What quote in particular?

**J:** Your suggestion that if you examine line-for-line a statement made by Mr Haughey you could, I think it said, 'only come to the conclusion that Mr Haughey no longer recognises the right of the Parliamentary party which elected him to remove him from office'.

**B:** That's right. That is an – that is from an interview. But I'm not going back over those interviews from years ago. If that's the way this interview is going to take place I suggest you cancel it.

**J:** Basically what we are trying to do is give to readers a sense of the man behind his role as Lord Mayor. To do that I must go into your history, as a politician, as a human being.

**B:** *[interrupts]* I really think we'll have to end the interview. I'm sorry, Joe, but you're only interested in controversy. I'm not getting into anything controversial. I was reluctant in the first place to talk to your paper because I've had the feeling, and it's been borne out by the manner of the questions, that you are only interested in controversy.

**J:** Actually I felt that as certain controversies you've been involved in have very much fed into the public perception of Ben Briscoe, they had to be addressed.

**B:** *[barely restraining his rage]* I'm going to answer you very straight. The public perception of this man in this office is that in every election since 1981 I have gotten in on the first count in excess of the quota. That is the public perception of this man. Thank you very much. And, as far as I'm concerned, that ends the interview.

**J:** I'll have to put all this in print.

**B:** You can.

**J:** If you change your mind you can contact us.

**B:** I won't change my mind.

**J:** Well, I'm sorry you responded in such a manner to what I see as just questions about issues you've been most open about in the past.

*[Mr Briscoe stands silently by his desk until the tape recorder is turned off]*

I looked at my watch again. It was 10.20 a.m. There was no handshake as the Lord Mayor walked me to the door of Dublin's Mansion House and said good day.

# 13    SOUND BITES
## 1988

'What really annoyed me about what Ben Briscoe said about gays is that groups like the Order of Malta help people whereas all we do is help ourselves. The youth group, for instance, is to help whoever needs us, whether they are gay or not. Some may phone and just want to talk because they are worried about their sexuality. Others may come here, stay a few Sundays then decide they're not gay at all. And, in the Hirschfield Centre, there was a Parent Enquiry which helped parents come to terms with gay son or lesbian daughter. Surely that's helping the community? Anyway, the gay community is part of the community at large, and Briscoe did say that as Lord Mayor, he was supposed to be representing everyone in Dublin, didn't he? He also said we shouldn't be getting grants, but we get no grants.'

'Clubs for the blind are for those who are blind, same with clubs for people who have cancer. Why does the Lord Mayor single us out? Why doesn't he like us? Are we really such a threat that he's afraid of us and all he can do is put us down? Maybe if he came to see us and talked to us and then went off and afterwards said that, I'd accept it, but he doesn't even know who we are.'

'Yet the prejudices you see in Ben Briscoe's comments are, after all, the prejudices we grow up with all our lives. That gays are just molesters, old men outside toilets. People like that make you believe that is the way things are. And it's only when you come to a group like this that you realise how much different the reality is. But then Fianna Fáil do seem to be very right wing on this issue. They've made no comment on it at all, whereas Young Fine Gael do have a policy of decriminalising homosexuality and Labour Youth do have a policy. But it's really hard to believe in party politics when you know that most of them are going to discriminate against you just because you're gay. Yet the worst part about people making comments like that is them saying or suggesting we shouldn't be proud of our homosexuality. Why shouldn't we? We have nothing to be ashamed of. I was brought up with the same morals as my heterosexual brothers and sisters. My morals are no lower, no less strict, than theirs. But I'm not gong to let comments like that, by him or anyone, make me feel ashamed of that. None of us here today has anything to be ashamed of. Nor has anyone who is gay.'

*(Members of a Young Dublin Gay and Lesbian Group, who used false names and didn't want the location of their Sunday meetings to be revealed, out of fear of 'gay-bashing')*

'I was pleased to hear young gay men and lesbian women speak in the last issue of *Hot Press* about how 'easily' some now seem able to publicly declare their homosexuality, but things were vastly different in my youth. Young people have all this information coming in through television and magazines and newspapers, but we never had that. In my day anything to do with sexuality was dark and shameful and sinful, especially if it had anything to do with homosexuality. Such was the power of the Church. The irony is that I now know at least sixteen priests who are out gay on the scene with their boyfriends or living quietly with someone, mostly in the Dublin area. Yet let's not forget that there was a time when even a liberal thinker such as Dr Noel Browne treated homosexuality as a 'very serious mental ailment'. And the World Health Organisation still considers it a mental ailment. Many gentlemen I know, in the evening of their lives, have been 'treated' in an attempt to 'cure' them of their homosexuality. Often where they had a friendship and someone died or left, they'd crack up, like any other person. But then in the older days you'd end up in one of the hospitals, they were considered more of a mental case because the break-up had been with a person of their own sex. And so, if they weren't classified as mentally unstable or schizophrenic, they were given aversion therapy. It consists of being shown pictures or slides of 'naughty' men in action, and every time this arouses your pulse they give you an electric shock. It's supposed to cause nausea and thus effect a 'cure'. It's still used. Back then most of it was apparently done up North: people were shipped up there for treatment, and apparently it is only rarely used down here. And when it is, it's the private hospitals and in a very, very hush-hush manner, understandably. I know many people in the higher echelons of society – civil-service, the law – who lived long happy lives with companions, and they never needed therapy. And in certain cases some were even magistrates, well aware that homosexuality was illegal, so there was even more pressure on them to keep it underwraps. But there was a form of freemasonry among these people. They took care of their own. I'm just glad I never had to depend on anyone else to help me through the years.'

*('Tom', an older man and his perspective on homosexuality in Ireland)*

'This is very much part of Irish life, violence in the home. A lot of it stems from alcohol abuse, and from the way that men are cossetted and spoiled by their mothers, and then feel they can bully a wife and children and get whatever they want. I think that such men are, in many cases, jealous of the children or of the mother's relationship with the children, because the children came on the scene and spoiled the cosy twosome it may have been. In some cases this can also lead to child battering. And, again, this is kept under covers. Sometimes the only ones who know abut it are the children, the partners, and the neighbours who live on each side of the house. And I am not just talking about working-class families. Wife-bashing and child abuse happen just as much in middle-class and upper-class families, but there's even more of a cover-up when it happens in those areas. But that form of emotional immaturity is common among men in all classes.'

*(Mary Mooney, politician)*

'There is class distinction in Ireland, though it's not as bad as it was when I was young. In the convent school I was the only from Charlemont Street, and that was kept a secret from everyone. Then later I'd put people on pedestals and be afraid to talk to them. And I'm not talking about God or the Pope! I mean musicians like Donal Lunny. I'd turn and walk away rather than talk with them, I felt so inferior. And that feeling goes back to like when I was in the choir ... after I'd get off the bus I'd be like Judas denying where I live, walking past the house until that bus went up over the bridge. But nowadays, I realise if you're not true to yourself, you're hardly likely to be true to people you're meeting. Now I am very proud of the fact that I came from Charlemont Street.'

*(Mary Black, singer)*

# 14 ANTHONY CLARE
## 1989

Anthony Clare has a bit of a problem. On the one hand he is a man who can be, by his own admission, 'verbally murderous', yet on the other he is a trained psychiatrist who cannot be seen to attack – or, it would seem, even to comment on public figures in any way that could be construed by his profession as an abuse of his role as psychiatrist. 'The one occasion they really gave me a bad time was when I said, in a jocose manner, that Margaret Thatcher was obsessional,' he says. And so, on certain subjects, he tends to veto his words. At least when he remembers to. But then that is another problem for Anthony Clare. He loves to talk. And when he forgets to set in high gear his own screening system or hits his stride on non-taboo subjects the words gush forth as frantically as a priest might flick for the first time through the pages of Alex Comfort's book *The Joy of Sex*. But no, even at the peak of the rushing rapids he will not release even one retaliatory comment about his recent savaging at the hands of Messrs. Eamon Dunphy and Colm Tobin in the *Sunday Independent*. Instead he jokes about it. 'I really liked the cartoons, I wonder could I get copies for my office?'

But the joke also reveals him to be a dedicated professional who has his priorities in order. Television shows such as *Irish In Mind* are very much just a 'hobby' to him. Psychiatry is his vocation. This fact is brought into sharp focus by his final comments on critical reaction to his TV series. 'The thought that even one of my patients killed herself and that others might, is far more real, more relevant to me than thinking about how some critics may be attacking the TV show.'

**Joe Jackson:**

You said that many famous people you interview are 'cannibals'. 'They live off other people', you suggested, be it their workmates or family. Is that how it is in your life?

**Anthony Clare:**

If I divide society into 'Christians' and 'cannibals', I think it is, yes. It's a crude image but some people do need other people to support them and others do the supporting. I am quite cannibalistic in that sense – not so much with my children as with my wife. She has played a remarkably supportive role, I wouldn't be able to do a lot of what I do without her. And I am conscious that if it gets out of balance one could devour her life. Fortunately she also has a clear view of this happening and we make great efforts to avoid it. And I did, in fact, once say to the producer of *In The Psychiatrist's Chair* that we should be talking to those in the background whose lives may be being cannibalised.

J: To Valerie Grove seven children indicated you might be 'addicted to fatherhood'. It also could suggest that you are highly-sexed. Are you?

C: *[laughs]* That's like the classic 'beating your wife' question! Put that way there is only one possible answer: highly-sexed.

J: Any problems coming to terms with that?

C: *[laughing]* No problems.

J: Psychiatrists are in the business of normalising what otherwise might be taboo subjects. To take an extreme example, does that mean they or you would also have 'no problems' dealing with feelings of being sexually attracted to your own daughters or sons?

C: *[pause]* It is exceedingly difficult to discuss parent/child physical relationships. There's a movie coming out of Hollywood, *The Good Mother*, which discusses the issue of what is reasonable sexual enquiry from a child to an adult. Is it reasonable sexual behaviour to have a child in bed with you when you've got no clothes on? Or to make love when you think the child is asleep? My wife and I watched this movie – I'd been asked to comment on it – and we realised we never discuss these things with our friends. Even eighty years after Freud allegedly freed us to talk about this, it still is a taboo subject. We're educating our children to look at sexual differences, to ask about your penis or vagina. But what if a child wants to touch it? What are the rules? Supposing the child, as in the movie, goes and tells that his stepfather let him touch his penis. Should all hell break loose? Where does ordinary sexual enquiry end and abuse begin? You are quite right to suggest that psychiatrists should have a better idea of where the boundaries are, but I don't know whether they do or not because I haven't discussed this with fellow psychiatrists either. Hopefully people will look at this movie and talk about the issue, and that will help somewhat.

J: You seem reluctant, in most cases, to talk about sexuality – here or during *In The Psychiatrist's Chair*.

C: I sometimes discuss it when it is appropriate. When Tibbett brought up the subject of his homosexuality it was appropriate because that was part of his general tendency to be an outsider. But it would have to be of crucial relevance to ask people to enlarge upon such things in a public interview. In a clinic I may but not during public interviews. It would be pointless, for example, to ask a man or woman what kind of sexual activity they engage in. It's no concern of mine.

J: And yet as a descendent of Freud, aren't you supposed to be dedicated to making taboo subjects non-taboo, as you suggest *The Good Mother* may do in relation to children's sexuality?

C: In fairness to Freud, he also realised that every culture needs taboo. A society with no taboos is a jungle. It means no trust, no shame, no privacy, no relationships, nothing. Everything is out in the open. Yes, Freud was keen to undo the bourgeois hypocrisy of Victorian Europe, but I don't think he would have defended the uninhibited, puerile permissiveness which occurred in small pockets of the United States in the 1960s. What we called permissiveness in Britain and in Ireland wasn't really that – it was just the long overdue undoing of hypocrisy and constraints. I think Freud would have approved of that but not gone all the way.

J: In relation to undoing sexual hypocrisy and constraints, would you advocate exploration of the full range of pleasures described by Dr Alex Comfort in the book *The Joy of Sex [at the time of the interview, banned by the Irish censor]*?

C: Bearing in mind that sexuality has some kind of moral context to it, I certainly would agree that adult sexuality is for adults and that what people get up to in their own lives is very much up to them, governed by their own moral and psychological view of themselves.

J: But the Irish state, influenced no doubt by the Church, has taken that freedom of choice out of the hands of its citizens in this specific case by banning *The Joy of Sex*.

C: Yes, and that is outrageous. Ridiculous. And because if anyone wants it they can cross the border or buy it in England. But the ban is also sad, it betokens still an immature attitude to pleasure and an awesome fear of sexuality.

J: Heavily influenced by the Church?

C: Yes, and I think the Church, if it wants to remain a significant force in Irish life, must come to terms with the fact that these kinds of preoccupations are going to damage it. And Irish society in general has got to accept that the link between sexuality and procreation is not now and never again will be as it was in the pre-Pill era. Therefore we have to look afresh at what sexuality is about and what sex is for. This is where the Church could be useful instead of reactionary, by looking at sex as another way in which people can express their personalities, build trusting relationships and make sense of their lives in a world otherwise occupied with material things like money and possessions. Ultimately the expression of sexuality is good and one should facilitate it and further educate a generation who will not be fearful of sexuality and who will not see it as something you engage in 'as a necessary evil'. That's the idea people had in the 1940s and 1950s in Ireland. Apart from its role in procreation there was just the hydraulic model of sex, you had to let off steam 'unfortunately'. But celibacy and virginity and the nonsexual life were the real goals and people were afraid of their sexuality and repressed it. And that is such a nature-hating, life-negating, guilt-enhancing view of sexuality that, bearing in mind Aids, illegitimacy, one-parent families et cetera, I still am prepared to take the risks of the opposite. I think we will go through a period of permissive bonanza till we reach maturity. That, rather than go back and become the frightened little children in our bedrooms being told what to do by a combination of Church and State.

J: But where do you draw the line between a healthy, necessary exploration of sexuality and acts of 'perversion' such as beatings?

C: Alex Comfort is insistent throughout his book that the defining element in sex is mutuality, two people mutually agreeing to some activity, as opposed to exploitation. That to me is the basis for adult sexuality. I have an absolute revulsion against exploitation in the name of sexuality. That's why so many of us feel bitter about past sexual mores in Ireland. Because within those restrictive and hypocritical positions was a great deal of sexual exploitation, particularly of women by men. Those days pre-television, 'before sex was invented', were not a halcyon time, as is sometimes presented.

J: Your scepticism about the Church is matched by the Church's long-standing, and, perhaps, understandable antipathy towards psychiatry. Or, more specifically, psychoanalysis. But do you ever feel that when you claim you can differentiate between valid and invalid interpretations of such nebulous things as dreams, longings, fantasies that you are, in effect, playing God?

C: Yes, I do. And psychiatry must stand accused of extending its area of expertise considerably. You've picked the area I agree with, such as dreams and fantasies.

J: But surely the real danger is that most of your patients don't realise that your theoretical formulations are not scientific data which can be weighed and balanced and monitored, for example, by a independent body.

C: Yes and no. There is an extraordinary split view of psychiatry. People are sceptical, there is the credulity you describe. But somewhere between these two views psychiatry has a small body of painstakingly developed expertise. But it is small and constantly being modified. The rest is just speculation.

J: As in the view of homosexuality. It's claimed that here in St Patrick's aversion therapy is still given to homosexuals. This presupposes that homosexuality is both abnormal and a disease. Do you think it is?

C: I thought the homosexuality debate had long been resolved by the view that homosexuality per se was an alternative biological status the consequences of which are often distressing and which psychiatrists can relieve. My approach would be that it is better to try help the individual come to terms with their homosexuality, not to try change it. And certainly the hospitals I worked in Britain have given up aversion therapy.

J: Would you then argue to have it stopped in St Patrick's?

C: I'm only here a month, so I haven't come across any such cases. But then my stance on this is very much an ideological position. What if a patient says, 'I'm not interested in your views on homosexuality. I've got homosexual desires and fantasies and frankly I don't want them. So is there any treatment you can give me?' What would I do then? I don't know. Maybe that's why the option is left open, if it is.

J: There were reports that when you came back to Ireland you'd be aligning yourself with Fianna Fáil. How sympathetic are you to Fianna Fáil?

C: Increasingly sympathetic. I didn't come out of a Fianna Fáil family. We had a middle-class Dublin view of Fianna Fáil, influenced, to be perfectly honest, by West British values and the feeling that Fianna Fáil was a peasant party, a rural party. Now, partly, because I've reassessed what I am, as an Irishman, I feel that Fianna Fáil, despite its many irritating aspects, is, at least, the national party.

J: So you suspect you will in time publicly align yourself with Fianna Fáil?

C: I don't know because Fianna Fáil has got to take Ulster Unionism on board if they really are an all-Ireland party. They've got to stop seeing it as something that has to accommodate itself to them – it won't. But I do know that only Fianna Fáil can deliver on Northern Ireland. Of course, maybe I couldn't stomach them because of the way they've dragged on issues like divorce and women's rights. Would I say so were I part of the party? If I did would they throw me out? How tolerant is the Fianna Fáil of the 90s going to be? I think they'll make a mistake if they stay a kind of Stalinist party.

J: Are you saying that Charles Haughey is a Stalinist dictator?

C: *[laughs]* No. In saying Fianna Fáil is a Stalinist party I mean it has a rather inordinate driving ethos which probably has something to do with the 'holy grail' of Republicanism. And a long line of personalities from de Valera to Lemass to Haughey acknowledge this and in doing so become larger than themselves in a way that Fine Gael or Labour don't. Fianna Fáil exploits this force, suggesting it is the residue of a purity other parties have compromised on. And that's conveyed down through the leadership in a way that I relate to Stalinism, because in the Soviet system they continued to do that even after the unsullied nature of the original ideology had been demonstrably proven to be false and the connection was broken by Trotsky and others. There are similarities in that respect.

J: Is one similarity the danger that if leaders overdose on that driving ethos, be it real or illusory, they may turn into monsters, often without noticing until it's too late?

C: There is that danger, yes, and Charles Haughey should beware because you don't see it happening. But the great protection against Charles Haughey becoming Stalin is that Ireland isn't the Soviet Union, it is a democracy and there have been and always will be enough people ready to tell him if he is going too far in that direction.

J: Some suspect that your reasons for joining a major political party have more to do with a need to feed your own insatiable appetite for power. Could you become a Stalinist dictator? Are you, here in St Patrick's?

C: *[laughs]* There also would be many people quite ready to point it out if I was. No, the appetite I have is for getting things done.

J: That sounds a shade too noble. Aren't there also ignoble motives seeping through your psyche? Would you admit it if there were?

C: I will admit I get great personal satisfaction from pulling levers and I know that satisfaction fuels certain people, irrespective of what the levers do when pushed. I could become addicted to that. But then I don't think one has to have a fastidious dislike of power – just of the abuse of power. Yes, I am medical director here and there are 500 people involved and I am involved in public affairs because I like to influence things. In Britain I had influence in certain areas, and that raised the question: do I want to have it? Was I all that pushed about what happened in Britain, particularly when so much of what I believed in – like the BBC, the NHS, the university system – all were under siege? I thought, 'Jesus, it's one thing to fight this battle and lose in your own land, but here? Why should I bother?' Then I saw contemporaries of mine in Ireland and the battles they were fighting and I thought 'Damn it, it does matter to me what happens in Ireland, maybe I can help.'

J: What about the suggestion that *Irish In Mind* reveals you to be politically naïve and somewhat ignorant of the true complexities of politics in Ireland?

C: I'll agree with that, it would be politically naive of me not to. I am aware that coming in and out of Ireland regularly over the last nineteen years is not sufficient. This country is very complex, very hard to read. And I may have been contaminated by a certain English naïveté.

# 15 CHARLIE McCREEVY
## 1989

**Joe Jackson:**

It's said that in your argument for coalition you suggested that U-turns and selling out are part of Fianna Fáil's history from the beginning, such as in the way the original party turned its back on the IRA and entered the Dáil.

**Charlie McCreevy:**

My point was that the leader in those days had tough unpopular decisions to make but what they did was in the best interests of the country. Dev did go into the Dáil having major problems with the Oath of Allegiance. That was a tough decision. In 1932 Sinn Féin canvassed for the government, yet in the 1940s we allowed these people to die in jails, executed people who had fought side by side with us because that was in the best interests of the country. That was a tough decision. And that was my point.

 **J:** But hard-core Republicans in the party would have seen that and the recent coalition as another example of Fianna Fáil selling out on its original principles.

**M:** Yes. And even more recently hard-core Republicans had trouble with extradition. But now you've hit on what troubles the very soul of Fianna Fáil these days, that great dichotomy, our being totally torn in two directions. We are the nationalist, Republican party and yet we've had to do in government things that tore at the heart of the old organisation and the party. Deep down and going way back, as with many Fianna Fáil supporters, I'm one who believed that having anything at all to do with the Brits was a tearing at the very heart of the party. Yet as a national party in government we have to do what is right for the Irish people and internationally and that includes having an extradition treaty with Great Britain. But in my own psyche there is that tension, that battle going on between what I call the 'breeding' side of my brain and the side that is logical. And that dichotomy is brought into sharp focus when it comes to Northern Ireland. The birthright was 'Jesus Christ, we're always against the Brits and have to get a United Ireland'. Yet the logical side now says 'We must have talks, must negotiate, must have devolved government in Northern Ireland, must participate, must have extradition with these people'. And you don't, I believe, have to scratch Irish people very much to find this latent nationalism. We have 800 years of history to pull out of our psyches in just the last sixty years. Jesus, even twenty years ago when I was in school we were told in our history classes that all the oppression we suffered from the penal days, the famine and everything else, the Brits were the cause of it all. And in my home, as a child, I'd be told by my mother about the War of Independence, the Civil War and which family fought on what side. Stuff like that is deep in the psyche of the Irish people and many have great difficulty coming to terms with that, or looking at things from another angle, including myself.

**J:** In that battle between the 'breeding' and 'logical' sides of your brain, which side most often wins?

**M:** The logical, on most occasions. That's why I understand Charlie Haughey so well. I know he experiences the same problems and has the same tensions, absolutely. That's why I also understand, as I'm sure he does, those who are reacting against the coalition.

**J:** Is part of your breeding support for the IRA?

**M:** Look, I know people who are so peaceful they wouldn't slap a dog on the bum to get him out of the way yet after six pints when the Wolfe Tones start singing *A Nation Once Again* they're up on chairs, and if you say 'Let's march on the border now and take over' they would. Or if an IRA man commits a horrible crime and the Brits want him extradited the same people are up in arms saying 'No'.

**J:** Including you?

**M:** Yes. I have a problem with extradition, I won't deny that.

**J:** Are you the kind of Fianna Fáil TD who supports the IRA cause but can't support their methods?

**M:** I've changed. In the 1960s I was a rabid Nationalist defending what I saw as the cause our fathers fought for. This was before there was an IRA as we know it today. But you learn to accept that you can't achieve anything by force. At least that's the logical argument. But if we're all honest with ourselves we have to ask ourselves would any progress have been made, including the Anglo-Irish Agreement, if there had just been politicians talking and no violence? Maybe I shouldn't say that, but it's true. In all our dealings with Great Britain in even our century, there's never been a decade where there hasn't been violence because of the armed struggle. And as long as there is partition on this island you'll always have young Irish people prepared to take up arms. The British government will not finally fix it. And there's really no point in my thinking one thing and saying another. As a Constitutional politician I have to say I abhor the fact that people from all sides have been killed. I abhor what the IRA do but maybe if I'd been born in Derry I'd have been drawn into the armed struggle. Maybe if I'd been born sixty miles further up the road I'd be in Long Kesh today. And though I don't condone the thuggery and violence and killing, I do feel sorry for people who are drawn into it. But there always will be people who'll say 'The only way to get the Brits to see sense is through the barrel of a gun', and that's the saddest thing of all. The IRA can say that 'If you want to take Constitutional politicians further down the road' et cetera or 'If we didn't do this there'd be no progress at all'. And that's what's wrong about it all. And here I'm just speaking about a historical fact, not condoning violence.

**J:** If you can accept that Fianna Fáil has failed in relation to its original aims in terms of reunification and the restoration of the Irish language, do you also accept that at this stage in our history most voters don't give a damn about either of these issues?

**M:** Most voters don't give a damn, I agree.

**J:** Does that make redundant Fianna Fáil's base, and very basis for being?

**M:** No. If you didn't have Fianna Fáil, a Constitutional party articulating what is fundamentally a Sinn Féin or IRA cause, the reunification aim, then there would have been even more continuing violence throughout our century. We were the party that gathered that form of electorate together. As for the restoration of the Irish language, the only way to revive it would be to ban it! If we banned it we'd all learn it. Apart from that, no, we haven't been able to restore it as the spoken language of our people.

J: Some suggest that Fine Gael's involvement in the instigation of the Anglo-Irish Agreement means it has, in a sense, become the Republican party, at least in terms of its commitment to finding a political solution to the question of reunification.

M: I don't see things that way at all. The facts are that Charlie Haughey was the person who initiated with Mrs Thatcher 'the totality of relationships' between these two islands and that got things off the ground long before the Anglo-Irish Agreement. He put relationships onto the plane that then led to the Anglo-Irish Agreement.

J: Which he and Fianna Fáil then violently opposed.

M: We did, and that was a mistake.

J: Do you believe that the traditional Fianna Fáil supporters merely pay lip service to supporting the Anglo-Irish Agreement?

M: Yes. But it would be wrong to portray it as a big issue in Fianna Fáil people's minds at all, nowadays. And those who are paying just lip service probably do so because of the dichotomy I referred to earlier. But I would say that if Fianna Fáil is not prepared to change with the times, we will become redundant as a political party. People have to accept change. Politics no longer is as it used to be when we'd just wave the green flag and everybody did come out and vote for us. Those days are gone.

J: Patrick Pearse once said: 'The man who, in the name of Ireland, accepts as "a final settlement" anything less, by one fraction of one iota than separation from England, is guilty of so immense an infidelity, so immense a crime against the Irish nation that it were better for that man that he had not been born.' Are you one of those politicians who now no longer regard such texts as holy writ?

M: I'm familiar with that quote and all I can say to it is that I do still believe that the reunification of the country is our most important aim. That partition is the cause of violence in the country and so I will always want to get rid of it.

J: But some revisionists believe it is the severity of such edicts and the intractable positions they impose on believers, be they de Valera or Haughey, which limit the party's potential for evolving in the way that even you seem to agree is necessary.

M: I don't believe it's that which will stop the party from evolving. But such beliefs do form the one thread'running through us all. Most Fianna Fáil supporters mightn't summarise it as you did there in that quote by Pearse but that's the very kind of thing we believe makes us what we are and makes us different from all other parties. That type of thread has always run through the Fianna Fáil organisation. My father had it, his people, my people and that's the kind of thread that binds us. If we lose that what have we got?

J: But revisionists don't ask that you relinquish it, merely suggest you stand back and examine all such threads and ask are they really as relevant, should they really be seen as sacred in 1989 as they were in the early part of this century? Shouldn't Pearse's contribution and Dev's continually be critically reassessed or must they always be the inviolate 'sacred cows' of Irish history?

M: No. No. No. *[fumbling for words]* I must admit here that I feel that the 'breeding' side of my brain is responding to these questions rather than the logical side. Jaysus, I once said of my own home that if my mother had to choose between God and Dev I wouldn't be sure who'd get second preference. So this is a problem for me. It is, I'll admit, difficult for me to even apply the phrase 'sacred cows' to the people you mention. I can't.

J: Does this mean there is a lack of judgement when you assess, say, Dev's contribution to Irish society? Can't you see the negative effects he had?

M: It's not just a lack of judgement, it's simply hard for me to look at things that way.

J: Would you say the same thing applies to most people in the Fianna Fáil party?

M: It probably does, yes.

J: But surely you, as a disciple of the need for change and evolution within Fianna Fáil, must see how this might be crippling the party's potential for growth? Surely the first phase in stepping beyond the shackles of history is to re-examine the 'sacred cows', shoot them down if needs be, then move on?

**M:** You lodge a strong argument, but I still must say to you in all sincerity that this is one of those 'sacred cows' I have the greatest difficulty dealing with.

**J:** Pearse or Dev?

**M:** What they both embody.

**J:** One commentator said of Dev that 'The creation of a virtually homogenous Catholic state, of which he was the prime architect, proved to be the greatest hindrance to the prospect of Irish unity'. Can you even consider that possibility?

**M:** *[pause]* I believe that Dev's idea of involving the Catholic church ethos in the Constitution has been a stumbling block but no more than that. The Unionists have used the idea of us clinging to that Catholic ethos as a stick to beat us with, that's the real problem. You have these two trains, Nationalists and Unionists, and no meeting point.

**J:** Some might say that's because of the chasm that has developed because of the influence the Catholic Church had over the Irish government, mostly in the shape of Fianna Fáil.

**M:** It is a chasm, that I agree with. And yes, I do believe that any Constitution should be non-denominational and I must accept what you say about the Irish Constitution. The Roman Catholic ethos of the time was imbued into Dev's philosophy and it's definitely not what I'd embody in a Constitution. But I do not accept, to reply to your quote, that this was the 'greatest hindrance' to progress we could have made with getting to grips with the Northern Ireland problem. Besides, everyone knows that the influence of the Catholic Church has been loosening, especially over, say the last twelve years.

**J:** Do you think it might loosen even more as a result of the new coalition and the fact that this may signal the end of single-party government in Ireland, specifically Fianna Fáil?

**M:** I hadn't thought of it in that sense but if that does happen it will be another healthy consequence of the coalition.

**J:** It's also said that Fianna Fáil, as a party of pragmatists rather than ideologues, is fundamentally out of step with developments in European politics and that, as a consequence of this, it might 'vegetate in the bogs of history'. Do you agree?

**M:** There is that danger, yes. That's why I've often compared Fianna Fáil and, for that matter Fine Gael, as roughly the same brand of washing powder; because we don't have an ideological base. Whereas the Worker's Party and Labour do. And because they have I believe that sometime in the future the centre-right parties will be forced into an alliance and we'll then have the necessary ideological base of being a centre-right, Free-enterprise *laissez-faire* conservative-type party. Ireland has resisted that change but can, no longer. Then we will finally end up with a clear left and right division in Irish politics, as with the European model. And yes I do agree that if Fianna Fáil doesn't develop along these lines it just may 'vegetate in the bogs of history'.

# 16 HENRY MOUNTCHARLES
## 1989

Henry Mountcharles still seethes with rage when he paraphrases a comment made about him by junior minister Maire Geoghegan-Quinn. 'She said there was no place in Ireland for people like me. "People like me"? What the hell does that mean? I certainly intend to press her to explain precisely what it means when I meet her.'

The comment angers him partly because the mention of his name, particularly if prefixed by the word 'Lord', has led to him receiving death threats, veiled or otherwise. At the time of the first rock concert that was held in the grounds of his castle at Slane he received a note which read: 'Irishmen are tortured to death by your British friends. Your class have an easy ride of it in Ireland. Call off this vulgar festival you're promoting while brave men are dying, you British Toad.' It was signed 'Militant Tendency, Meath.'

**Joe Jackson:**

Did you have any sympathy for the sentiments expressed in that note?

**Henry Mountcharles:**

I did feel that the hunger strike was a terrible waste of human life. Everything associated with the hunger strike: the black flags, the intimidation. That note is only an example of what I received, though it is representative. But those were the tactics used by the National Socialists in Germany in the 1930s and I reject that absolutely.

**J:** But could you feel any sympathy for the anger expressed in the note?

**M:** Yes, I do have some understanding of the rage and frustration that exists. People should ask themselves why eighty to a hundred thousand people in the North of Ireland vote Sinn Féin. That's an awful lot of people. Why do they vote for an organisation that openly advocates the use of murder on one hand and the ballot box on the other? Why is Danny Morrison finding a receptive audience? That's the question we should be addressing.

**J:** Why do you think he does?

**M:** Because there is serious discrimination in the North of Ireland, there is an appalling misdirection of resources, there is a failure to produce a political solution. I want to see a United Ireland but there's no use in saying just that. It's a perfectly fucking meaningless phrase now, to just say that you want a United Ireland. What you want is to find a way to produce a harmonisation of the relationships between the people living on this island before you start looking at a federal solution. And every goddamn politician who fails to address themselves to that problem is failing in their job as politicians. The national question is still the most crucial question facing this state, but it is being marginalised by the media and by politicians because it is so huge an issue they don't dare confront it. Failure to address the problem is bordering on being a political obscenity. As is human lives lost, families blown apart, despair, destruction and the hatred that exists on this island. There are very few politicians in Leinster House who take this on board. We've had so much shadow-boxing, and Green Republicanism in all this present nonsense, where elements in Fianna Fáil are saying that the party's 'true Republican heart' is being sold down the river. Fuck that! Where are those same people when they should be up on the rooftops shouting about how we confront the national problem, the fundamental problem on this island? Arguing about roads down in Ballyporeen? When will they stand up and be counted on the issue that really matters?

**J:** Taking a position against the bombing in Regent's Park in 1982 you wrote, 'This was not the first nor was it to be the last time the name of Ireland has been tainted with blood by the callousness of the IRA.' Did you ever make similarly worded statements about the UDA?

**M:** Yes, but obviously, because of where I'm coming from, the media would latch onto the criticism I make of the Provos. I condemn violence from whatever quarters, including the UDA. I have as little time for Ian Paisley as I do for the likes of Gerry Adams. But I can't remember the last time I was asked by the media to comment on an act of violence that might have come from the Protestant tradition. But you see whereas the connection between Sinn Féin and the IRA seems to be strong in the public consciousness, the Protestants associate themselves only by loose implication. Robinson is particularly clever at playing this. The Clontibret episode was a clear attempt to associate himself with the violent extreme wing in the Protestant tradition in the north, while at the same time leaving, himself able to stand back when it suited him. He then can criticise Adams and fellow travellers by saying, 'They're patched in, I'm not.' But his clothes are sullied too, though not directly.

**J:** What about the view that the British government is waging, and has waged, a campaign of physical and psychological violence on all Ireland, specifically the North, and that your forefathers were at the spearhead of that campaign? And that for that, you too must be held responsible?

**M:** That's a racist view. Are the sins of not just the fathers but the forefathers to be perpetrated upon their sons? I have often encountered that view but it's so blatantly absurd I don' t humour it at all.

**J:** Do you feel any sense of historical responsibility?

**M:** Well, of course there is an element of that, yes, in relation to my family's record. One member of my family had an appalling record during the Famine, the things that were happening on his land holdings were horrendous. So in that sense I would be appalled, but I am not burdened down by guilt or anything like it, because that is so unproductive. Of course I encounter that argument but people coming to me with prejudices that stretch back hundreds and hundreds of years – surely that is an encapsulation of so many of the problems we have: What was done then wasn't my doing. I don't feel guilty or that I personally was responsible. Nor was my father, my grandfather, or great-grandfather. We're talking about going back four or five generations, am I to be held responsible for that?

**J:** Nevertheless, you have, for example, described as 'tragic' the fact that the English performed an act of 'linguistic imperialism' in Ireland.

Would you therefore support those people in the North who are reverting to Gaelic and breaking the law by putting up Irish street names?

**M:** Yes. But with the qualification that an expression of cultural identity should not develop a chauvinistic element to it. Then again even with the question of a cultural statement becoming a political statement, I have a problem with that because it brings us back to the fundamental question of defining Irishness. If you get a group of people who feel so alienated they have to politicise their culture in an aggressive manner that, in itself, tangentially, alienates somebody like me. I feel distinctly Irish but I don't feel I have to immerse myself in the Gaelic language to feel Irish.

**J:** Can you appreciate why Nationalists in the North feel the need to do that, as a form of symbolic gesture?

**M:** Absolutely. It's reactive to the sort of strident Unionism they're confronted by. The struggle does take place in these areas, which is something people tend to forget. In relation to schools, symbols, language soccer versus Gaelic football, et cetera. It is in those areas people define themselves.

**J:** But let's push this to its logical conclusion. If you support the action of those Republicans who do to want to get rid of British street names, do you also have any form of sympathy at all for the cry of 'Brits out'?

**M:** But who are the Brits? That's a load of garbage for a start. That's just a slogan. And there is too much sloganising. I've had 'Brits Out' scrawled on my wall. I don't consider myself a Brit. I could go up to the guy writing that and say 'Who is the Brit here?' And who is the Brit up North? I firmly believe in what Donal O'Sullivan once said: 'This island is a sea fed by many streams.' I am as much one of those streams as somebody who feels the need to immerse themselves in any form of chauvinistic expression of Irish culture in the north. Yes, I do come from what you might call an Ascendancy background but that, in itself, is the challenge. The Anglo-Irish tradition, the Protestant tradition, was not only supposed to have been absorbed, but actively involved in the political system in the South, that was the concept from the beginning. That has not happened. Yet the fact remains that the involvement of people from the Protestant tradition in the South in the political system here would do a lot to help solve the problems in the North. It's this fact that makes so insulting comments like Maire Geoghegan-Quinn's 'We've no place here for people like you'. That is absolute crap. Anyone who says I have no right to speak out on political issues here, or have no place in modern Ireland, is living in the past. Quite the opposite is true. Because if there really is any aspiration towards uniting this country, people like me have to be integrated into political life in the South. Otherwise there isn't a hope in hell.

**J:** As a symbolic gesture would you consider giving back part of your fourteen hundred acres to those some might see as their rightful owners?

**M:** Who the hell are the 'rightful owners' for a start? My family have been in Slane since 1701 and that acreage I have held on to, and managed in a manner I consider to be sensitive to the responsibilities that were cast upon me. It is fulfilling a worthwhile role in the community and I absolutely reject that kind of garbage.

**J:** How did your family originally come by the land?

**M:** Bought it.

**J:** From whom and was it at a reduced rate or a rate that would have been out of the reach of most Irish buyers at the time?

**M:** I don't know what the purchase process was but after the Battle of the Boyne there was the Willamite confiscation and land was put up for sale by the then government and it was acquired by Henry Conygham. He acquired it, we actually bought it. We were Scottish settlers that started off in Donegal and moved down to Slane a hundred years later.

**J:** But you still are the beneficiary of British Imperialism.

**M:** But I'm not British, I'm Irish. And I just find that argument so fucking ludicrous. But okay, let's try to knock this fucking thing on its head once and for all. I'll say it again: who are the 'rightful owners'? Are they our 'unflawed' Bord Pleanála? The government? The politicians? Why should my land be nationalised any more than Charlie Haughey's? Should Charlie Haughey hand back Kinsealy to its rightful owners? Who are the rightful owners? The logic is perfectly ludicrous.

**J:** Might the local people feel they have some territorial claim on the land?

**M:** Some might and there are people who have called me a 'robber baron'. I totally reject that. I used to be intimidated by that kind of thing but no longer because the accusation has no foundation at all behind it. One whole section of the land has been bought back since I was born, so who are the rightful owners of that? I honestly can't go along with that, this whole argument

**J:** Someone suggested that a lot of the 'anti-Henry' feelings locally are based on party loyalty, that you'd have had an easier time if you were part of Fianna Fáil.

**M:** Yes, I've heard that. By that they mean I then might be 'one of the lads'? Maybe. But I would never even consider joining Fianna Fáil until it puts itself into a position where it is producing policies I could agree with.

**J:** You'll hardly make yourself potential Fianna Fáil material when you're publicly declaring: 'I have no time for the narrow-minded nationalism of Charles Haughey... no time for the pious lip service he pays to Irish unity'. Still feel that way?

**M:** I do, but CH seems to have mellowed. He's in a coalition government with Dessie O'Malley, for Christ's sake! He also has not pulled the plug on the Anglo-Irish Agreement. Re 'lip service' to it, I think there still is a residual tension there because it was instigated by Fine Gael. But I think he sees his role now more as the architect of the South's economic revival. That's the way he'll go down in the history books. I think he may have abandoned the idea that he could be the architect of a new Ireland, North and South. But Fianna Fáil has sold out. There have been so many U-turns in respect to every other policy, so why not the North?

**J:** You joined Fine Gael in 1982 believing Garret's election indicated a new departure in Irish politics. Yet you feel he has failed miserably too, don't you?

**M:** Yes. But what was interesting about Garret was that here was somebody in the mainstream of Irish political life who was saying that you don't have to be covered in green paint and be a fluent Irish speaker, what I call a 'stereotypical Irishman' to feel Irish. And while he failed in the sense that his government presided over a lot of economic disintegration, he gave things a sense of direction, he got the ball rolling. So he was a noble rather than a miserable failure, and time will prove that to be true. And most importantly of all, one of his prime motivations was to actually produce a solution to the national question. Garret FitzGerald is much more an ardent Nationalist than Charles Haughey has ever been.

**J:** You once said to your father that he was an anachronism, that he should get rid of the title. Does the same apply to you now?

**M:** Sitting here, at thirty-eight and having learned to live with it, I think now I should wear the title on my sleeve.

# 17     SOUND BITES
## 1989

'The ultimate criterion for success would be to be accepted as worthy of being part of the divinity. Politics, for me, is about absorption into other people, which I now see as a gradual evolution of the spirit in that one direction. And I do think the spiritual life is an area too many Irish politicians ignore. Leaders should not just be about structures, Semi-State bodies, grants to industry. It should also be about something deeper in people, and leading that out to something greater than they are.'

*(Michael Keating, Progressive Democrat TD, who has since retired from politics)*

'In many ways, I've always been a very right-wing, reactionary sort of person, a let's-kill-the-Commies kind of thing, which is appalling, looking back on it as a Christian. But those were the mores of the 1960s. In relation to my own immediate background, I came from a Dublin professional family who were traditionally apolitical, never involved in a struggle for independence or anything like it. We would have been seen as 'Castle Catholics', in collaboration with the invaders. My father, for example, tended to be anti-Franco, but I was pro-Franco. Looking back on that too, I see I was totally wrong. He obviously was a bastard. And obviously I've changed or I wouldn't be in the Greens. But a lot of us were raised on that "go off and fight for Christ in Spain against the atheists" propaganda.'

*(Roger Garland, Green Party spokesman)*

'It is a deeper and more complex issue than "Brits Out". What would happen if they did? Civil war? Because the roots of the problems go back so far, everything's been fucked up for so long, there is no simple solution. It's really so far above my head like a dark cloud. Besides, guys smarter and better informed than me have been working to sort it out and can't.'

*(Mickey Rourke, actor, questioned about his naïveté in relation to Northern Ireland)*

'She didn't like me doing stuff like "House of the Rising Sun" at all. Jesus, she was so religious she wouldn't talk to me for six months because I was playing Judas in *Jesus Christ, Superstar*. "Anyone but Judas!" she'd say.'

*(Colm Wilkinson, singer)*

# 18     FINBAR FUREY
## 1990

'U2 are the biggest rock band in the world,' says Finbar Furey before pausing then adding, without the slightest trace of self-consciousness, 'And we – the Fureys and Davey Arthur – are the biggest folk band in the world.'

Make of that claim what you will, but the Fureys do, at least, have one distinct advantage over the aforementioned U2. All (excluding interloper Davey Arthur, of course) are brothers. Mind you, not everyone knows that, as Finbar explains. 'We were doing gigs in New York at the time and one day we suddenly ended up in the middle of Harlem. Not that we knew exactly where we were. But anyway we're dyin' for a drink and we see this club but before we can step inside, this black guy blocks the door, says, "Sorry man, only brothers allowed in here." And Paul says, 'But we are brothers. That's me brother Eddie and that's ..." And the black guy pissed himself laughing.'

The story may sound apocryphal but Finbar swears it's true and tells it with such relish, as he lounges back into a chair in a Dublin hotel, that it doesn't really matter whether it is or not. Yet underpinning the tale is the inescapable fact that Finbar, George, Eddie and Paul are essentially, brothers, bound by blood and flesh rather than just their love for music. Cut one and all bleed. Cut one and you'll probably bleed. And it certainly wouldn't be over-romantic to suggest that growing up in Ballyfermot in the 1950s, as part of the first generation of travelling people to live in fixed homes, music was about as much as Finbar and his family could be sure they 'owned'. Finbar's mother, Nora, who played banjo and accordion was, it's claimed, 'the fountainhead for songs and stories from their earliest childhood', and his father, Ted, was known primarily as a 'famous fiddler who collected songs and airs' from all over Ireland.

'Well, I meself was born in the Coombe but my people were mostly circus-y people, related to the Fossetts and the Duffys and such,' smiles Finbar, an easy sense of nostalgia settling on his face. 'My father really was a gifted man, highly intelligent but, I imagine, deeply frustrated because he never got the education he needed to draw that out. But he always had the music. Like, he'd play banjo in the circus tent then next night traditional in the local pub. But me dad's biggest love was traditional music and he was deeply loved by all the musicians who came to stay with us, like Seamus Ennis and Felix Dorgan. Jaysus, you'd wake up and find dead bodies all over our house. And fiddles and flutes. You'd have to watch where you're walking, or you'd step on some guy's flute. Either of his flutes!' he laughs.

Recalling Sunday mornings when he'd count up to thirty people littered round their home in Ballyfermot, Finbar says, 'You gotta remember our house was no mansion! In fact it was so small you could dip your bread in the fella's soup next door without leaving your own dinner table. Jaysus, you'd be afraid to take the kettle off the gas in case it was being boiled by his ma.'

Let Finbar Furey wax lyrical about his Dublin childhood and you'll soon find him tangled in ribbons of laughter or fighting back rivers of tears. However, madcap laughter is very much his mode as he makes a Proustian leap from tales of soup and tea to his one abiding memory of margarine.

'It was great for the 'oul hair when you hadn't got Brylcreem,' he recalls. 'So I'd slap a clump of it in me hair and off I'd go boppin' at the local, Lucan hop. There I'd be ravin to the Beatles or the Stones and the marg'd be drippin' down my face and on to the suit I'd gotten for £2.50 from the Iveagh Market. And some poor girl'd think it was her that was turning me into hot stuff.'

Whatever about the shortage of kettles and Brylcreem in the vicinity of the Furey household, there was no shortage of uileann pipes. Finbar and neighbour/buddy Paddy Keenan were known, locally, as 'the incredible twins' because of their precocious talent on pipes. 'Paddy's from travelling people too and I remember clearly when Tommy Moore'd teach us staccato twice a week he'd invite all his friends round to hear these kids, one twelve, the other eight, and they'd all be amazed at us, saying 'Bejaysus, yer man has twenty fingers on each hand ' But my strongest, and fondest memory is of playing in the Piper's club, at fourteen, and Leo Rosen throwing a quid on the table and saying to me father, "Johnny Doran was the greatest piper of all time and it's like you dug up his body and put his spirit in a fourteen-year-old boy." I'd never heard Johnny but later me an' Paddy heard him on the wireless and got so excited, saying, "Did you hear what he did with that thumb?" So that's where we came from, that's who we are.'

Finbar Furey sees this as a pivotal moment in terms of how a people can define themselves according to their music. 'That's exactly how it felt to us. We felt mighty, so proud, thinking, "Now we know who we are." But what really pisses me off now is the fact that although he was a brilliant piper and he kept piping alive during the war years when it was in danger of dying – him and Rosen – there's no memorial built to either of them. There should be. People like me didn't go to the Municipal School of Music. I learned from great, natural teachers like me father, Paddy's da, John and Tommy Moore. Yet what official recognition do those musicians get?'

Finbar Furey believes that the government, through its bodies such as the Arts Council, doesn't do enough to either honour or chronicle what he describes as this 'neglected core of Irish culture'.

'Instead, as our cultural heritage what's kept on record are the so-called "posh arts". So there's a whole body of work that hasn't been officially recognised. Meself and John Faulkner have gotten the go-ahead to do a series of six ninety-minute programmes on Gypsy music in Europe, but we had to get the grant for that from a university in Yugoslavia. Yet we're damn well doing it, covering countries like Yugoslavia, Germany, Spain, England, Scotland and Ireland extensively, because we both feel that this is a part of our culture, as Irish, as Celts, that has not been recorded. But the Irish government itself should give us the grants. This is our bloody heritage, not ballet.'

The core of truth in Finbar's claim about the link between his music and 'our bloody heritage' can be gleaned from the following review of his work: 'Finbar Furey ... plays the uileann pipes in a manner that draws out its very soul of poignancy and its full dancing life'. Does he agree that this blend of sorrow plus a love of dance is quintessentially Irish?

'Absolutely, especially the last part,' he says. 'If you asked me to describe my music in one word it would be "wild". Martín O'Connor, when he plays the accordion makes my ears dance! The same with Frankie Gavin. He goes for everything, no holds barred. And these men didn't learn this music from a book. It comes from deep down inside them. I'm the same with the pipes. I go for everything, even if I don't always get there. We hold the wildness of this music in our souls. And you can't capture that on, or working from, paper. Take Liam Óg Ó Flynn, for example. He's the golden-haired boy of the traditionalists among pipers because he does what he's told with the pipes. It's sweet, beautiful but straight out of a book. That's because he – like Paddy Moloney – went to the Municipal School of Music. But you can't compare Liam's imagination with mine, so it's wrong to compare us as pipers. I'm a total fucking lunatic as a piper. And Paddy Keenan is the same, and Davey Spillane, who is our pupil, is living proof of that. What it all comes down to is the simple, central fact that this is the travelling people style of playing music, which has never been tamed.'

Referring back to the time when he was rejected by the Pipers' Club, Finbar elaborates on the experience, which clearly was a turning point for him and which left its mark. 'I'd been the golden boy up till then, my Dad'd bring me in and they'd all stand to attention. But after I did the single of 'Her Father Didn't Like Me Anyway' they turned their backs on me in that Pipers' Club. They went to Paddy Keenan and he said, no fucking way. They put a weight on your shoulders. They've put that weight on Liam Óg. He's carrying that weight. He's the nice, clean-cut hero they want, and good for him, but it's not for me. I can't be their nice-boy ever again because my hair is too long, I wear earrings and I curse and swear and drink pints. But in all this I honestly believe I am true to the soul of the Irish people, the travelling people. And I won't let anyone fucking tame me. Or break me. I really feel if I allowed that to happen I'd be betraying myself and the roots of my people so I'll never, never let it happen.'

Finbar pauses, then laughs. 'You can't put a dickie-bow on traditional music. I firmly believe that. This music is the music of the working-class people of Ireland. They kept it alive. It's our way of crying in music. It wasn't written by Lord Lucan or Lord God knows who. It wasn't even originally written down. It was passed among the ordinary people of Ireland, the travelling people. These songs are ours. And if many are sorrowful that's because so is our history. How could that not be poignant? And the dancing element is part of the same thing. Dancing in the face of despair. Or death, like at wakes. Or famine. Or emigration.

Or oppression. And what's really Irish is that the best of the music contains both these elements. I can play a reel and make you weep or make you dance, depending on how I feel at the time. That's our heritage and our true culture and we must keep that alive.'

# 19 FRANK McGUINNESS
## 1990

Frank McGuinness's latest play *The Bread Man* opens with its protagonist shadow-boxing. It's a fitting metaphor for McGuinness himself, a writer who, according to at least one commentator, is in danger of burning himself out if he doesn't find a balance between the 'contrasting forces in his own nature'. Yet if ever there was a playwright who tapped these opposing forces, and turned potentially destructive energy into art, it is Frank McGuinness. As a male writer he attempted to explore only the female mind/feminine perspective in his first play, written nearly ten years ago, *The Factory Girls*. As a Donegal-born Catholic he also set himself the task of exploring a Protestant perspective in his award-winning play *Observe the Sons of Ulster Marching Towards the Somme*. And in *The Bread Man*, set in Donegal in 1970, he examines the dual crisis which besets a man when his faith in Nationalistic politics is fragmented and he suffers what McGuinness describes as a 'crisis in terms of his sexual identity'.

**Joe Jackson:**

It's claimed you spent much of your childhood creating, and living in, fantasy worlds. Why?

**Frank McGuinness:**

I was extremely lonely as a kid. Partly by choice, as I wasn't terribly keen on other kids and they weren't too keen on me, so by mutual agreement we stayed apart. But then I really did prefer my own company and imagination, right up to my mid to late teens. I was very much a loner living in fantasy worlds. Yet a lot of the isolation, being self-imposed, was more positive than negative. I used that time constructively. Of course my parents didn't approve of that. They wanted me to be less of an oddball! But overall I had their protection and support so I'm not one of those Irish writers who seem obsessed with their childhood. I was more influenced by puberty because that's the time Derry exploded. I was fifteen, sixteen and, if anything, that's the time I have hang-ups about. When my sexuality was developing and there was a war going on all around me. That's the time that really shaped me.

**J:** Was there also a 'war' within you, sexually?

**M:** Like all kids going through puberty I had no idea what was happening to me. It was the late 1960s but the so-called 'sexual liberation' in relation to Ireland was a myth. I personally had a lot of hang-ups and repressions that I had to work through and I'm still working through. But you have to be careful how you use the word 'war'. I'd call what was going on inside me a 'struggle' and that continues.

**J:** In what way?

**M:** *[pause]*. I'm never really content in relationships. I tend to give people a reasonably hard time. I find it difficult to be at peace in a relationship and that stems, I think, from the sexual struggle within myself. And it permeates into all areas of my life. I don't feel I've settled, in any way, even at my age. The only sense of security I have is the teaching job in Maynooth. And I've a terrible fear of ending up homeless. In ways like that the overall struggle goes on.

**J:** You have said that a person can be 'obliterated' by love and suggested that once you love that deeply, and lose, you never recover. Has that happened to you?

**M:** Well, I have been 'obliterated' by the loss of love, yeah. *[laughs]* But someone pointed out to me on reading that comment at the time: 'Honey, you never recover from lung cancer but you do recover from the loss of love.' Maybe that's a more realistic way of looking at it. So let's just say that I no longer break down on hearing the song 'I Get Along Without You Very Well'.

**J:** There is a scene in *The Bread Man* which strongly suggests that even potentially bland love songs by the likes of Perry Como can be a life-affirming force in moments of despair. Is that what music has meant to you?

**M:** Absolutely. Music of the 1960s really kept me going when I was growing up. I'm still mad about Cilla Black and Dusty Springfield and other girl singers from the 1960s. I really loved that stuff. Of course it wasn't considered terribly 'manly' but, in a way, I enjoyed being not terribly 'manly'. And part of the force I now feel I tuned into was the voice of an oppressed species, woman. Hearing Lulu's 'The Boat that I Row' even today, and placing it in the context of the 1960s, can still be a shock to the system. Those songs are very much about oppression and denial. Yet they also are about immensely strong women unafraid to feel those depths of anger, frustration, rage. Listen to 'Anyone Who Had a Heart', it is a tremendously angry song and it was that I identified with as much as anything else.

**J:** You've also described your first visit to the theatre, at nineteen, as 'a shock to the system', yet can you still identify with young people who see theatre as a farce, politically, socially, emotionally irrelevant, as you may have done in your teens?

**M:** Completely identify, yeah. But once you give theatre a chance, as I did, that 'shock' can change your life. And I think it's sad that the majority of working-class people, in particular, don't try theatre. Some may even be intimidated by some of the buildings but they should just go. And they must too, for the sake of theatre. Because the real energy in this country comes from that particular class. If the theatre is to survive it has to draw from that area in terms of designers, actors, writers, all levels. Where did Noel Pearson come from? Look what he's done. Look at Jim Sheridan. But there is a very strong middle-class bias in theatre in Ireland and that's got to be broken down. And it has to be done by working-class people themselves insisting on their right to go. I was very intimidated going to the theatre at first but I just kept on going, me and my bags of crisps, because the first play I'd seen – Brian Friel's *The Gentle Island* – had such a profound effect on me. It was, and remains, a crucial play. And when I got into writing plays a few years later, Friel remained an influence, along with writers like Synge, Hugh Leonard, Rattigan, Coward and Shakespeare, of course. But it really is a wondrous world to explore and to become a part of, in any way.

**J:** In the diary he kept while writing *Translations*, Friel suggested that the play's theme – 'the eradication of the Irish language' – should remain a 'public question', an 'issue for politicians'. He wrote that 'The play must concern itself only with the exploration of dark and private places of individual souls'. How does that relate to your work?

**M:** In a play like *The Bread Man*, which deals very much with public issues and private dilemmas, I demand of myself, as a writer, that I do not live in an ivory tower. It's so tempting to look at what's happening in this country and shout 'A plague on both your houses'. But the point is that we live in this country and must try in any way we can to eradicate the plague. So as a writer, in my work, I have to involve myself in political questions. That's where my politics lie. I don't like talking politics outside the plays. The plays are my political statement. *The Bread Man*, for example, concerns itself with Nationalistic questions, the crisis in Fianna Fáil and the failure of Nationalists to act during that crisis in 1969/70. But then it's also very much concerned with sexual politics, with the politics of heterosexual men. So I don't hold with Brian's tenet, in relation to my work.

**J:** Yet an observation about Friel, and writers like him, who steer away from political statement, preferring instead to 'show through the homeless lives of his people the failure of social and political institutions to accord with their needs' very much relates to a play of yours such as *The Bread Man*.

**M:** That's spot on. And it is very much where I stand at the moment. I really couldn't add anything to that to describe my work right now, politically.

**J:** Yet writers of agit-prop might try to take from that, and your work, by suggesting you cop out, exhibit a lack of balls, politically in that you don't put yourself on the line, say 'These are the targets, the people and/ or political parties who have left us this way.'

**M:** I do not suffer from a lack of balls but I'm not about to show them to *Hot Press*! *[laughs]* But, seriously, if someone said that to me I would feel morally obliged to disagree, and to point out to them the error of their creative ways. I find agit-prop too easy to do. It can be radically effective yet it's a form of theatre I couldn't take on and have no desire to.

**J:** One critic suggested that in your best-known play, *Observe the Sons of Ulster Marching Towards the Somme*, you explored the notion of struggle as an end in itself, that struggling is the glory. Is that premise central to your theatrical vision?

**M:** Very much so. That, in fact, is ultimately what *The Sons of Ulster* is about. It was a celebration of the heroic efforts of those men, and I do have a deep respect for those who work hard and fight with all their might for their own corner.

**J:** Is it true the play had its roots in a poem you wrote at that fatal war monument in Enniskillen?

**M:** It came from two sources. I was teaching in Coleraine at the time and I'd never really looked at a war monument so yes, when I visited Enniskillen and stood there something clicked which later became the story I addressed in *The Sons of Ulster*. So you can imagine how I felt after the Enniskillen bombing years later.

**J:** In an article you wrote at the time you said, 'All is changed after Enniskillen'. Was it that decisive a turning point for you?

**M:** Yes, definitely. I vowed after that I would never, and could never, think of a United Ireland again without remembering those people. For me it was as black a day as Bloody Sunday, where the British opened fire on the Irish. But this was the Irish opening fire on the Irish and I'll tell you it really was the one time I felt I could stop writing. I know that plays don't change anything and should be a justification for their own existence, but it was as though *The Sons of Ulster* was utterly pointless. As if it had never been written, or heard. So yes, for me all was changed, utterly changed after that day at Enniskillen. I really felt as though I'd lost my own. And I felt far more in common with those standing at that war monument, celebrating their dead, than I would ever do with those fighting for what had always been one of my dreams, a United Ireland. It was at that point I knew I had to forfeit that dream.

**J:** And lose hope in any form of political solution?

**M:** Absolutely. And whereas in *The Sons of Ulster* I, as a Catholic, had attempted to understand the Protestant perspective, in *Carthaginians* I looked at it from a Catholic point of view. Yet even taking that double perspective I still can't see any solution, any light. *Carthaginians* ends with a miracle, which is basically just another day dawning with the people forgiving themselves. The hope lies in the fact that they take responsibility for their lives and that is a massive moral and spiritual step for a Catholic to take. Catholics are trained so much to let other people do their thinking for us, put the blame on us, lead our lives for us. As in the Christ-figure. As in Rome. And that's not on any more. Not for adults. And that too is what I was exploring in *Carthaginians* – people who have been damaged by their faith. But at least they do wake up in the end and see a new day dawning. Sometimes I really believe that's all we can hope for.

**J:** At the time of the Enniskillen bombing you said that a lot of the rage you felt was directed towards yourself. Would you see any point in attacking those responsible, be it the bombers or those that created, and sustain the overarching political context for such an atrocity?

**M:** I wouldn't. But my plays make it clear where I stand in relation to violence and to the campaign of violence on both sides. But there was one question I wanted to ask in the article I wrote on Enniskillen and I didn't at the time, because I felt I had no right to. But now I would. I wanted to ask Republican prisoners, 'Is it for this you are enduring jail? And, if not then speak out loud and clearly to everybody in the IRA to stop it.'

**J:** In *The Bread Man* the personal dilemmas slowly but inexorably take precedence over the political context. Is that deliberate?

**M:** Absolutely. *The Bread Man* is going through a dual crisis, which is the Nationalist crisis and his own sexual crisis in terms of 'Who am I, what am I?' He learned the failure of his own political rhetoric in the course of the play, and having learned the failure in that he is left with the final challenge, which is to make absolute sense of why he is on this earth. If the Nationalist politics don't provide him with the answer then he must find the answer within himself. And that answer is political in its point in that he finally learns he is alone.

**J:** Does it bother you that people tend to equate the phrase 'political plays' only with plays about 'party politics'?

**M:** Absolutely. An awful habit of Irish people is to identify politics only with 'jokes about Charlie'. There's far more to it than that. All my plays are studies of sexual politics in a way. That is a reflection of the time I grew up. When I came to be an adult, feminism was a very exciting, very innovative way of perceiving things and that certainly shaped me. As I suggested earlier in relation to female pop singers, it struck me in the context of outsiders, women taking control of their lives and challenging the way we live. Inevitably I couldn't be at the centre of that but I learned from it and that's how I work rather than direct involvement. And I really hope that I give back, in some ways, through my work.

**J:** Nevertheless, some might say you project your sexual uncertainties onto the characters of your plays in ways which make them misrepresent broader realities, less disturbed lives, perhaps.

**M:** That is a fair point but I do continually ask myself am I doing that. Then I look at my characters and see that some, in fact, have a lot more hang-ups than I have. *Caravaggio*, for example, is a damn sight more disturbed than even I am; *The Bread Man* too. And I do try to end the plays with a kind of talk, a healing touch to show that the people involved have, at least, taken one step forward. But I certainly am aware of that criticism.

**J:** What about the suggestion that unless you personally find a balance between the contrasting forces in your nature you will eventually burn yourself out as a writer?

**M:** I won't do that. I'm much too determined to keep going. I may decide to stop but I certainly won't burn myself out.

**J:** Do you agree that the seedbed of your creativity probably lies at a point defined by those conflicting forces within you?

**M:** It probably does, yeah. And the creativity is an attempt to find that balance then, having found it, paradoxically enough, disturb it in the work. And if I'm not writing I am, as I once said to someone 'edgy, moody, irritable, no company for a dog'. Dreadfully unhappy in fact. So, in the end it is both my lifeline and the way I choose to live my life. Without the writing I really don't know what I would do.

# 20 MARY COUGHLAN
## 1990

Mary Coughlan rejects as 'parochial' the criticism that by doing music that was so self-consciously European on her album *Under the Influence*, she was selling out on her Irish roots. 'That "selling out" accusation is crap. I'm an Irish singer, amn't I? Isn't that always there in my voice?

'"My Land Is Too Green" was directly political, saying "fuck the country", and I got a lot of flak for that. Particularly from journalists who said, "Hey, you can't slag off your country. It's been good to you." My response to that is fuck that. Criticising my country doesn't mean I'm not being good to my country in return. Why do people criticise things if not in the hope they may be able to bring about changes? Fuck the taboos. I'll sing about drink, drugs, sex – anything. Though when it comes to sex, I got a lot of hate mail after I did 'I Want to Be Seduced' on *Kelly's People* on TV in Northern Ireland. One letter said: "Ten men at our drinking table agree she is rude and vulgar." And that I was a "Southern Irish, Catholic, lesbian, feminist bitch"! Fuck them! But in terms of political songs, I'd have to identify with the political point being made. I couldn't sing it if I didn't feel it.'

One battle with which Mary Coughlan intrinsically identifies is the fight students are waging against SPUC [Society for the Protection of the Unborn Child] to ensure freedom of access to information about abortion. 'I went down to the court and I sang and stood outside and shouted with them. And it really was like a breath of fresh air to have people out on the streets protesting again. There doesn't seem to be the same fire and vigour among young people nowadays. And students have become very conservative and right wing and fascist. I was amazed at the number of universities that took the line SPUC was taking,' she explains.

Has Mary any sympathy for the line SPUC was taking?

'No. None at all. I do, however, believe that to have an abortion is to end life. I don't agree with those who say there is no life there until you cut the umbilical cord. I do believe that you are terminating something that is alive. I've had three kids and I know what I'm talking about. I've also suffered the devastation of miscarriages, so I am painfully aware of the mental and emotional upheaval involved in such things.'

Did Mary Coughlan ever need to seek advice on, or have, an abortion?

'Both. So I am speaking from the centre of the experience. That's part of the reason why my position on the issue is so strong. I've never said that before in an interview, but the bottom line is that I've had children, had miscarriages and had an abortion, so I know the agonising that's involved in all three. The decision to have a child is not easy; nor is the decision to have an abortion. Women need advice.'

Mary angrily suggests that the lack of advice before an abortion and the absence of aftercare is 'the most disgusting thing of all. It's bad enough having to have it done without any real advice beforehand, but it's worse knowing there will be no advice afterwards on how to cope... Obviously your family doctor has to give you a check-up after six weeks – if you can approach your family doctor – but that's not enough. And in any of the [family planning] centres they can't say anything because they never can tell who SPUC may have sent in to set them up.'

Mary shakes her head, unclenches her fist and turns to look out the hotel window. She pauses before continuing. 'That kind of things really is fucking disgusting to me, so how can I have any sympathy for people who would do something like that? As we speak there are women in deep crisis wondering should they or shouldn't they, and unable to talk to anyone about an abortion. Or girls coming back to Ireland after an abortion, having nowhere to go. And imagine how the women in the Well Woman centres feel, unable to help? It's horrendous. Though they did help me, as it was a long time ago now that I had my abortion. But it's repulsive that help is now denied to women who are going through such trauma. It certainly helped me to have advice, before and after.'

# 21 **PAUL DURCAN**
## 1990

It's no secret that one of the proudest moments in Paul Durcan's life occurred when President-elect Mary Robinson quoted from one of his poems during her recent victory speech. And not just because she used his poetry, or mentioned him by name, but because by drawing on the words of a writer who is relatively young, forward looking, heavily politicised and very much 'the people's poet', she was further fuelling the faith he'd shown by publicly supporting her. 'In electing Mary Robinson we've elected ourselves,' he said at the time. 'We've said yes to life. Instead of rejecting change we've embraced change. On November 7th we grew up.'

Furthermore, Brendan Kennelly has suggested that certain poems in Paul's latest book *Daddy, Daddy* are 'essential reading for politicians'. Specifically 'Poem Not Beginning with a Line from Pindar' which castigates both Durcan's late father and the party that appointed him 'President of the Circuit Court/Of the Republic of Ireland': Fine Gael.

'There is a strain running through the book, particularly the last section, which I refer to, in that poem, as "the history of fascism", and the connection is very much with the Fine Gael party,' Paul explains. 'And I'm not referring to just the Blueshirts – which is an easy cop-out interpretation for their own people. I'm referring to something that's much deeper and much more in their bloodstream. Part of what's at the root of it goes back to the Civil War then leaps forward, for example, to Garret FitzGerald very deliberately introducing to Sean Duignan, on the six o'clock news, the allegation that Mary Robinson should not be voted for because of her attitude to the Anglo-Irish Agreement. That, to me, is a continuing context for the fascism within Fine Gael. The hypocrisy of it. Over the bodies of tens of thousands of dead people in Northern Ireland Garret FitzGerald deliberately twists a knife in this woman who has done her level best to confront our nightmare in Northern Ireland. And this he did just to try get his Fine Gael candidate in. Unsuccessfully, as it transpired. But that's not the point. No man is lower in my estimation right now. And he is the one who spoke of "flawed pedigree". "Punk-yuppies" is the phrase I use in that poem to describe these guys in Fine Gael. It's a different thing again to the kind of cowboys and Indians we see played in Fianna Fáil. It is fascistic.'

Does Paul perceive John Bruton as carrying on this 'fascistic' tradition in Fine Gael?

'No. His first public statements as party leader were like a breath of fresh air and they suggested, to me, that he too has been changed by events in the last couple of weeks. There were echoes of the energy in Mary Robinson's campaign in John Bruton's whole demeanour and in the content of that statement, at least in relation to his remarks concerning civil liberties in Ireland – specifically divorce. That a new leader should take it upon himself to mention that at the start stunned me. And there was a certain ease about the way he spoke, an absence of that old rigidity, which to me strongly suggests a willingness to embrace rather than fight change. Though I suspect it will be a long time before the fundamental fascism in Fine Gael loosens its grip.'

Reflecting further on his involvement in Mary Robinson's presidential campaign, Paul Durcan says: 'Since then I've been told that all my remarks about Mary Robinson were "politically naïve", particularly, perhaps, my "We've elected ourselves" statement. But it still seems to me that even if you accept the preposterous proposition that Mary Robinson will now do nothing other than put her feet up in Áras an Uachtaráin for the next seven years, the fact that we elected her was a radical change in Irish history. And with all due respect to, and affection for, Mary Robinson, her election really had more to do with us than it had to do with her. Of course you can't disassociate the two but what it most reveals is the single, central fact that we voted her in. Quite a few people thought that the same rigid reactions that predominated the divorce and abortion referenda would reoccur, but they were proved wrong. And I'm still dazed by the fact that we did vote her in. And by the fact that a candidate of such a calibre and integrity should come forward in the first place. Some people suggest to those of us who have been celebrating that we should calm down, but those are the very people who are still holding on to that old, old Ireland, with its rigid rules like "You can't enjoy yourself, you mustn't". But for far too long we've knuckled under the cult of failure and the cult of darkness and dictates saying we mustn't celebrate what's good, spacious and hopeful. It's partly an outgrowth of the influence of those other, old grey men in the Church, telling us not to celebrate life, just to sit quietly in a corner and wait for death. Well, we've had enough of that. Of course I know – and we all know – that one person in the Phoenix Park isn't going to change Ireland totally; no one is that naïve. But to hell with the cynics. They too are part of that old, dying Ireland, I hope. This is something to celebrate. And in my heart I believe it is our response to the tide of Glasnost sweeping Europe. It must be clear to anyone who can perceive the truth, that in electing Mary Robinson we are breaking out of civil war politics. Those who can't see that are the ones who are politically naïve.'

# 22 SOUND BITES 1990

'I believe that the type of people who joined Fine Gael when I did, in the late 1970s, early 1980s, were not part of a repeat of that. The Civil War doesn't mean anything to me, really. When I get up on Monday morning it doesn't inspire me one way or the other. In fact I think the agenda I set out for economic reform and in terms of modernising institutions and effecting social change is more where it's going to be at in the future. And unless we can perform on those levels we are going to become a redundant party. You've got to change with the times. I'm not so tied to the past that I can't see several integral changes taking place in Fine Gael, in terms of structure, type of party financing name, philosophy, old parties merging to create new parties, whatever. The point of politics is to serve people and if you're not doing that because you're locked inside something that has no contemporary relevance to people then you deserve to become redundant.'

*(Fine Gael TD Ivan Yates, on the suggestion that one of the problems for his party, Fine Gael, is the need to establish that it has a raison d'être other than being doggedly anti-Fianna Fáil)*

'I've despaired of Charles Haughey since 1987. I had some belief in the possibility that he was what he maintained himself to be. But I don't believe him any more. I don't believe he has any great, deep conviction about anything. In 1985 the whole party as articulated by Charlie Haughey came out and slammed the Anglo-Irish

Agreement, left, right and centre, declaring that it copperfastened partition. With that, I entirely agreed then, and I still agree. And I can't stand the idea that he operates it despite that. The man is obsessed with power, with status and position. And each and every contradiction that he has been seen to be a part of, every U-turn he's done has been aimed towards him retaining that top spot. That's what makes the man tick. And I don't think it matters a damn at this stage, the cost to the party or anything else. Certainly the party doesn't matter a damn because he has wrecked it. Charlie Haughey has betrayed everything he ever stood for. Or, perhaps that's being much too charitable. He's betrayed everything that he led a traditional Fianna Fáil people to believe he stood for. He's sold Fianna Fáil out lock, stock, barrel. And with that any semblance it ever had of being a Republican party of the nature that was founded in 1926. Fianna Fáil, without its ideology, isn't even a third-rate political party. There never was any need for Fianna Fáil if it wasn't for logical assertion with regards to the unification of the country and the scrapping of partition. There wasn't any need for it to be formed. And the day they departed from that – which they now have – they became really third raters. Now they are only doing what others have been doing as well, or better, before them. And I would stress that I'm saying all this not just in relation to the National question. I'm thinking now specifically of the way we're preening ourselves and prancing around Europe at the moment claiming to be doing such a 'wonderful' job in terms of financial rectitude, budgets and reduced inflation and such. Inflation is on the rise again. And what about the national debt, which is also on the way up and which we're keeping so quiet about? What about the scandalously high unemployment, the unbelievably emigration? All these things are of the essence in terms of the well-being of any nation and yet here they are in total disarray and this is the country we're boasting about in Europe? Anything that we are achieving at the moment is at the expense of the poor bastards that have been chased out of the country and the others that are living on a shoestring in the country. It's all blood money. And I'm sick of Fianna Fáil, so sick of them. And no, not even to myself, can I glean hope from saying, "There is the one" who could change things.'

*(Independent Fianna Fáil member Neil Blaney)*

'That's just one of many similar assumptions. Another is that you are Gaelic, but things are changing. The World Cup epitomised that. There is a whole body of people under forty who are more modern and cosmopolitan in relation to their perspective on what it is to be Irish. And I think that the traditional values of the church, Fianna Fáil and the GAA don't have the grip on society they once had. Things haven't changed completely, but they will in the 1990s. The institutions that were known as controlling our society will have changed.'

*(Fine Gael TD Ivan Yates, elaborating on an earlier claim that he deplored the presumption that if one is Irish one automatically must be Catholic)*

'A central sorrow in the lives of all Irish people – one of which I am acutely aware, being Donegal-born and raised – is the situation in Northern Ireland. It was that feeling we tried to evoke in 'Harry's Game' which really does capture the true soul of Clannad. We tend to draw back from political statements in that sense, particularly about Ireland, but I honestly, deeply believe that music is a unifying factor, politically. And we do make a political statement just by singing Gaelic songs in the Royal Albert Hall. We're showing people there is more to Ireland than their possible, or probable perception of 'The Troubles', particularly, culturally. And 'Harry's Game' was our clearest statement about Northern Ireland because it doesn't show anyone winning in the end and that, to us, is the country's 'core sorrow'. But for the rest of my life I'll always remember singing that song in Belfast and being overcome by this truly magical, and healing feeling of unity. And it was, I think, Brendan Kennelly who said that Irish music, and Irish art in general, has so much to do with 'expressing the inexpressible'. Especially now, after centuries of oppression. That is very much Irish. And sometimes the achievement is in even trying to express such things. And that, plus maybe healing and unifying in even our own small way is, I hope, what Clannad achieves with the music.'

*(Maire Brennan, of Clannad)*

# 23   KENNETH BRANAGH
## 1991

It has been suggested that Kenneth Branagh's experience of originally being mocked for his working-class Belfast accent when he moved to England, plus a concomitant striving to be accepted by English society, may have led to a desire to reappropriate classic English roles once played by Laurence Olivier and Co. In other words cultural reappropriation à la James Joyce. 'Certainly I was deeply traumatised by the displacement anyone would feel leaving home at the age of nine,' he admits. 'And later, having discovered the theatre at sixteen – delving into the past and realising there is a history of acting and there is that classical tradition – that certainly did give me a sense of having found a great club I could belong to. But whether going after those classical roles was an attempt to legitimise myself is something I honestly don't know. Perhaps subconsciously it was. But in my mind it always seemed to be because I've a strong gut-reaction to those plays, the power, the dramatic poetry. They sound, taste, feel, look wonderful and are quite magical to act in. Because when Shakespeare is well done to me it is utterly real. But as I discovered when I presented Shakespeare in a school in London's East End, so often this great big, fucking wall comes down – this cultural divide – and it's "You're not educated enough to enjoy Shakespeare". That's the kind of cultural reappropriation I've always been trying to undo.'

Despite sharing what he describes as 'that Anglo-Irish sense of belonging nowhere', Branagh, for all his seeming 'Englishness', describes himself as 'an Irishman in spirit'.

'And I think this manifests itself in ways such as a certain love of words, a certain wildness and a maverick streak. I'm slightly outside it all,' he says.

'I was in Hollywood making *Dead Again*, but I wouldn't live there, I'd rather come back here. People think of me as a classical actor but I'm not in the National Theatre and I formed my own Shakespearean company and all that has to do with a very independent, romantic Irish view of life and of acting. It's the pursuit of something higher, of a more honourable way of life. We all fucking compromise ourselves left, right and centre but I really have never been in it just for the money. Though perhaps I do need it because I do feel so rootless. If I could just accept that this is my permanent state of being and not whip myself because I haven't fucking settled down anywhere, maybe then I'd be more at peace with myself.'

It was, ironically, Branagh's Belfast base which got his first major break as a professional actor, in the play *Too Late For Billy*.

In his autobiography Branagh claims that the play was deeply loved by his own family and by 'the Province'. 'There was a universal quality to the way in which it caught family relationships,' he elaborates.

'It caught a certain slice of working-class life which, while seeming to be soap-opera, somehow transcended that base because of the power of the writing, which streamed largely from someone with a desperate need to write about the situation. Everything was meant, everything was informed by personal feeling. And there was something very generous about the way it was unleashed, the realistic delineation of how tough the divisions between men and women are in that working-class environment. That all touched a chord all over the Province; especially there was something that responded to the fact that the drama had transcended the thing branded "Northern Ireland drama", integrally involving the Troubles. This was a "Protestant" film but the troubles were more of a backdrop for a story about the human condition that really covered a lot of people's experiences.'

Kenneth Branagh may as well be talking about his own family in particular when it comes to the question of 'the Troubles' being just a backdrop in their lives. In *Beginnings* he reveals that although the ratio of Protestants to Catholics in his street was two to one, the area was relatively free from sectarian violence until the night he watched 'wild-eyed Protestants from Shankhill Road' terrorise the area. How did that experience effect the young Kenneth Branagh politically? Did his family distance themselves from the developing 'Troubles' by moving to England in 1969?

'My father was a Protestant but never a member of the Orange Order, never involved in any of that. My parents' priorities always were to do with having enough food on the table and earning enough money to see that this was the case. And there always was a true neighbourliness thing in York Street and the surrounding area and everybody knew each other and were united in hardship because no one had much money. So their concerns never moved much further than the family, immediate and extended,' he says. 'So it seemed to me that there was that culture and a quite smaller yet very influential and powerful culture expressing political discontent. But the divisions were quite strong on both sides. So my parents' "political", if not apolitical, position didn't change when they left. It had always been a, perhaps simple, yet deeply held belief in common sense. They never talked about things politically, it was more about individuals who had suffered because of it all. But I never heard in our house any form of resentment based on religious prejudices. In fact I had cousins who were beaten up quite regularly for not joining the paramilitaries. Yet this was an absolutely inbred stance in that family, a resistance against people coercing them into doing what they didn't want to do. And that I inherited, absorbed. Ours was a very matter-of-fact even-handed approach to life that would not broach any political stuff.' And yet Kenneth Branagh is quite aware that Laurence Olivier's movie *Henry V* was used as propaganda during the Second World War, designed partly as a cinematic rallying call for England. Was Branagh afraid that in the post-Falklands 1980s his movie might be read as a clarion call for continuing colonialism, British rule at all costs?

'I think the ambiguity the play had, outside of the very special circumstances of the Olivier film, has to revolve around the action of a man that Shakespeare presents as invading another country on what seems clearly to be a political pretext. And a man who writes a play at the end of which his final words underline the irony of having invaded that country and lost it all. Shakespeare was very explicit about the ways he presents these facts and the way in which they are to be interpreted. What we did was to give all of this space in a way that couldn't possibly be seen as propagandistic. It was always clear to me that some people would look at it and see the film for what it was in the 1944 version – which is a tribute to the "Great British Invaders" and colonialist. But to me it's an ambiguous debate about the nature of war and the nature of leadership which, uncompromisingly, does not point the finger but literally leaves it all exposed, saying, "You are feeling sympathy for this man but look at what he's done." Am I to feel sympathy for this man too? Yet it also says, "Isn't he moving, even though he has killed all these people?" That's what I see as its core ambiguity. I certainly didn't see it as it was presented in 1944.'

And yet in his book Branagh says he wanted Henry and the English not to be seen as 'thugs'. Many people 'Irish in Spirit' might say that this position is a historical lie and that Ireland is continuing proof that the English can act as thugs.

'There have undoubtedly been English and Irish thugs throughout history. But I don't think you can label an entire race like that,' he says.

'There were thuggish deeds done in Irish history, there is no doubt of that. Yet what I wanted in *Henry V* was for the English to be seen not simply as thugs. I wanted them to be, as Shakespeare puts it, in the context of the whole man. In other words if you have to consider *Henry V* and the English as, on the one hand, brutes, then on the other hand you have to see them as people capable of deeds of generosity and passion. As we all are. Certainly as I am.'

# 24

# TOM MURPHY
# 1991

Tom Murphy is one of Ireland's leading playwrights, sharing the ever-shifting top position with fellow thespian Brian Friel. Indeed, there are those who believe that Murphy holds his cracked and shadowed mirror up against the Irish psyche, and reflects the *Zeitgeist* of our time, in a way that is rarely as consistently matched by any of his contemporaries.

**Joe Jackson:**

> You've claimed you grew up feeling 'like a Martian'. Isn't that a beneficial, even healthy perspective for an artist/playwright?

**Tom Murphy:**

> I would say it is now but I wouldn't wish it on anybody. I wouldn't want that to be the price of writing a few plays. But there is about many writers I know an element of the orphan, and the orphan complex. There is also a large element of exhibitionism involved, probably stemming from that 'Look at me – no hands – I exist – I belong here too' syndrome. And in many families, mine in particular, there was this tendency to compare the youngest member with somebody next door so that no matter how intelligent, or stupid, or how much of an achiever you were, there was that degree of sensitivity and of feeling like an ET.

**J:** You apparently invented a twin brother as a buffer against perceiving yourself as the underdog of the family. Would you describe that as one of the original impulses that later led to you writing plays?

**M:** Yes, but tellingly enough, when I did create a twin brother I made him younger than myself. Not so I could make him the underdog but so I could give him good advice and build up my own sense of self-importance. But other inclinations towards creativity showed themselves in the fact that at the age of nine I wrote a history of heavyweight boxing. There also was the huge influence of radio. There was one radio in the street – 'Mrs Ford's radio' – and a chosen few of us would visit her on Sunday nights to listen to the news, to a tenor named Billy Thompson singing songs like 'The Snowy Breasted Pearl' and finally to the Sunday night play. That led to a fascination with the disembodied voice, which has existed to this day. But if Mrs Ford had the first radio on the street I was the second. There was an old gas stove in our yard and I could fit in the oven of that and my feed man, who later wrote *On the Outside* with me, Noel O'Donoghue would twiddle the knobs on that gas stove and I'd sing. That's probably where it all started. Then later, in second year at school, I found I really could net a captive audience by reading to them, between classes, a novel I'd written. So, in a way, becoming a writer now seems to have been inevitable.

 **J:** Wasn't cinema also a huge influence?

**M:** Absolutely. My generation, my background, had more to do with film than stage. We saw McMasters only occasionally – I saw him twice – but I got to the cinema once a week and longed for it. I remember seeing a film of *The Glass Menagerie* and walking home with this couple who seemed elderly to me, they said, frowning, 'What was all that about?' and I said 'I thought it was great'. I couldn't tell you why it got through to me on such an intrinsic level but it did. Then a few years later I got a copy of Williams' *A Streetcar Named Desire* and reading it certainly became a punctuation mark in my life. I'd read Chekhov, Ibsen, Strindberg and so on and they were chalk marks on the wall but Williams was, and is, so exciting because he is so poetic and charged with an energy that Arthur Miller, for example, could never achieve. I'd never heard anything like the language – I could hear it – and I recognised the person, the human being, in Stanley. He wasn't just a character and the overall impression, rather than sense of comprehension, that play made on me was truly a liberating force in my life.

**J:** Evident from your own first play *On the Outside* is a sense of social divisions. Was that partly rooted in the fact that you'd crossed the class barriers in moving from a Christian Brothers secondary school to a tech in your teens?

**M:** Absolutely. I became very much aware of the working-class/middle-class divide because of that change. And that certainly was another input into the need to assert that 'I, Tom Murphy, am as good as anyone else' because there was a huge stigma attached in going to the tech – which was assumed to be for the stupidest and the poorest. I was one of the five in my class in the CBS who'd passed the Inter so they, naturally enough, wanted to hold on to me and when I told the Superior I was moving he said, "You can go to hell or you can go to the tech". In truth I had been in hell with the Brothers and I was very, very happy in the tech – even if I did become acutely aware of the class divide.

**J:** Why were you 'in hell' in the CBS?

**M:** I know it's a tired old story but I did live in terror of them. It was not unusual to go into school at nine or nine-thirty and already see boys lined up against three walls of a room waiting to be beaten. That whole landscape has left a terror that has rarely been matched in my life. And to describe another major difference in the tech I'd invert Goldsmith's line of 'the children reading the day's disaster on the master's face'. You could also see the teacher's reading the previous night's disasters that happened in our homes, and their sympathy and understanding. They had a life experience that included rows and conflicts within families of their own whereas the Brothers clearly couldn't give you that sense. And in terms of work the tech did prepare you for the sugar factory in Tuam, which had kept the town going for years. And it was there I began serving my time as a fitter-welder.

**J:** How would you describe the time you spent working in the sugar factory?

**M:** Well, the first year certainly was a honeymoon period. There was tremendous camaraderie there and suddenly, instead of the cinema we lived for the Sunday-night dance. The fitter I was with had a car and seven of us'd go to Seapoint on the Sunday night and six of us'd be left in Eyre Square at six o'clock in the morning waiting for the fucker to come back from having gotten off with a bird somewhere.

Then, during the tea break in the factory the next day there'd be a lot of talk about scoring. I remember one guy, who claimed he'd gotten off with five women the night before, was presented with this heavy lump of a chain as a symbol of his 'achievements'. In many ways it was a blissful time of my life.

**J:** You draw on those factory experiences for a play like *On the Outside* and yet still you've always denied that your plays are autobiographical. Aren't they, in a subterranean sense, as with Williams's work?

**M:** They are. And I think I've been too rigid in my denial of the autobiographical dimension until now. Most of the plays I've written are very autobiographical – in mood. And in terms of certain autobiographical details. Like in *The Gigli Concert*, the Irishman is forced by JPW to talk about his first sexual encounter and that is an autobiographical detail. A lady of perhaps fourteen, fifteen took me to the end of our garden where the potatoes were, took me on top of her between the drills and kept putting sweets in my mouth while she was trying to get my mickey into her. Yet, as I say in the play, I enjoyed the sweets, but my mickey was too young to enjoy her treat! But one of the reasons I've hitherto been denying an auto-biographical element is because ultimately a play has to transcend not just me but the characters themselves. The pendulum in life swings very fast on me and I deeply resent being a total victim of moods or feelings, old or new, being a puppet of anything. So in retaliation I recreate the feelings and reshape the experiences and then say, I created them, I'm now in control. Yet more than this core form of retaliation against life I must also hopefully, turn the feelings and experiences into some form of work of art. The ultimate retaliation is that the writer becomes the creator and if he, or she, achieves transcendence then you end up presenting a shared autobiography rather than just your own. That, always, has to be the goal.

**J:** Your father was a tradesperson forced to work abroad and your first major success, *A Whistle in the Dark*, opens with the impending arrival of the father of a train. Did the absent father syndrome lead you to believe that broken families are the natural order?

**M:** I don't think that a broken family is the natural order. I still believe very much in the family unit provided that the members of the family aren't trying to kill each other within that unit. A unit can become a bloodknot and then it's better to explode that and let the individual units pursue their own destiny. But to me the family is astonishingly beautiful and I do deeply regret that the economics of the time were so severe that my father had to emigrate when I was nine and that I was twenty-six before he came back. Indeed I'm conscious that already, since you and I began speaking, I've already mentioned my mother and, probably 'my mother's house' and that is like lifting the male figure out of the landscape where he became almost obliterated. But a seventeen-year gap is a long time. My father disappeared and my greatest moments of anticipation, and despair, were at that railway station in Tuam. But that only prevailed for the first three years. Then my father became redundant to me, which is sadder for him than for me. He was forced to emigrate and he must have felt totally unnecessary and that is a sense shared by many fathers that the man really is unnecessary. But it was heightened in my life because of the circumstances that forced my father to emigrate.

**J:** Was there a reconciliation when he returned in 1961?

**M:** In a way there was nothing to reconcile and there was little time anyway. He came home and I emigrated six months later and we kissed and cried together. But the difference was that by 1961 some of us could choose emigration rather than have it forced on us.

**J:** Your plays are political in the broadest sense in that they explore lives that have been blighted by emigration, poverty and other failures of the state. Yet does this mean you lack faith in any particular political ideology or party?

**M:** No, I lack a particular interest. But it's not solely that I don't want to be a political commentator in the narrow sense. I don't think I've got that sort of talent. And if I had I'd probably try to get rid of it because I do want to achieve some form of permanence in my work. There is a great danger of ephemeral being the net result when one tries to write about a political, or social, situation that is prevalent at the moment. A certain type of play being written now has so much to do with just sociological aspects that I always feel if the stage was a newspaper those plays belong on page twelve. I don't see the passion behind such work, or the life. It's not that all plays have to aspire towards music or poetry but I don't see that indefinable type of wonder in those works, which turns a piece of propaganda, or a political thesis, into art. It's the Williams/Miller divide again and I'll always come down on the side of Williams.

**J:** Many critics, in Ireland and Britain, suggested that *A Whistle in the Dark* was needlessly violent, exposing those dark, primal forces in the Irish psyche which most would rather see left unexplored.

**M:** When that play was done I was twenty-five. I'd been to England on a few occasions and that was just me absorbing a situation and giving it back with truth as I saw it. The English response I find glib and in terms of the Irish reaction, though it's claimed that de Valera and his comely maidens dancing at the crossroads are dead forever, they are not. If people react, not just to my play, but to that truth about themselves then they are denying a core truth about humanity. I'm Irish and I choose to write about a race I know but I can't be held accountable if some people are so immature that they refuse to acknowledge the dark, primal forces in our own nature.

**J:** Do you see that tendency as a consequence of the Christian desire to venerate the good/Godly and vilify all links to 'Satan', the other side?

**M:** Absolutely. The Christian lie we live is that if Christ was the magician he's supposed to have been why did he have to shed his blood? Surely he could have redeemed mankind with another trick? Secondly, part of Christian understanding is that we're all brothers. That's patently absurd. We have proved time and time again that we are not brothers and that, yes, is a refusal to admit to Cain and Abel. We will read about Cain and Abel as the first murderer yet we see it as a fairytale in the Bible. That is a base denial. If we agreed to the primal scream that Cain and Abel gave at each other, and that Cain killed Abel then we'd have to agree that the power to kill, and similar forces, are within us all. But instead we live the lie that we are brothers, 'civilised', 'a Christian people'. Yet it would be much healthier if we could accept that, yes, if you take a swing at me I will probably kill you. But people do deny that core truth as past or Christian mythology. People do try to deny the presence of the darkness. Look around Ireland, in particular, and see the psychic wounds that has led to. Many writers are described as 'dark', 'depressive' but we do at least confront and celebrate the darkness, as well as the light colours. That, in a very fundamental way, is an affirmation of the life-force and perhaps too, another form of retaliation against that potentially damning bias in Christian teaching. And in society at large. The greatest 'liars', in this context, are Californians and their culture certainly tries to deny that there are any dark shadings in life. That is lethal and something we, ultimately, must never yield to.

**J:** In *The Gigli Concert,* J.P.W. King finally turns to the 'devil' to pray. Must one go to that extreme to deny the lie in Christian teaching?

**M:** He responds that way because he finally realises that God doesn't exist, that God is people. Us, we are God. In the play J.P.W. says 'God created the world in order to create himself'. Part of this play, indeed many other plays I've written, is that we ourselves are the people who can fly, and will, eventually. We won't through appealing to something that isn't there. We, collectively, are the thing that is 'up there and/or 'down below'. We are the union of both forces and we don't need all this mumbo-jumbo about 'talking to God'. But no one needn't go to the extreme of turning solely to the dark force. That's the same twisted ideology turned inside out. But maybe it's a first move in accepting both.

**J:** You were once a devout Catholic, even serving at Mass at one point. Is part of the anti-clerical, anti-Christian element running through your work also based on a rage against the loss of having once been centred in one's faith?

**M:** You're dead right *[laughs]*. When people talk about how different my plays are from each other I immediately see the same threads running through my work. And frequently a character emerges who, in the play, is the most harsh, violent creature, yet it is he who was originally the most innocent and idealistic believer of all. Totally centred in one's faith, however you choose to define it – religious or otherwise. And when the disenchantment sets in it is then the person becomes increasingly dangerous as he, she kicks out in agony against the loss of all those certainties. Or, yes, of a central certainty. Perhaps that is part of what happened to me. I did shift from being a person who was supremely innocent to being extremely cynical about life.

**J:** What were the positive advantages of your base in religion, say, in relation to the concepts you draw on for your plays and the language you use?

**M:** Both those elements are definitely influenced by my base in Catholicism, of course. There also is an overarching ritual involved in religion which does, at least, bring people together in a gregarious, celebratory way. But all those formulas, and the emphasis they put on how to get into the next world is, fundamentally, a denial of this world, our potential in this life and that, finally, I cannot accept at all.

**J:** Catholicism also propagates a denial of the life-force, as in sexuality. Did you have many problems moving from the enjoyment of sweets you mentioned earlier, to an enjoyment of sex?

**M:** *[laughs]* The basic insult to the body, in Catholicism, was definitely a factor, yes. In Seapoint at those dances I'd occasionally stand on the balcony and look down at dancers, anything up to two thousand people. There was great, natural attraction between young men and women but most of them knew if they ever got into a situation where they actually had to expose themselves to each other that was a bigger sin than blowing off in your pants! So a lot of sperm was shed over desires fired on that maple floor in Seapoint. And doorways and cars in darkness became the place to discover the 'joys' of sexuality. They weren't, and couldn't ever be seen as 'joys' because the whole thing was seen as irredeemably dirty. People can't be screwing each other indiscriminately, especially these days, without some form of protection, but my mind boggles at the attitude that prevailed in the 1950s towards sex. It was anything other than celebratory. And like most young people of that time I had to fight to break free from that infantile reading of sexuality, in relation to a sense of my own, and women's bodies. Now I firmly believe that 'naked we come into the world' and that I apply as a core philosophical position in relation to sex, class, politics.

**J:** You said in 1985, 'My generation was brought up with the idea that a woman belonged on a pedestal or on her back'. Do you now see that either view is offensive to woman?

**M:** Yes. Both are equally offensive. My own coming of age, in this sense, has happened only over the last ten years. I seem, increasingly, to be trying to write for women, with, hopefully, a greater understanding of their psychology.

**J:** Were you wounded by the critic who suggested, early in your career that you 'knew nothing about women'?

**M:** That was said to me on my first ever first night and it has remained in my mind to this day. So clearly it wounded me, yes. Not in relation to my personal life but it is something I frequently think about in terms of my work.

**J:** Can you draw a distinction between the two? Looking back on your life, would you say that this admitted ignorance damaged your relationships with women?

**M:** *[laughs]* I feel that I am an evolved form of the Tom Murphy I was in Tuam. If I wasn't I should be shot. But I would hope that the learning process I've been involved in throughout my life, particularly in this context, through the roles I wrote for women, has lessened the danger of my ignorance damaging my relationships with them. But yes, when I started writing I used to view woman as a race apart. But in my own defence I must say that since that comment on that opening night people, particularly critics, have been very complimentary about the roles I write for women. Some suggest 'It's because you know Mary-so-and-so' but my secret is that those roles now come, fundamentally, from within me. I feel I now can adapt to the biologism of the female from within myself. And, more importantly, to the female within myself. Males shed too much of their 'femininity' as they grow older. I certainly did. But now I'm sick and fucking tired of the masculine role that was forced on me for most of my life. So in ways I'm trying to return, to reconcile all I once was with what I've become. But as to the idea that the union of masculine and feminine was the original state of being and it's that we're all trying to recapture I really can't focus on that because a blanket comes down over my mind's eye when people apply that kind of pure, philosophical reading to my life, or my work. But I would stress that this is not to say that such a theory isn't true.

**J:** Is a need for reconciliation with the original woman in your life – your mother – a need revealed in the fact that your play *A Crucial Week in the Life of a Grocer's Assistant* has been described as 'a savage attack on the Irish mammy'?

**M:** I was a man who, as I explained earlier, grew up almost without a father and so my mother was the figure of authority in the house – she was the matriarch. And I lived in that house, more or less, until I was twenty-seven. I recall that in the last five years of my life there when she made attempts to start conversations I just said yes or no – I know she wanted more conversation than that from me but I'd found a civilised way of dealing with a pressure that she, as the figure of authority, was putting on the house. And it was too much. So yes, certainly, in terms of feeling, there is an element of autobiography in *A Crucial Week*. Also I found when I was growing up a great hardness in Irish women – even if there was a beauty in the younger ones. Hence the fact that I married an Englishwoman made total sense to me. But subsequently, when I wrote a play called *Famine* which was the first time I tried to explore distinctions between the husband and wife, I decided, like O'Casey, that the woman was the real heroic figure. And in exploring mentalities of Irish people that had been twisted by their history I found I began to understand more about women, and the roles that had been forced on them by life, particularly here in Ireland. It was at that point I began to also understand a little more about my mother. But yes there definitely was an original need to rebel against her authority for a definite period in my life. But the real point in all this is that I was an extremely quiet man and the rebellion was happening inside. Yet when I began writing plays I realised I'd found a natural form of therapy for myself and a weapon against the silence that had dominated those years in my life. It was catharsis. One became a writer to have an outlet that is not banging doors, saying shit or fuck off to your mother. It's sitting down and working it out on paper.

**J:** Have you ever been punched back into silence by critical reactions to your work? You 'retired' at one point in the late 1970s.

**M:** By choice. And I was deeply depressed that Ireland didn't go into mourning! But no there is such a total selfishness about the writing that you forget there's a woman bleeding in the street and through that process you also forget negative responses to your work. And positive. You forget everything

**J:** Is that the reason your marriage failed? Must everyone – wife, children – remain bleeding outside your door while you get on with the work?

**M:** *[pause]* That's certainly a question I've thought about. I don't want to sound like the crucified writer but at times it strikes me that writing seems to be the only thing I can do. Yet I don't know that writers and artists hold a monopoly on domestic crises or marital breakdowns. I can think of a number of reasons, outside my work, why I separated from my wife and family. But yes, the creative business is conducive to destroying the bond that exists with one's dearest. When one gets into the deepest process of writing a play it is a totally selfish business. Writing is a solitary, antisocial game, yet the problem is that frequently the writer works at home. He locks himself in his room while domestic life goes on all around him. He has his ups and downs in his home, things that, in other professions, happen on the building site, in factories, in the office. These ups can be as mysterious and meaningless to his family as the downs. The family wonders what colour his mood will be when he comes out of his room. Frequently he's silent for long periods. The work, like a disease, can be all-embracing. He carries it, mentally, with him to the kitchen table. A family – wife, children – can interpret this antisocial behaviour as a reflection of their failings. They can celebrate an up with him – but at his dictate. It is inhumanely selfish, despotic and unfair. And it's difficult for any marriage, or relationship, to survive such extremes. I'm not saying every writer is this way but it's pretty close to what I'm like.

**J:** Does that mean you have to find a companion, or form children, who can cancel out their human needs while you're committing your life to that process?

**M:** *[pause]* That's a very dangerous question and I must admit I hadn't thought about it that deeply because I'm always, still, so involved in the process. But there is the feeling, in terms of human relationships, the question: 'Am I so treacherous that if it comes to it I'll go for a minor degree of ecstasy through my involvement in art rather than try meet the demands of an ongoing human relationship?' There is no single answer to that. But I do know that the twenty-five or so stage plays I've written are of nothing when I look at one of my children. I can't speak for other members of the family in terms of us living apart but I do know my love has not diminished and in relation to friendships with members of my family I now feel that the friendship is stronger. But I do ask myself what was I giving while I was there? That kind of solitary confinement I mentioned earlier can last for anything up to two years – with weekends meaning nothing. And it doesn't cease when the play is finished because at that point you feel like a dog that's been locked up all that time and once you're released you start to chase the wind. Hence the artists that go crazy around town, shouting, fighting, drinking. But the point is that the last thing you want is to have to meet the domestic needs of the family, even though the immediate have been waiting patiently for the emergence of a social animal. Instead all they get is a wild dog.

**J:** Is part of this 'chasing the wind' an indulgence in drink, for you?

**M:** Certainly there is an attempt to numb the skull, to a degree, to kill the feeling of guilt one has about the family because they have put up with the bear for so long.

**J:** Are you in control of that pattern or is it in control of you?

**M:** I'm in control of it to the extent that I do seek release that way and have almost always done that. Equally I've also carried a guilt with me for doing that. I've no control over the guilt but I must indulge myself in some sort of debauch of socialising after immersing myself that deeply in the work. But the single, solitary light of redemption, I hope, in all this is that there is a point, when I'm writing, where I forget not just my nearest and dearest but also myself. I can get up at 4 a.m., start work then look at the clock and it's suddenly ten past two. Time has no meaning in that context. I've stepped out of time. And if I have an ability to do that, which I achieve rarely, then that is what I'm continually seeking. This transcendence of the self, writing the play, can also mean I may hit that target when the play is staged. In that sense the larger, aggregate self becomes of more importance than any immediate consideration in terms of the needs of loved ones, or my own needs. I have been, and am frequently sorry and guilty about my chosen way of life but if I changed, mended my wicked ways and sacrificed the plays I'd probably be sorrier and guiltier.

**J:** Patrick Mason describes *The Gigli Concert* as having people in conflict, wrestling with the 'dark angel' yet some critics suggest that your later plays, overall, mark a point of resolution in your work, of the unremitting tragedy of *A Whistle in the Dark* giving way to a glimmer of hope.

**M:** More than a glimmer of hope, I'd say. And in terms of wrestling with the 'dark angel' I've been told I tempt sanity in the way I approach my work. And it is like wrestling, say, with the darkness of a disease, saying 'I'm going to get the better of this play, it won't beat me'. Sometimes it does. The real darkness, depression, comes out of trying to get a first draft. Like when you're working on something for weeks and nothing is happening and you ask, 'What could this mean to myself or to anyone else? Nothing', and you stay in bed for two weeks, grind your teeth at the ceiling and say 'If that's how life wants it then fuck life'. So I do go into a form of combat but one has to go down into the abyss to reach the source of more than a glimmer of hope – the springboard beyond the self. That's the wonderful paradox. As a character in one of my plays says 'rock bottom is my basis'. That is the area you have to travel to. I'm not saying I do it every time. I don't have that kind of courage. But what we're talking about here is a state of total unselfishness a writer who is saying 'I'm ready to lay down my life for this'. Joe, I really don't want to make myself out to be a martyr for my art or suggest that the writer is on a higher plane than anyone else. Not at all. But this is the creative process, as I know it. This is what playwriting is to me.

# 25 CHRISTY MOORE
## 1991

In 1987 Philip King described Christy Moore as 'singularly the most popular entertainer in the country'. Four years later, as the century slides into its last decade, one could suggest that Moore also is the single most important Irish singer/songwriter of our time, largely because his best work operates as a blend of both poetry and political polemic. Indeed, at some point in the future, when cultural analysts seek to find a popular art form which will most profitably reflect the social/sexual/political changes over at least the last half of the 1980s in Ireland, it is to Moore's work they should turn. His emotional power, his perceptions, sense of humour, history and of self makes him a true barometer of his age.

And yet, if Christy Moore is quintessentially Irish, he also has embodied some of the more questionable traits of his race, such as his one-time tendency to define his 'Irishness' solely in accordance with his propensity for alcohol, his patriarchal perspective on women and his heart-first-and-maybe-the-head-will-follow approach to politics. And if the latter, for many, is undermined by the lack of a base in political theory that too is a characteristic which frequently defines Irish nationalism.

However, as Christy Moore himself says, 'It all begins and ends with the music.' Donal Lunny, a friend of Moore's since childhood, has written in *The Christy Moore Songbook* that 'sessions of music were frequent in his family – his mother Nancy loved, and still loves, creating opportunities for people to sing and play. Thus encouraged, albeit initially in a more genteel direction, Christy flourished.'

'"Genteel" is not a word I would have used!' laughs Moore. 'It suggests something cosy and inoffensive and decidedly middle-class. There was a touch of that but the first songs I ever learned were things like "Kevin Barry" and "The Meeting of the Waters" and hymns and such. It wasn't traditional music I was into in those early days. There always was music there but it was show tunes and pop songs. I remember popular music before rock 'n' roll.'

Christy Moore reveals that although he was a bit of a 'teddy boy' in the mid-50s he wasn't bohemian enough to rip out seats in cinemas as he watched *Rock Around the Clock*. 'I saw the film in Newbridge and Naas and Celbridge but I wasn't into that,' he laughs. 'Yet I certainly was aware of the birth of something new. I was very into rock 'n' roll and Radio Luxembourg, 208, from the moment it all hit Ireland. I bought Elvis 78s from the beginning. I remember the thrill of buying 'Hound Dog' and later the trauma of having to change over to 45s, getting the first one – Elvis's 'A Mess of Blues'. I also remember having an amazing time dancing to those early rock 'n' roll records. It was wild,' he recalls.

Was 'Christy the Ted' also a bit of a 1950s wild-boy in terms of 'wimmin and de drink'?

'Of course that was part of it,' he smiles, almost coquettishly. 'I started drinking very young and there was always a lot of lovely women around and it would have been weird seeing Kildare women and not trying to get off with them! Strangely enough my Catholic school upbringing didn't really leave a mark on me in terms of sex. I worked very diligently to break those particular chains! But then by the time I started getting off with women I was no longer worried about mortal sin. By that stage I only worried about mortal sins when I wasn't committing them.'

Christy pauses before continuing. 'But it is true that I had no problem at all with my own sexuality from the point of view of the Catholic Church. The only problem I had with sex and the Catholic Church was that it prevented me from having all the sexual experiences I wanted as a young man. But that wasn't because of any conflict between the Church and me. It was more a result of conflict between the Church and the people I wanted to have sex with.'

More seriously Christy adds, 'A lot of Irish women writers have written about this from the other side, how women had more problems than men had in the 1950s, 1960s, coming to terms with their bodies. But I wouldn't have been aware of this, or sensitive to that side of the argument at all, at the time.'

So how has Christy Moore's attitude to women changed over the years? Was it originally sexist, chauvinistic, thoughtlessly placing the man's desires, on all levels, above the woman's needs?

'Yes, guilty on all counts,' he answers unhesitatingly. 'And as I've achieved liberation from my attitudes towards women, as I've become educated over the last fifteen years, I've realised that I was tremendously sexist when I was younger. But those were the attitudes that were normal at the time. Who, in Ireland, in 1961 believed women were equal to men? Even women didn't, or if they did they weren't telling me. So if I was to give a more considered answer to your question about the influence of Catholicism on my attitude to sexuality I'd have to say that part of the root of that attitude to women stemmed from my upbringing as a Catholic. The patriarchal perspective, the belief that women definitely were not equal in the eyes of the Church and that they were, in fact, totally different people. People who were there to serve, sexually, and in every way. And it was years before I broke away from those shackles. But then my attempts weren't helped by the fact that for a long time I was working in folk music. I remember getting a shock once when I heard Gay Woods on the radio saying that the whole folk-scene was so macho and male-oriented that it was ridiculous. She's right. She also said, "All these men singing 'Fine Girl You Are' but I never felt like a 'fine girl'." That brought me down to earth and made me realise that the folk world is totally a male-dominated ethos. But such realisations were far from my mind when I began singing folk music in the early 1960s.'

So, why had he abandoned rock 'n' roll?

'Because, although I was listening to Elvis, Buddy Holly, Terry Dene, Gene Vincent, Cliff Richard and Tommy Steele up until 1960, I then heard the Clancy Brothers and – end of story! Or, at least, suspension of Christy the rocker's story.'

And yet Moore clearly had absorbed more than just a rock 'n' roll attitude. His breakthrough album *Prosperous*, though intrinsically true to Irish traditional music, was also fired by what one commentator described as a 'youthful exuberance' and a fresh approach to the genre – particularly in the album's opening salvo 'The Raggle Taggle Gypsies/ Tabhair Dom Do Lambh'. It also contained Woody Guthrie's 'The Ludlow Massacre' and Dylan's 'Tribute To Woody', the latter's inclusion explained by the sleeve note by Christy which said: 'There is very little I can add to what has been said about Woody, except that for me he was the man.' Twenty years later, however, there is more he can add to that hymn of praise.

'The approach Woody Guthrie took was a revelation to me when I first heard his songs, particularly the fact that he could take something that was specific to an area and turn it into a song that had universal resonance, as in "The Ludlow Massacre". You can sing those songs seventy years after the event and they are still relevant because, at base, they are about injustice. On this level other songs of his inspired, for example, my "Stardust" song which is a memorium to the people who died in that fire yet which also asks questions about a society that would allow that to happen. That's something Woody Guthrie had and that's how he influenced me, fundamentally. The seed was sown in 1966–67, but it wasn't until ten years later that I really started producing work in that mould. I'd played with Planxty and recorded a lot of albums before the Guthrie/Ewan McColl influence bore fruit. But part of that influence, when I was with Planxty, was that I reached a point where I no longer felt satisfied getting up on stage and singing with the band. It was a big high for the first three years. Playing in the Carlton to two thousand people was fucking amazing. But I needed something that was more substantial in my work. I needed songs that had more contemporary influences, that had their roots and their reference points in the present, rather than in the past. And, primarily, songs that were political. I felt an obligation to sing such songs because no one else was singing them at the time.'

Christy Moore has always claimed that it was the nuclear power plant issue, brought into high-profile in Ireland courtesy of the Carnsore controversy in 1978, which led to his 'politicisation'. Why wasn't he similarly effected by the escalation of civil unrest in Northern Ireland in the late 1960s or, for example, after the Bloody Sunday massacre in 1972?

'There were political awakenings in 1967–69, but it was a few years before I became involved on a personal level and subsequently through my music. I wouldn't have begun to describe my position as "republican", for example, until 1972–73, but it was a slow evolutionary process rather than waking up one morning and saying, "This is what I am". Yet I never studied politics in my life. It was always a gut instinct. But the reason I didn't speak out in 1972–73 was because I was too wrapped up in being with this big band, the success of it all,' he says. 'And there was always a lot of paranoia in Planxty in terms of political issues and making political statements through songs. "Only Our Rivers Run Free" was about as radical as we got! This was a dictate within the band, it was part of the deal. And, as I say, I had to leave because I needed to make political statements through my music.'

Yet Christy Moore admits that he had been making coded and counter-productive 'political statements' through the style of his solo performances in England from 1966–70. 'When I was performing there for a lot of the time, to my shame, I was the stage Irishman who went on and sang sexist, bawdy songs. At the time I wasn't aware that this political consequence of this was that I was feeding into the stereotypical image the English had/have the Irish. Toward the end I became aware of it.'

Revealing that at this point in his life, and throughout the 1970s he was 'filled with hatred', Christy Moore admits that this feeling frequently found a point of focus in his audience. 'There were times I was obnoxious on stage,' he says. 'Sometimes I hated the audience as mass of people and occasionally, though not often, I'd even come down off the stage and take someone on, usually coming out second best. I also got a few hidings after gigs and I'm sure I made many enemies during those days. But I was drunk all the time and that's how it came out. I hated every fucking thing. I hated the world and I hated myself most of all. And the point is that I never had that sense of hatred when I was younger. I don't remember being filled with hatred when I was a young man or when I worked in a bank or went to England in the first place. I was full of the joys of life. But I became dependent on drink and some time in the 1970s I lost touch with all realities other than my desire for drink. I was a very confused person, very fucked up.' He sighs.

Looking back on the gigs he gave in those days, particularly in the late 1960s, Christy says, 'Drinking was such a crutch for such a long time that I couldn't go through a day without a drink. For ten years of my life every time I went on stage I was drunk, even though it may not have seemed that way. I certainly was drunk by the end of the night. And although at the time I thought I was delivering good gigs I now realise I wasn't as assiduous as I could have been. It was the same in the studio. On the third Planxty album Phil Coulter plays keyboards on the track where I didn't turn up because I was so pissed! That was 1973–74. And that's no way to remain a functioning professional musician, or a functioning anything. And I was very lucky to escape from all that and to still be creating music. It was a long process breaking the dependency. For many years I tried to stop drinking and never quite managed it. It's only over the last three years I've finally kicked off the shackles of alcohol and found it's possible for me to carry on a life without that crutch, that weight on my back.'

Moore claims that both Planxty and, later, Moving Hearts 'evolved from discussions he had with Donal Lunny. In his book on Irish rock Mark Prendergast claims that one problem for the latter band was that initially they 'were very much perceived as an overtly republican group [and] this led to a lack of airplay, record company support and financial rewards.'

'Politically, we were, by and large, ideologically unified,' says Moore. 'And what happened was that the first year of the band saw the lead-up to the hunger strikes and in the second year the hunger strikes were happening so we had to sing about that. The whole country was effected by it and as we all had similar feelings about such issues there was, in this case, no problem about making political statements through the songs. And there never was a lack of record company support, in Ireland. WEA released anything we wanted to release. They released material that no other record company in Ireland would have released at the time, particularly "On The Blanket", which was recorded the night Martin Hurson died. And we were doing a gig in Castlebar when Ciaran Doherty died. So we were affected by all that.'

Around the same time as his breakthrough solo album *Ride On*, Christy Moore recorded a 'bootleg' album *Spirit of Freedom*, which was originally released in what he now claims was 'a limited issue of 500 cassettes'. If 'limited', why was the album later officially released by WEA and is it true that the profits from the project went to 'the republican cause'?

'The money was to go to prisoner's dependants to buy a vehicle to ferry them back and forth, that was the original intention,' explains Moore. 'And in my naïveté I thought that I could release the album and WEA wouldn't get to know about it. But six months later the then MD, with a copy of it in his hand, said "What's this?" According to the terms of my contract it was their property so I had to give them the master tapes and they released it as an album.'

In such a situation, or initially, could Moore oversee the project, insist that the profits be used for buying that vehicle rather than, for example, for purchasing arms? 'I didn't physically oversee the project of the tapes but I would have handed them over and said, "This money has to go to purchasing a vehicle",' he says. 'But then how does anyone know where money from anything goes? Suppose I make an album for WEA and a subsidiary of the company is involved in the production of arms for the arms race, what way have I of knowing whether or not that subsidiary of Warners in America is, or isn't, using the profits from *Ride On* to develop new weaponry? So the answer to your question, as in that scenario, is no, I didn't know where the money was going and if I'd examined it eight years ago, in this context, I don't know what my answer would be. I don't know how much weaponry costs, but profits from the project must have been in the region of £10,000, which would have been the approximate cost of such a vehicle. I don't know how much weaponry you'd get for that but I suspect it wouldn't help carry on any kind of war for long.'

Yet would Christy Moore raise moral objections if any weapons were bought with the profits from his records?

'Now I would,' he says. Meaning that in the early 1980s he wouldn't have objected? 'I don't know,' he replies. 'I can't put myself back to 1983 and say this is exactly what I would have felt. All I can say is that now I would have an objection.'

At times such as the Enniskillen bombings, how deeply does Christy Moore question his definition of republicanism? 'At times like Enniskillen, if not all the time since, it is a constant process of re-definition,' he says. 'And bringing it up to date, thinking of how Tom Oliver was killed and how a kitchen porter was used in a proxy bombing, I find I've reached a point in my life where I can't fucking take it any more. After Enniskillen, and now, I find I no longer can support the armed struggle. It's reached a point of futility. It doesn't seem possible to carry out an armed struggle against the enemy. It's an armed struggle in which too many "little people" are blown away. And you can extend this view with attacks on the enemy. On the one hand the enemy of the British are the little people in the republican movement and in the Nationalist ghettos in Northern Ireland, and on the other hand, the enemies of the IRA are squaddies in the British army. Guys who end up in the armed forces because they are unemployed and sick of hanging around job centres in Tyneside, or wherever. These are the people who are dying. So I have all these conflicting feelings where it once seemed to be so clear cut. Then, of course, I also have the feeling of "Where am I at?" Here I am ten years after the hunger strikes and I no longer can support what I supported ten years ago.'

Do those he supported ten years ago accuse Christy Moore of 'selling out' or 'having lost his guts'?

'I haven't encountered that yet but when I do I'll say it can't be helped. This is how I am, how I feel in 1991. You must tell the truth, whatever the consequences. Of course I still can't tolerate even the thought of one side of the community in Northern Ireland being able to suppress the other with the presence of a foreign army. It doesn't seem right to me and never has, since I was a child. Nothing has happened over the past twenty years to make that more palatable to me and I can't handle it. I can't handle it when I go up North and I am stopped by British soldiers. I can't handle the fact that the view we have of the North, in Dublin, in the twenty-six counties, reflects no understanding of what's going on up there. All we ever hear about is what the IRA is up to. Let's examine closely what's happening on the other side. They're talking about internment again! There have been thousands of republicans interned, hundreds locked up for possession of weapons, yet we never had a British soldier charged for shooting children with rubber bullets. That causes deep confusion within me, and anger. I can't handle it. And as I talk to you now about it that old sense of hopelessness sweeps over me and I see no way out of it all. I understand why the struggle goes on but I can't see where it will end. But the point is that I'm not subsumed by it as I used to be. There was a time in my life when I was preoccupied with the war in the North. But I'm not preoccupied with it any more. I really do bring it down to a question of all the little people who are suffering and dying. That, to me, is the bottom line.'

Christy Moore's core concern for the common person runs, like a silver thread, through all his solo albums from 1984's *Ride On* to 1991's *Smoke and Strong Whiskey*. Songs about oppression and strip-searching in Northern Ireland sit alongside songs that highlight political injustices in South Africa and in Dublin. 'My songs must be viewed in this wider context,' he claims. However, Moore is angered by the suggestion that his last album *Voyage* too often veered near presenting the kind of 'romantic escapism' he once seemed to be attacking by writing the politically explicit 'The Other Side' in reply to Paul Brady's 'The Island'.

Eamonn McCann has suggested that Christy's 'spot-on reference to Paul Brady dreaming his Troubles away on the strand is the most perfectly aimed piece of musical polemic in history'.

'When I heard "The Island" it sparked off in me a need to write "The Other Side (of the Island)" because I feel differently about the same place, but it certainly wasn't a musical polemic against Paul and I don't think he took it that way,' he says. 'And as for the suggestion that certain songs are inferior because they are more in the mode of "romantic escapism" than political polemic – though both are far from mutually exclusive – I no longer go along with that. It's a kind of intellectual or political elitism. And I now feel we have to give people the right to choose what they listen to. One can be critical of what other people do listen to but I now see it's intrusive for me to even suggest that people who like mostly love songs are being exploited by the singer. Or to suggest that hat singer is, wittingly or unwittingly, in the service of the state, using "romantic escapism" to blind people to other political realities. I no longer see things that way.'

Addressing the criticism of *Voyage*, Christy Moore says: ' "Farewell To Pripchat", which is about the Chernobyl disaster, could hardly be described as romantic escapism. Nor could "Missing You". But yeah, a lot of people were angry with me for recording "The Voyage" because they felt it wasn't a "Christy Moore-type song", which means someone out there is making the statement that I cannot write/sing a song of love for my family. Seemingly some people consider expressions of love as wishy-washy and I myself would have gone through a long period of my life very uncomfortable with terms of affection. My macho codes wouldn't allow me to say "I love you" or "I'm afraid" or "I'm a coward". Apparently it's fine in folk/rock culture to express hatred and rage. But I've had enough of that. Expressions of love are another facet of self-expression that I should have the right to choose. And I do, through songs like 'The Voyage'. And there are other people whose albums I'll always buy, just to hear what they're doing: Shane McGowan, Dylan, Elvis Costello, Leonard Cohen and Van Morrison. I wouldn't listen to them in relation to my own work, I just love the way they sing. They touch me, move me, have that power we spoke about at the beginning of this interview. I really love the way Van Morrison sings.'

The voice/music of Van Morrison is very much defined by the singer's continuing spiritual quest, yet if Moore does identify with Morrison on that level, he claims that his heart attack in 1987 did not reunite him with his 'original Catholic-based concept of God'.

'Until quite recently I was spiritually bankrupt,' he reveals, smiling slightly. 'During a whole period of my life I believed I was God. Not in the David Icke sense, more in the sense that I believed I knew everything and that no one could tell me anything. But now I believe there are powers outside of me. Yet it's not at all a return to the old faith, or its core concepts. I've no trouble with the concepts believed in by Catholics, Protestants, Jews, but none of that is for me Yet what I have is the tolerance to allow people to have their own space – provided they don't ram it down my fucking throat, or down anyone else's throat. I've learned tolerance for other people's beliefs, which I didn't used to have. There was a time I considered it most uncool to be a Catholic and I wouldn't allow people that right. Now, as with other areas we've talked about today, I respect other people's right to choose. And I do have again a spirituality in my own life, which I must have had as a youngster, yet lost somewhere along the way. But then I was forced to go to Mass and to believe in ever-fucking-lasting hell. I had to rebel against that. Yet now I see other, more positive sides to the story. I realise that having a base in Catholicism equipped me with a language in terms of concepts like spirituality and grace and aspiring towards something higher, better. Elements of that very much mark my writing and the works of many Irish writers.'

Pausing to reflect on what would have been his artistic legacy if that heart attack had killed him in 1987, Christy Moore concludes: 'I've probably written a couple of hundred songs but I've only recorded about twenty-five of them. Maybe 'Lisdoonvarna' is the best song I ever wrote. A lot of people don't think it's a serious song, but it is and it's serious piece of writing. It originally painted a picture of a particular point in my life yet I can perform it anywhere in the world and it seems to also paint similar pictures for other people. It's plugged into something so it must be a good piece of writing. I don't sell it short any more, whereas I used to say "Oh it's just something I rattled off". It's not. It's a song of mine that has passed into the tradition. It's the same with certain other songs I do. People shout lines from these songs at me and I know they have a resonance beyond just my life. Songs like "Vive La Quinte Brigada", "Derby Day" and "Delerium Tremens" for different reasons to different people. And a song like "Ninety Miles to Dublin" – whatever anyone thinks about it, is a very descriptive song about what led up to, and happened during, the dirty protests. The beatings, the methods of torture. It's not the kind of song you'll hear on MTV but in terms of presenting a historic perspective it is true. And it's the same with regards to "On the Bridge", which describes strip-searching; and "The Time Has Come" which, though seen by some as a simple love song, is about hunger strikers dying. And perhaps, though it may be too soon to say "Whacker Humphries" from the new album 'Smoke and Strong Whiskey', which could be describing an inner-city drugs situation that applies anywhere in the world. I do have a style of writing that is peculiarly my own, for better or worse, and I'm proud of it. And in terms of what I leave behind I believe some of these songs of mine will surely live longer than I will. That, in itself, is a gratifying feeling. To know that even a handful of my songs, in years to come, will mean to other people what certain songs meant to me when I started singing. Those songs were written by people whose names I don't even know. And although it may seem trivial or simplistic, it has occurred to me that someday people may sing one of my songs and not know who I am. My name, my memory won't come into it. That too is an appealing thought. You can't leave more behind, artistically, than the fact that the song finally matters more than the singer, that the song finally became part of the people and, hopefully, will remain so after the singer has gone.'

# 26 SOUND BITES
## 1991

'There's a huge reservoir of compassion and concern for people in the Catholic tradition, and, indeed, in other Christian traditions. The one I'm most familiar with is the Catholic tradition and I think there is a tremendous amount of good in it which needs to be developed into the political field. Not in the sense that the religious viewpoint should proscribe what politicians can do, but in the sense that one can draw on that as a reservoir of thought and human experience and inspiration. But I wouldn't claim myself to be a very religious person, I'm not religious at all. To be truthful I couldn't claim to be very spiritual. It's an important, but not dominant part of my life. So, if, for example, the Pope phoned in relation to the divorce referendum and said 'you've got to keep Ireland Catholic' I'd say that's not my job as a politician. Likewise, I'm totally in favour of changing Articles 2 and 3. I don't think that in the Europe of 1991 the Constitution of one state should lay claim to any territory that's not already in its jurisdiction, within explicit regard to the people living in that territory. Our Constitution contains a claim on an area which basically puts territory before people and to come back to that core Fine Gael view, if, 'every person counts', then every Unionist counts. And our Constitution shouldn't proceed on the basis of claiming territory regardless of what the people believe there. And that, in a sense, is a very fundamental difference between Fine Gael and Fianna Fáil. We take the view that it's what people can live with that's important, not some theoretical map or image. So, yes, Fine

Gael are now relinquishing claims, as a right, to territorial unity with the North. We would not claim a right to rule the North on the basis of words in our Constitution. We would hope that circumstances would be arrived at, in which the majority of people in Northern Ireland would want to form a closer political connection with people on the rest of this island. But not on the basis of something that would be imposed as a right, but rather as a voluntary decision. As long as we're making a claim there's no chance of any voluntary coming together. And there's no coming together that's worth having if it isn't voluntary.

'And in my first speech as party leader I said, "The defeat of the IRA will remove the primary cause of violence in this country." I still believe that. I don't accept the counterview, that historically, the primary cause of violence in this country is the British presence. Because I think that, in reality, the British would agree to any solution that the communities in this island could agree to. I don't believe that the British have any strategic interest in Northern Ireland as such. It's costing them a lot of money and once we, and they, move closer in the European community they will become even more indifferent as to what sort of political future Northern Ireland chooses for itself. I think, however, that the campaign of violence initiated by the IRA, first against the security, then gradually spreading out to effect all of the Protestants, has led to counter-terror on the part of the Protestants. But if the IRA campaign stopped it wouldn't be long before the Loyalist counter-terror would also stop. And, in that sense, I think the IRA is the primary cause – not the sole, but the primary cause – of violence. We've got to start now to move forward. And, in my view, the British presence in Northern Ireland is not there because of any British wish it's simply there because there isn't agreement between the people living in Ireland.'

*(John Bruton, soon-to-be Taoiseach of Ireland)*

'Of course events in Eastern Europe have created a major debate within the Workers' Party but before those events ever happened, Proinsias De Rossa, in his first address as President of the Party, made very clear a number of points pertinent to this revisionist view:

namely that there is no such thing as socialism without democracy and that democracy must lie at the heart of socialism. We have set up a committee which will have a document ready for the next annual conference and it will clearly take into account the fact that the centralised, standardised model of socialism practised by the Soviet Union is dead and finished and failed and is simply not workable. I, and most members of the Workers' Party never believed that it was an ideal model for socialism. But you don't throw out the egalitarian principles because of the failure of the Soviet model. The principles of the French Revolution, of liberty, fraternity and equality, are as pertinent to our society today as they ever were. Look at the way the First World is raping the Third World, forty thousand children dying every week of malnutrition. In a global sense exploitation is still at the heart of politics. Describe that in whatever revisionist modern language you want it is still exploitation. That is the role of the noble, socialist ideal and how it will be expressed by us in the future, is what the public will make their decisions on.'

*(Pat Rabbitte, Workers' Party TD)*

'It's because I believe there is no future for the Labour Party if it sells out on its core values and moves unduly from its existing position. There are other parties which represent people in the upper echelons and let's not forget that the only reason for the formation of the Labour Party is that no political party was representing people that needed representing at the lower end of the scale. And if it does move from this core position it's moving into an area that is already catered for by Fianna Fáil, Fine Gael and the Progressive Democrats. What the Labour Party must do instead is restate its commitment to its natural constituency which is that third of the Irish population on, or below the poverty line. Then it can seek to increase its attraction to the electorate in other sectors, who would broadly share its concerns. That is one of the lessons we must learn from Mary Robinson's election win. But unless the Labour Party remains anchored to its natural constituency it will in time become irrelevant, redundant, just one more party of the centre.'

*(Joe Costello, Labour Senator)*

'You see U2 graffiti everywhere in the world and that reminds you that four guys can come from a small city like Dublin and make themselves known across the world. That fact alone definitely is a source of inspiration because when you're growing up you realise that your only goal, as a band, need not only be playing the Baggot Inn, that you can reach any audience in the world. Not in terms of selling product but with your music. That is a magnificent thing to inspire. But, at the same time, I get sick and tired reading of how all us other bands supposedly plunder U2. Every band learns from imitating, every artist does, whether you want to call that plundering or not. That's what you do until you find your own voice, your own style. So I really get bored with the U2 connection. Especially in Europe. Because it's so easy, so lazy a point of reference for Irish bands. Do they really think we all grew up listening to only U2 records all the time? That's not the truth. Charlie Mingus also comes under the heading of what Irish people listen to. It's not a case of one country-one group. The fact that we're a four piece does lead to the "next U2" quotes but it strikes me that any band that seems set to do anything in Ireland automatically becomes "the next U2".'

*(Ger Whelan, lead singer with An Emotional Fish)*

'The two necessary conditions for 'coming out' are that you be financially independent and that you live away from the town where your parents were born. I suppose a lot of Irish people who emigrate are more easily able to come out and that probably is a contributory factor in relation to why they leave this country.'

*(Edmund White, novelist)*

'Songs like "Slow Dancing" and "The Common Tongue" are, essentially songs that celebrate sexuality, irrespective of gender. I see peoples' inability to deal with sex in artistic terms as a major block in the Irish psyche. When artists become explicit about sex it tends to be in a negative way, implying that psychologically there is always something problematic at work. That's not true and it's one of the lies we've always tried to erode with *Hot Press*. So I see it as totally legitimate, artistically and politically, to present songs that are deliberately, shamelessly celebratory about sex.'

*(Niall Stokes, editor of* Hot Press *and songwriter with The Brothers)*

# 27     EDNA O'BRIEN
## 1992

One suspects that if Edna O'Brien was writing and setting her first novel *The Country Girls* in the 1990s, it would end with one, or both, of its leading characters leaving Ireland not to begin a new life in England but to have an abortion. Published more than thirty years ago this tale of two young women attempting to come to terms with sexuality captured to a previously unparalleled degree the process of growing up female in Ireland during the 1950s. Indeed the psychic nerve she hit in this country and, even worse, the sociological truths about Ireland which she revealed to the world led to some outraged citizens publicly burning the book and to it being banned by the Censorship Board.

The same fate befell many of her novels during the 1960s, including *Girl with Green Eyes* and *Girls in Their Married Bliss*, which carry to a conclusion the story of Kate and Baba, the leading characters in *The Country Girls*. Of course part of O'Brien's notoriety stems from the belief that she herself is the leading character in her own literary landscapes and that subsequent novels such as *August Is a Wicked Month* and *Johnny I Hardly Knew You*, and collections of short stories such as *A Scandalous Woman*, were largely fragments of autobiography in disguise, manifestations of their author's seemingly endless quest for love. Or, in some people's minds, simply for sex.

Tales of her moving to London in the early 1960s and 'drowning in a sea of men' recently resurfaced in an article about her latest novel, *Time and Tide*. Unfortunately, all this attention paid to Edna O'Brien and sex, in its most basic sense, obscures the fact that her desire was to escape from loneliness and longing. From the outset, novels like *The Country*

*Girls*, written when she was in her late twenties, also present women struggling to break free from patriarchal power structures, particularly those that have their roots in Rome. In ways, her art, and life, crystallises at least one strand in the evolution of Irish women during the second half of the twentieth century.

Not that Edna O'Brien is seen as a suitable role model by feminists. On the contrary. Many regard her tendency to see guilt and sex as synonymous as an unnecessary relic from her own background as an Irish Catholic, and argue that when Rome eased its hold on her body, romanticism stepped in to take its place. Julie Burchill, in a scathing attack on Edna O'Brien in 1989, wrotO: 'I'd have her shot for crimes of collaboration in the sex war', and asked: 'Is there any more treacherous, parodic prostitutor of the condition (always terminal in her books) of being a woman? The way she wears her romantic wounds – like Victoria Crosses! I bleed therefore I am.'

More recently Stan Gebler Davis described *Time and Tide* as a cheap, cannibalistic re-telling of the story of Edna O'Brien's marriage to his uncle Ernest Gebler, 'the class of drivel written by neurotic housewives who wish to escape from Wimbledon.' Wimbledon was originally O'Brien's home in London, which she shared with Ernest Gebler and their two sons, Carlo and Marcus. Now resident in Chelsea, Edna O'Brien was born in Co. Clare in 1932.

**Joe Jackson:**

> Both characters in *The Country Girls* were, you've said, opposing sides of your own nature, with Baba the wild girl you always wanted to be. But were you yourself really the stereotypical, father-fearing Catholic good girl?

**Edna O'Brien:**

> I was, and to an extent still am. I was endowed by God, and by my background, with a rather merciless sense of conscience, and conscientiousness in terms of time and work and duty. Combined with that I had a father who, let's say, had a temper; and a mother who was judgmental. Added to this was the Church, which compounded the dominant atmosphere of "Thou shalt not" or you will be punished. That was the whole ethos of the time and it effected everybody. But I took it more seriously than a lot of people.

**J:** How much was determined by a desire to escape from the shadows of patriarchy?

**O:** To escape from the shadows, period. Not just from patriarchy, from matriarchy as well. But that is something I've come to realise only later in life. But in the early days, yes, it was male authority, male rage, male violence that terrified me. Those things still do. But even in terms of the physical differences in size as a child you are in a precarious position in danger of, at any minute, being annihilated. I felt that at the time and those feelings never go away; at least not completely.

**J:** You've suggested that despite the family bond you and your father were 'chemically ill-suited'.

**O:** Yes and I do believe that our friendships, affiliations and our love-affairs and hate-affairs are chemically informed, definitely. But I think my father was a deeply restless man who didn't realise himself and therefore in many ways I now feel sorry for him. He didn't know what the cause of his unhappiness was. He wanted a much more glamorous and extroverted life than being a farmer. He wasn't cut out to be a farmer. He should have been on the stage. He was a great storyteller and he gave me that talent, as did my mother. I thank them both for that, and for disturbing me so much that I am fired by a need for self-expression. But you really do only see the positive elements in all this later in life.

**J:** Were there Sylvia Plath-like tensions between you and your father? Were you attracted to his darkness?

**O:** I'm sure there were those tensions, yes. But I was probably more stupid than Sylvia Plath at that time, but I'm not so stupid now! *[laughs]*. I'm sure that I was drawn to the darkness, the demonic force in his nature, absolutely. And I do identify with Plath. Indeed, someone reviewing *Time and Tide* in *Newsweek* said that my writing is 'beautiful and harsh, like Sylvia Plath'. But the difference is that she lived in a more enlightened home, went to university and was educated. I wasn't, in that sense. Therefore I only now see those aspects of myself and my childhood which I didn't see when I wrote *The Country Girls*.

**J:** So you couldn't, as an Irish Catholic girl, have dealt with, for example, the subject of being sexually attracted to a father, as Plath did?

**O:** Forget it! You'd be locked away in Our Lady's Convent! *[laughs]* But in any society the shadow on incest hangs over us all and this is the subject that even the most educated and enlightened are least willing to discuss. I know now that the figure of my father, a very tall man, good looking, definitely impregnated me in terms of the kind of men I am attracted to. The physical appearance of him maybe more than the mental, psychological make-up. But the latter played a major part too, being drawn towards someone to be afraid of. All these aspects of my relationship with my father have lingered throughout my life.

**J:** If he set that pattern in place, do you therefore almost automatically associate love with fear, darkness, punishment, self-immolation?

**O:** I certainly did. But you can change your patterns, definitely. An analyst I once went to said the most wonderful thing to mO: 'There is your first nature and your second nature, you can change your second nature.' A lot of my handicaps are my second nature. My original nature, I've found, is a much braver person. Your first nature basically means before they fucked you up, as Philip Larkin put it. And for a great deal of my life I have been attempting to change my second nature, to reconnect with that original state of being.

**J:** For Irish Catholics in particular, such a journey is often made more difficult by the fact that Catholicism tends to divorce a person from a guilt-free sense of her or his own sexuality. Was that part of the landscape for you?

**O:** Definitely. I remember that even words like 'breast' would send me into a fever of shame. Everything of the physical world was taboo. People still say to me, 'It wasn't like that in those days.' and I can only say, 'Maybe not for you, but for me it was.' I am not exaggerating, or inventing my fears, guilt and sense of suffocation about those aspects of the physical, sexual side of life. But I also now see that a lot of that came from my mother. Her own feelings about sex and the body were very complex and dark and I breathed that in. So there was the Catholic hierarchy and the domestic hierarchy and the blending of both really oppressed me from the outset. Many women blame only patriarchy for this. I did in the beginning, as I said earlier. But now I see there were two different types of coercion at work.

J: Darkness induced by the abuse of alcohol plays a major factor in relation to the father in *The Country Girls*, and many fathers in Ireland. Was that also part of your family life as a child?

O: My poor father is dead, I don't really want to go into that. But the point about alcohol is that it is no harm to like drink, the trouble with us is that we feel guilty about it. A French farmer fond of his wine in Normandy would drink as much as my father did but the method was entirely different. My father would go out of the house to go on a binge and that took all the joy away from drink and turned it into another ogre. We really had a society then in which anything that gave pleasure was instantaneous sin. This would be compounded by whatever dark feelings would rise then when my father would return to the house. But he was unlucky in that he was the kind of person who was gone after two drinks. He didn't even have to drink to excess to get drunk.

J: How has all this affected your attitude to drink?

O: I love drink! I can't drink spirits and such but I love a few glasses of wine.

J: Is there any danger that you might become an alcoholic?

O: I don't think so. I have too much conscience. I sure have had hangovers but I've never been part of the alcoholic syndrome. And I'm not one of those writers who seems to need a drink to write.

J: You had at least one known LSD experience, with R.D. Laing. What is your response to philosophers, songwriters, theologians who use the claim that drugs can be an aid to creative thought, creative writing?

O: I wonder how many of those people say that of LSD? It's no accident it's called acid. And if you take a pan of acid and pour it on the texture of anything, let alone the brain, it scours it. And I seem to have gone the whole way that once, taking the whole pan of acid in one day! I was that vicious in my folly! But it was a horrendous trip indeed. I couldn't come back for hours and hours and flashbacks I got for years. It certainly was a sobering experience. I didn't stop taking white wine or champagne but I wouldn't take cocaine or anything now. I'm terrified I might go on another trip like the one before. And in terms of writing I write immediately after waking, as close as possible to my dreaming state, and that would be ruined by anything other than the old reliable cup of tea. That's all I need to get started. I don't mean to insult songwriters. I can just hear Van Morrison begin to growl! But maybe you can write a song on a high but a novel is a longer journey. And I really do believe that there already is a little inbuilt drug in the psyche of creative people that causes one to get into a more heightened state of awareness. I certainly feel that way when I'm writing. Some people suggest I live that way most of the time.

**J:** Doesn't living in a constant state of heightened awareness make you a prime candidate for a nervous breakdown? How do you maintain your balance, keep from tipping over into the pit?

**O:** By the grace of God. But yes, I do live on that edge. I'm very highly strung and live with that constant sense of wanting to get everything perfect. That makes you impatient with what is laughably known as 'ordinary life'. If there is a bunch of flowers, for example, they must be beautiful, they must be arranged the right way. I don't mean that I'm bourgeois, I'm not. But I like perfection, which is a very different thing.

**J:** That also could make you very difficult, if not impossible, to live with. Does it?

**O:** No. Because I'm good-tempered. But maybe you'd have to ask my children and their friends that question!

**J:** What? If you like to keep them in vases looking beautiful in a certain light?

**O:** *[laughs]* Maybe that metaphor was wrong. What I mean is that as a child I must have longed for paradise and I want everything to have some of that element. But with regards to living with me, my biggest failing is that I withdraw. I'm very pleased to see people but then the moment comes when I must be with myself, otherwise the writing won't come. And children will accept that, whereas maybe a lover won't. Both of my children are glad when that happens! They know I'm always there, even though physically sometimes, I withdraw.

**J:** In relation to your lovers, one reads of you going to London in the early 1960s and 'drowning in a sea of men'. How do you reconcile that image with the suggestion earlier that you were sexually oppressed as a young woman?

**O:** When I read that recently I thought, what on earth is this? When I first went to London I was unhappily married and writing *The Country Girls* and crying my eyes out. I don't know where that idea came from. I don't have to defend myself to anyone but it strikes me that these days people like Madonna make a great deal of money if they parade their promiscuity. I am not capable of promiscuity, simply because I feel things very intensely. When I am in love, boy I'm in love and it lasts a long time. So it isn't a question of humping from pole to pillar.

**J:** Do you ever regret that aspect of your own psychology, or part of your view of sexual politics? Many women fight to break free from what they see as all that romantic baggage and want to happily hump from man to man, woman to woman, whatever.

**O:** No. I want depth. I want quality rather than quantity in my relationships. So I don't regret it at all. I am, in fact, very proud of my point of view on this. That may seem Catholic and smug but it isn't. It's the vitiation of feeling. Our relationships are precious and unique and must not be damaged by being taken for granted or treated in a dismissive way. Those we love and have had sexual relationships with should be extremely important to our lives. I wouldn't want to have a sexual relationship with someone I couldn't remember. And this really is something beyond being Catholic.

**J:** Is it not just romanticism taking the place of religion, in your case Catholicism.

**O:** Romanticism is a branch of religion and yes, it may well be that romanticism took the place of Catholicism in my life. But the focus of power is my heart. I want my heart to be with whoever I love for as long as I love that person. So it's not a moral stricture imposed from outside forces. And as for those who do say they want to behave, sexually, as men have, the point is that men haven't been made that happy by their promiscuity. Men feel guilty about their adulteries, in a different way than women. So to have slept around a lot isn't necessarily a guaranteed ticket to happiness or self-fulfilment. Certainly for me that's not the path I'd want to follow. And I'd seriously wonder whether it is genuinely the route for other people or whether it's something done because this is the modern way or it's done to get even with a husband or a lover or men in general. I'm all for sexual relationships but for me it must be in a holistic sense. That, to me, is what it's all about. And always will be.

**J:** But was that always the way you viewed sex? One reads of you originally having walked up to your ex-husband Ernest Gebler in a bar and said, 'You're very famous, aren't you?' That sounds like a young woman who is sexually very confident, maybe even a literary groupie.

**O:** Doesn't it! *[laughs]* But it's not true at all! I didn't even know the man when I was introduced to him. It's a myth. Or rather a rumour that doesn't deserve the status of myth.

**J:** What was your response to Stan Gebler Davis' recent attack, where he suggested that *Time and Tide* is just a cannibalistic recycling of your marriage to his uncle?

**O:** Sadness. I felt sad on reading those accusations and so did my children. Partly because he almost implied that my children and he were friends and that the only good thing that has come out of this is his love of his two cousins. If they saw Stan Gebler Davis now they would knock his teeth in. What he wrote is a malevolence and it's also untrue. It is very easy for someone to hang out laundry in public. I could have done it. I could have replied to that in a manner that would really shake him but I ain't gonna do that because my pact with my public is through my writing and in that I give them my soul and my heart. And my readers know it. So I'm not going to enter the domain of the gutter press. It's degrading. And the point is that if you get someone who has no concept of truth and does not care about truth there is no way you can have a debate with that kind of person. And that is the truth.

**J:** But one of his accusations, namely that his uncle Ernest virtually wrote *The Country Girls*, has been in circulation for years. There also is the suggestion that instead of, as is often claimed, you leaving while cooking dinner one day, broken by marriage, you became so arrogant after the publication of *The Country Girls* that you abandoned him and the children. How much of all that is true?

**O:** Firstly: if my husband had written my first book how come he didn't write anything of his own, since he is a man so zealous to be published? Secondly; anyone reading my first book, any short story of mine and my twelfth book would immediately recognise that the same voice, the same talent informs all the work. It's laughable to hear anyone making such a claim. It is so stupid that people would even consider believing that. If I wasn't able to write my first book, how come I've written so many more? And with regards to leaving the house, I did leave the house in the middle of cooking the dinner – under some terrible threat. And I was never arrogant at the time of the book. I lived in digs and had the most awful time. My money was taken by my husband and so was the house. I hadn't sixpence. So I'm presented by these people as some kind of ogre and it's just not true. It's so untrue.

**J:** But isn't it also tragic, for all concerned? As with the husband in your new book, Ernest Gebler is now suffering from dementia and detained in a nursing home. Does all this add to your core belief, to quote Joyce, that 'one has not lived unless one conceives of life as a tragedy'?

**O:** Yes. But my husband's temperament is not of my doing. The man was like that, probably as a result of his own experiences in childhood. He is a tragedy. But I didn't create his tragedy. He did a hell of a lot to try and create mine. When Stan Gebler Davis published that article in the *Sunday Independent*, my sons and I talked about my publishing a suitcase of letters from my husband, written to me during those times after I left, that are of the most violent and vile nature. But I ain't going to. I have failings but they ain't those failings.

**J:** How deeply was the fear of men which has run through your life shaped largely by your feelings towards your father and your experience in that marriage?

**O:** Very deeply. Until I took LSD, then it changed.

**J:** Into a fear of a different type of man?

**O:** No, as we talked about earlier, attraction to a different type of man. I no longer went for domination. And I don't go for domination.

**J:** Do you hate men? In her attack on your work, and life Julie Burchill suggested that the 'main function of O'Brien's work, for at least the past twenty years (her first book had something but then Ernest Gebler claims he wrote that one) has been to make men feel like right bastards'.

**O:** I wonder what she feels about men! *[laughs]* I think what she is trying to say there is that I can't write. And a few lines into that attack, the first time I heard about it, I remember thinking, boy, I induce a lot of jealousy. And I could see why. But no, she's totally wrong. I don't hate men. I love men. I love the company of men and I love my sons. If I hated men I wouldn't be able to write *The Love Object* or *Baby Blue*. These are love stories. If I hated men I'd be writing totally different books. All my world is impregnated with longing for men, or for a man, or the man, or the God–man union.

**J:** Is that not just romantic idealism? Isn't it possible that if he really arrived in your life you wouldn't want him?

**O:** I would. I would, believe me.

**J:** In *Girls In Their Married Bliss* Kate is sterilised. Some women might see sterilisation as the ultimate act of defiance against being perceived as merely a carrier of children for men, or for society.

**O:** They might. But I think it was a punitive act. It was annihilation or mutilation rather than defiance. She should have just gone and taken the contraceptive pill and thanked God for Marie Stopes, rather than removing from her body one of the most central zones of her self.

**J:** Do you think women in Ireland should have full access to information on abortion, and access to abortion itself, in this country?

**O:** They should have every right to have an abortion. It's very easy for the Pope to travel around the world and pass down his dictates. If he was living in Gardiner Street and had eight children perhaps his point of view would be more humane. What is always overlooked is that, for the most part, for a woman to have an abortion, for whatever reason, is a painful and traumatic experience. It's not like having a gin and tonic. It's not something she enters into blithely. So those people who call themselves pro-life (a) don't take that into account and (b) for a lobby of people who profess to have such feeling and tenderness towards unborn life, I'd like to see them show a little feeling and tenderness towards born life. That is, for the mothers who might, for whatever reason, not be able to have this child. I couldn't have an abortion but only because of my own, very perilous grip on sanity/insanity. I'd like to have had more children but I had only two. I never had contraception, I was meant to have only two children. But of course it should be allowed and the worst part is that those who proclaim themselves to be 'pro-life' seem to think an abortion is something people use instead of the pill, as a way out of paying the full price for their promiscuity. That's just not true. And it grieves me to even think of anyone looking on abortion in such a small-minded way.

**J:** You yourself were ostracised in Ireland during the 1960s for divorcing your ex-husband. Has that experience also left you favouring the right to divorce in this country?

**O:** Absolutely. I feel that everyone marries in good faith and for the most part remain married. If something is untenable then for the two protagonists, and children to grow or live in a state of acute disharmony, even hatred, is far more destructive than anything else. And in talking to you today I am not on a soapbox saying 'Let's have abortion, let's have divorce'. I am fiercely thoughtful about these things and feel we all have to examine society and decide what, in the end, creates the least harm or disaster.

**J:** With these, clearly thoughtful views on relationships between men and women, how do you respond when someone like Julie Burchill calls you 'a treacherous, parodic prostitutor of the condition of being a woman', allegedly always depicting them as victims?

**O:** The kindest thing I can say about her is to suggest that she should become a social worker for a month, in a poor district, and she might find out then what women's lives are like because she clearly doesn't know. What she writes sounds rather clever but really its a meaningless little barb. Or rather it's only meaning is to serve Julie Burchill. I have written about many women, and they are not victims but survivors. They go through rough lives as most of us do. And let us hope Julie Burchill does. She obviously needs it. Other than that I really can't address her accusation intellectually because it doesn't deserve it.

**J:** Comparing the thirty years of writing between *The Country Girls* and *Time and Tide*, the major development, highlighted in the latest book, is that the relationship between the child and mother is now central, rather than that between the child and father, which has more often been a key feature in Irish literature, art.

**O:** That is true. *Time and Tide* in that sense is *The Country Girls* come full circle. That was everything as seen through the eyes of girls, and overshadowed by the father and parents. *Time and Tide* is the mother as child herself and as mother and as casting a shadow but seeing that shadow in a deeper light. And a sadder light.

**J:** So you still believe 'One has not lived until one conceives of life as a tragedy'?

**O:** Tragedy is always part of great literature. Think of Shakespeare, Tolstoy, Dickens, Flaubert, Faulkner. There are comics parts but yes, fundamentally, I still believe Joyce was right in his observation of life, and, by extension, art. I am a joyful woman but mostly, perhaps, because I have known darkness.

**J:** Your earliest memory is of feeling 'stranded' in a cot. Do you also fear your memory of your last moment may be the same, you as woman/child lost and stranded?

**O:** Yes. Because I do have a great fear of being stranded. Part of it may have to do with that early memory. As the daughter says to her mother in the letter in *Time and Tide:* 'There is always a darker secret beneath the secret we unfold.' Who can tell what secret lies beyond death?

# 28 CATHOLICS AND SEX
## 1992

Authors Kate Saunders and Peter Stanford could hardly have known how perfectly timed their latest project would be. Three weeks before the Bishop Casey story broke, they were in Dublin to publicise their book and forthcoming Channel 4 television series which focuses on the thorny subject of Catholics and sex.

Novelist and journalist Kate Saunders was especially interested in the result of the recent case of the fourteen-year-old rape victim and the Maastricht debate suggesting that the latter issue in particular is sending signals to many people in Britain *vis-à-vis* their own position in Europe and what she sees as the 'attempt to bring us all in line in terms of a common aggregate social policy'. She couldn't, of course, foresee that within a month the revelation that one of Ireland's most highly respected bishops, Dr Eamon Casey, had fathered at least one child and used diocesan funds to pay off Ms Annie Murphy and her son Peter would also send shock waves all the way from Ireland to the Vatican. But she did discuss the claim made in *Catholics and Sex* that 'the exploitation of women by priests is a very real problem, the ugliest skeleton in the Vatican closet'.

'"Priests" women have been treated extraordinarily badly by the Church,' she says. 'One bishop wrote a letter to a priest who had resigned after getting into a relationship and having a child, and said, basically, "If you want to return to the clerical state, you must dump your wife and kid." It was not, "We'll take care of them." But then to avoid confronting the issue of female sexuality the Church tends to apply the

Augustinian method of painting every woman scarlet. All the blame goes on the woman, who becomes the whore who led the priest astray. In many cases we found the opposite to be true. One case we refer to in the book concerns a woman who, after the death of her husband, turned to a priest for support and soon found that this Father Michael was in her bed and that this was far from his first lapse from his vow of celibacy. In another similar situation a priest's housekeeper became pregnant and he didn't even visit her when she was in hospital for four weeks giving birth by Caesarean. Later a senior advisor of the Bishop offered her money but only on the condition that she would not "force" the priest to live with her. She refused and he just said, "May guilt haunt you". That is so representative.'

Saunders suggests that the situation is not helped by women within the Catholic Church. In the book she quotes a similarly 'representative' selection of letters from the Catholic review the *Tablet* last year (1991) which highlighted and difference of opinion between the National Board of Catholic Women and the more conservative Association of Catholic Women. The former had suggested that 'there are many good, loving relationships between women and priests – relationships which make a positive contribution to the life and work of both the priest and the women. Yet for the most part, these relationships remain secret and hidden'. The latter's reply should be quoted in full:

'If they are talking about a mature woman who freely enters into a sexual relationship with a priest, on what grounds are we asked to sympathise with her? Or are we asked to believe, near the end of the twentieth century, that there are still women gullible enough to act on the assumption that a priest who is ready to break his promise of celibacy will nevertheless keep a promise of marriage?'

'They describe such a woman as "gullible". Where in comments like that do they reveal any form of Christian charity or understanding?' asks Saunders. 'Most of the women who do become sexually involved with priests end up leading miserable lives because priests rarely give up their parishes for marriage. Some will, as David Rice did. But he went public whereas most priests don't. They just get some girl pregnant and in many ways that shadow hangs over her for life. In fact she's doubly damned, usually ostracised by the community, blamed for "leading a priest astray" and alone as a mother if she's allowed to keep the child – indeed if she is not forced to abort the child. And even in those circumstances the woman is terribly isolated because it is only very recently that anyone has admitted that any of this is a major problem. Until now she's probably been left thinking, "I'm the only woman in the world who's gone through this". She's not. It is a widespread problem. And, in terms of celibacy, Dr Roland Sipe, an ex-priest and now a psychiatrist, did a survey which revealed that 20 per cent of US priests were having sex at any one time and only 2 per cent were chaste. The rest were having sex. So it becomes a nonsense when people say "We have to change the rules and the priests can have sex." Priests are sexually active.'

In his book *Shattered Vows*, David Rice also suggests that the fear of excommunication need not necessarily hang over priests who have 'wives'. It seems to be more a matter of geography than theology, he suggests. And Kate Saunders agrees.

'That's part of the Vatican's hypocrisy on this subject,' she says. 'They oppose changes in the rules that relate to celibacy, yet the rigidity of those rules is undermined by exceptions and loopholes. As Rice points out, there are married priests living in full communion with Rome. Particularly in Peru where missionaries estimate that 80 per cent of the priests live with women and the Vatican turns a blind eye to that.'

According to *Catholics and Sex*, the Vatican also turns a blind eye to what the authors describe as 'the unlovely oozings which appear when the crust of celibacy is broken' in a more violent manner. To back the claim they cite the case of Canadian bishop Hubert O'Connor who resigned in 1991 after charges were pressed alleging that he raped two women, and the scandal last year in Newfoundland where four Christian Brothers and ten diocesan priests were found guilty of child sexual abuse at the Mount Cashel Orphanage. In Canada similar charges have recently been filed on 149 counts against nineteen past and present members of the Brothers of the Christian Schools. Another current scandal, in America, is the case of Dino Cinel, an Italian-born New Orleans priest who, allegedly, made pornographic videos of teenage boys in his rectory and sold photographs of the boys to pornographic magazines.

'Hypocrisy raises its head in that case as well,' claims Saunders. 'The Catholic District Attorney, Harry Connick, admitted in an interview that he had originally been unwilling to prosecute Cinel because he did not want to embarrass "Holy Mother Church"! But the priests who do commit acts of sexual abuse and violence have clearly hid behind the

Roman Catholic collar to exploit people weaker than themselves. And there is this touching faith among believers who say that as a priest is wearing a collar he is not a sexual being. As anyone can see from the Cinel case this could be a bloody dangerous point of view. People will say, "My little boy will be safe with the priest", but he may not be. And as long ago as the twelfth century, St Bernard was warning that the collective sex drive of the Church, if deprived of marriage, would burst out in all forms of unspeakable directions.'

The classic case of the love which dare not speak its name is, of course, homosexuality. In *Catholics and Sex* one unnamed theologian, speaking for the Lesbian and Gay Church Association, claims that roughly a third of priests are homosexual.

'The seeming sexlessness of the Church provides a safe hiding place for many men and in the case of some it seems to be an attempted escape from their homosexuality. One ex-priest we spoke to said he originally saw his vocation as a way of "defeating" his homosexuality and being "comfortable" with Christ. And he said it worked for a year, that he didn't even masturbate and would instead plunge his hands into boiling water as a sign of this intense love affair with Christ. But after a sexual encounter with one of his tutors he left the order. Another priest, happy to acknowledge his homosexuality and who counsels gay Catholics, claims he sees many priests who are extremely uncomfortable about their sexuality and deeply involved in that form of self-denial,' she says.

In their programme Saunders and Stanford also address the question of the 'overtly gay culture' which can dominate the life of a 'straight' seminarian. They quote David Rice in relation to what he describes as the 'snowballing effect' evident when young heterosexuals enter the seminary and are in time turned off by the predominantly homosexual lifestyle and feel obliged to renounce their vocation or to reroute their own sexuality under pressure. Saunders and Stanford also address the suggestion, made by one feminist, that 'there can be no doubt that homosexual cliques within the Church are keeping women out'.

'This is something that is very widespread in the Anglican church because of the debate over women priests. They don't want to let the girls in because so many become priests to get away from women. But there is also the belief, handed down through the centuries, that the priesthood is one big boys' club. There was Jesus with his disciples and they are always depicted only as men, which is not true. In the Bible you can read of the women disciples who gave him money and followed him. But as with all other areas of Catholic teaching, the role of women has been marginalised. And one of the ways this is done is by propagating the belief that women are synonymous with sex and ruin things. On the other hand the Church's view that sex brings damnation to us all and that the Holy Order is a sex-free zone also attracts women who are uncomfortable with their sexuality, straight or lesbian. And there is that battle within the Church now where lesbian nuns, for example, are beginning to assert themselves and have been so keen to embrace feminism, new theologies and enlarge their roles in the Church. And whereas one doesn't hear too many cases of nuns sexually compromising girls or, as the Association of Catholic Women once suggested, exploiting young males, one still reads about nuns and priests getting sexually involved with one another.'

Referring back to 'medieval times when nuns and priests were happily banging away at one another', Kate Saunders also suggests that the mere concept of a priest and nun locked in a passionate embrace would be anathema to most Catholics. Particularly those who buy the line that Christ was celibate. 'The paradox is that if you say Jesus Christ was either not human or not divine it's heresy,' she says. 'The official line is that he was equally the son of God and human. But if he was a man he had to have a human body. And it is this human body that people seem not to want to know about. A lot of people were outraged when we said in the book that Christ must have farted. He certainly talked about shitting in one of his sermons. So at the core of this denial of sexuality in the Church is the denial of Christ's human capacities, the fact that the original role model for all priests was a man.'

Pushing this line even further, does Saunders see how some female Catholics, in order to physicalise Christ to the fullest extent, could, like a woman in Padraig Standun's book *Lovers*, dream about what was beneath Christ's loincloth and fantasise about having sex with him? Or, as a form of substitute, with a priest?

'I can't do that. I even blush at the thought of trying to focus on Christ as a man at that level, but I can see why some women would have to go to that length to break the chain to Catholicism,' she says. 'But kneeling in the pew and fantasising about Our Lord and wondering what he would have been like in the sack is a bit far out for me! Likewise in terms of priests. Mind you, I do remember looking at that Benetton advertisement and thinking mmm, what a lovely-looking young priest. But one could argue that it is the Church's portrayal of Christ as only spirit and of priests as non-sexualised beings seemingly committed to the subjugation of women which makes some women feel they'd do anything they can, in fantasy or in fact, to strike back.'

Some of the trendier theologians suggest that if Christ himself had sex it probably was with Mary Magdelen. Kate Saunders claims that this so-called liberal perspective is little more than the age-old notion that women are either virgins or whores. It also could be seen as suggesting that if Jesus Christ choose to copulate only with prostitutes his representatives on earth can feel free to treat women the same way, she says.

'That's what I found offensive about *The Last Temptation of Christ*. They always assume that if he did make love it was with a whore. But it's a medieval sexual fantasy that the only woman Christ would want to have sex with was Mary Magdelen because she was "available". A Jewish theologian said to us that if Christ was a good Jewish boy – and he was – he would have been married at eighteen. Some believe he was. But the Church has even attempted to deny sexuality in marriage. Particularly in relation to women. In the gospel the virginity of Mary, the mother of God, is emphasised to prove Christ's holy paternity, to say he couldn't have been Joseph's son it had to be the Holy Ghost. Whether you believe that or not, the point is that in Catholic-speak this has been twisted into she had to be a virgin because if she'd had sex she'd have been a natural, normal woman i.e. unworthy of being the mother of God. In the Bible it says "Joseph knew her not until she had Jesus", but that too has been changed to mean that Mary never had sex. This is the core, and original denial of female sexuality. She's supposed to have lived only to give birth and that's the perspective which has dominated Catholic teaching since. Either that or woman is a whore to be treated accordingly. But it is just as likely that Mary and Joseph had sex continually and that Jesus had brothers and sisters. Yet all these dimensions to family life are denied in Catholicism.'

The desire to marry and raise a family rather than merely the desire to have sex is, says Saunders, another core issue neglected when the discussion turns to priests and marriage.

'The real crime, according to a lot of the priests we spoke to, is the denial of the love drive,' she says. 'Many priests also say that the loneliness, the lack of human contact, is almost impossible to endure.

Totally off the record, of course, some said it is a human right to be allowed one special person, one human relationship, and they feel bitterly deprived being told that all these needs should be met by their love for Christ and Christ's love for them. One priest said he ached with sorrow every time he held a child to baptise because he thought he would have been a wonderful father. And he probably would have been, but as a Catholic priest he is denied that right.'

It has been estimated that the majority of the 100,000 priests who have left the Church over the last decade did so in order to marry. With the patriarchal power structure in the Catholic Church also doggedly resisting calls for the ordination of women, one might suggest that we are bearing witness to the final days of Catholicism. Can Kate Saunders sympathise with those who might say 'Hallelujah if we are!'

'Feminists in particular do say let it crumble, but others remain to write their own theology and are holding services as we speak whether the Pope or the hierarchy says yes or no. That, to me, is a better approach,' she says. 'And the point is that as with priests the revolution has already started. People are making their own moral choices *vis-à-vis* sex. What we're saying to the hierarchy is, "Have more faith in the faithful". We're not writing this book or making the TV series to have people say "I always knew the Catholic Church was a load of crap". We're aiming all this at mature people who are Christian believers and we're saying that such people, from priests to lay persons, are living within a set of rules that are ludicriously outdated and lacking in compassion to a remarkable degree. But there is hope. The current Pope is stupid and blinkered in relation to sex, but the next Pope could do a lot overnight to change things radically. If he doesn't, yes, the Catholic Church will become more and more of an anachronism and more and more of a sad, sick, hypocritical joke – particularly to young people.'

# 29     SOUND BITES
## 1992

'The greater rape is what the state did to that girl. She is defiled by a man sexually and then, having suffered the original experience, she is defiled again by the state. And you know why? Because the Church and the state are so afraid that if they acknowledge the truth a hundred doors will burst open and they will lose control. But they are choking themselves to death. Because divine law is being broken here. First that girl's choice was taken away in rape and then it was taken away, to begin with, by the state. That is the sickness that cripples women, male-energy at its worst. And if we, as women, don't rebel against the way in which the Church and State have conspired to control our sexuality we'll never reach a point of self-evolvement. And evolution, in any sense, has nothing to do with enforcing guilt, with this horrific cross they have stuck between that girl's legs. Jesus Christ has nothing to do with that and it has nothing to do with Jesus Christ and don't let anyone tell me that it has. The cross has been used as a weapon, as it has been used against all women throughout the ages. And that's the greatest evil of all.'

*(Tori Amos, on fourteen-year-old Irish rape victim blocked by the courts from leaving the country to have an abortion)*

'I'm still a church-going Christian but I definitely realise there is so much baggage the Church needs to cast off. It's history of hostility to women and it's history of hostility to marriage. All its great spiritual leaders, like Thomas Aquinas and St Augustus hated marriage. They had a profound distaste for sexuality and for any forms of human pleasure. The model of marriage for them was a celibate marriage in which a couple lived together and once they performed the necessary duty of reproducing they stopped participating in sex for the rest of their lives. Overall I really think that the Church's attitude to sexuality is so off-the-wall that it's not in a position to give lectures any more. A thousand years silence on the issue is the least it could do as penance after two thousand years of oppression. But celibacy is only a side issue in relation to the overall need to completely restructure the notion of priesthood. The first job of a priest is to celebrate the Eucharist. But there shouldn't be a Eucharist in a church of two thousand people. There should be a Eucharist in every identifiable local community, celebrated and presided over by whoever that community picks. The structures in the Church are daft: hierarchical; authoritarian; male-based. They all need to be thrown out the window. For example, it took the Church a long time to acknowledge that women were anything other than the carriers of male seeds. They didn't acknowledge for hundred of years that women were actually part of the process of generation; the idea was that the male seed contained the fullness of creation. Suddenly they discovered that her body was half the process so, yes, the Church has always denied female sexuality in the broadest sense. Yet I've stopped wondering about how the Virgin conceived. I believe in Christ. I believe God intervened in history. But whether that was through a process of human sexuality or not I don't know. But I have no doubt that Christ had other members in his family. The idea that his mother and father lived together for years in a totally celibate relationship is so offensive and so un-Jewish that it's plain stupidity. But the whole point is that the gospels were written, and glossed over, by the Church. St Paul brought his wife with him on all his travels yet that, for example, is changed to saying "he brought his wife as a sister" to suggest to us "look at St Paul – he gave up sleeping with his wife to serve the Lord' simply because they so detest the concept of marriage. So it is a denial of woman on every level."

*(Brendan Ryan, senator and ex-priest)*

'Let's talk about Ireland today. My mother is still saying, "Poor Bishop Casey". But all he ever did was sit on his fat arse; chuckle on

*The Late Late Show*; live in his palace and fuck this woman, have a son and then deny them both. And what really gets me is that the bishops still haven't gotten off their high horse on the issue of abortion. I've read their latest statement on the Maastricht debate and hear all this stuff about their "new-found compassion" – that's bullshit. Basically they're back belting us with their crosiers again, denying a woman's right to make up her own mind.'

*(Mary Coughlan, singer)*

'I've always thought Bishop Casey was a bogus old windbag. All that chucklesome stuff always got up my nose. But what really got me is that today I heard a nun say that it is terrible for the boy, having to be denied. He didn't have to be denied. Casey could have acknowledged him when he was born but now it's only being acknowledged because Casey was found out. And if it's true that Casey treated Annie Murphy's new fella abysmally, downgrading the woman, when he was trying to effect some kind of reconciliation between the Bishop and the boy, then that is a typical Irish male attitude to women. It's the whore or the saint syndrome. The saint is your mothers and all the others are whores. But yes I do sympathise with the son if he finally felt he had to fight to make the whole thing public and to be acknowledged. But then I've always hated organised religion and priests and I'm not shocked by this. It just disgusts me more than I was disgusted before. So people will and should come out and let the full facts be known of how much of this goes on in the Church. But it is a dreadfully hypocritical aspect of being priest or something similar. You can work for Trocaire and heal the sick as an abstract commitment but when suddenly somebody says to your face 'give me a little love and a little charity' you say 'fuck off'. That's what's happening in the Bishop Casey case. And this shagger, but for an act of choice, could be a cardinal. In other words could be a candidate for the next Pope. And he behaves in this inhuman way.'

*(Hugh Leonard, playwright)*

'I really want to see it to make up my mind on the issue as I am particularly interested in representations of "Irishness". And there are also Irish stories I want to do, which I know, in Hollywood, they are scared of doing. They are good stories but they do deal with the IRA. The IRA are a very frightening people and what we have in Northern Ireland is a very delicate situation, but one is a great story about violence, by Brian Moore. I wouldn't have any problems doing a movie that deals with the subject, and I hope I can. I certainly don't want to make propagandistic movie for the IRA, or for anybody. That's why I'm a bit taken aback by your original question on James Bond, in terms of his character carrying what you see as imperialist codes. And what Gabriel Byrne sees the same way. I wouldn't want to be party to those kind of messages at all. I never really thought about it from those angles, at least, obviously, not as deeply as Gabriel.'

*(Pierce Brosnan, actor, responding to questions about controversy over* Patriot Games, *which had been described as presenting stereo-typical images of Irish characters, including a psychopathic IRA killer)*

'I was asked recently why I didn't go to art college or university and the reason is that the fucking Christian Brothers told me I'd never make a living out of art and I thought you had to be rich to go to college. Nobody told me I could go. And even today, when John Waters writes his book, it's all Dublin 4, Dublin 4, Dublin 4. Anyone who has a brain seems to be Dublin 4 whereas the rest of us are depicted as slobs. That's why I hate the way *The Commitments* presented Northside working-class people. I come from the Finglas/Ballymun area and I fucking know that the working-class people in that picture were pure caricatures. I was in Germany recently and people are saying "you come from a place that looks like Beirut and all young people do is curse and eat and drink?" And I have to say "It doesn't fucking look like Beirut, now fuck off". Sorry Roddy, sorry Alan Parker, but to me *The Commitments* was degrading and offensive. I hated it.'

*(Gavin Friday, musician)*

'I've had people ask why I don't record in English, saying "if you did we could play the song on such-and-such a show". My answer is "If I was French would you ask me to do the same thing?" I sing in Irish because it is my first language. It's the language I express myself best in and feel most comfortable with. And it's very important that when a language is in decline you should fight that. Ironically, people in Europe have no problem with me singing in Irish, whereas people in Ireland do. And as Ireland becomes more Europeanised, and music becomes more of a global industry than a form of cultural expression, the need is greater than ever before to remain in touch with our roots. There is an "Irishness" to Irish music, irrespective of the instrumentation or style and it has to do with spirit. It's as if a people who were, until recently, forbidden to express themselves in ways that were natural to them, are saying 'try stop me now'. And Altan is very much part of that tradition rather than just, as some say of us, people intent on highlighting the riches in Donegal music. So we do get terribly discouraged when people say, "Altan" just play diddlyeye music and are living in the past. We're not. We look at what is happening now in traditional music and haul it forward by playing with the same energy and drive you encounter in rock. Of course we have the source and we keep one foot planted in the past but just as important is to keep the music alive, ensure its future by remaining open to new ideas.'

*(Mairead Ní Mhaonaigh, Altan)*

'Sometimes I have people say, "What gives you the right to come over to Ireland and play Irish music?" My answer is that I see my role as an extension of a long historical process which began in middle and eastern Europe as far back as 500 BC and anyone here who thinks they've got a corner on the Celtic tradition is blocking out a couple of thousand years! That doesn't mean I don't empathise with the sense of territorial, and cultural protectivness at work in a country such as Ireland which has such a long history of oppression. But the Celts also went to places like Canada and the cultural bias where I grew up was much closer to Scots/Irish than to any indigenous native North American culture.'

*(Loreena McKennett, Canadian harpist)*

'Why is it that there hasn't been an acknowledgement of the millions of records the likes of Foster and Allen, the Furey Brothers and Daniel O'Donnell have sold throughout the world? I'll tell you why.

Because there is a feeling that these people are somehow inferior, that they are not really in the music business at all. And a lot of it has to do with the imposition of a rock 'n' roll orthodoxy which, though evident around the world, seems to be more prevalent here. And, basically, it all comes down to money. It is international record companies who write the agenda and that agenda is slavishly followed by broadcasters and by the media who, sadly, often like to think that they themselves are setting that agenda and leading the trends. And I know that a lot of musicians out there are deeply angered by the implication that whatever U2 or Sinead O'Connor are doing is the be-all and end-all of the Irish music industry. And justifiably so, in my opinion. This aspect of the Irish music business irritates me immensely. People like The Dubliners, The Chieftains, De Dannan and Stockton's Wing attract an incredible amount of people to this country because of the element of Irish culture that is reflected in the music. One specific area in which you see this happening is in relation to summer schools. So this is obviously another area that needs to be acknowledged, and developed. The problem is that we in this country have never had anybody who has the political clout, or enough vision, to put the arts and culture in general onto a higher political plain and give it, as a voice of the people of Ireland, the status it deserves.'

*(Pascal Mooney, senator and broadcaster)*

'There's a notion that there's a lotto in operation in Ireland in relation to the music business and all you need to do to win is get one hit single or album and you're set for life. That's a lethal notion to have caught on. And I think some of the parasite industries that have grown up within the music business – such as massive music seminars – deceive people into believing this is true. It's not. And the point is that even after a decade of that kind of hype no other group has followed U2 onto the world stage, to the same degree. So too many Irish musicians waste their lives away waiting for "the deal", hoping some cigar-chewing A & R man is going to sign them. That happens so rarely that the whole concept really is a lie.'

*(Bill Whelan, composer)*

'In Belfast we have a strange identity which is almost identity-less. We have the problem about where you come from on a national level and where you come from within Belfast, plus the usual religious and class schisms. You're almost open to any identity at all. The first single I ever did was "Religious Persuasion" and the first line of that single was "Protestant or Catholic?/ Cried a voice from the crowd/ ". The last verse was "Someone's got to stand up/Or nothing's going to change/Until religion is rearranged". From the first moment I have tried to confront head-on what I feel we all have to confront in Ireland – the national question. And although everyone writes about the two great themes, love and war, when you come from Belfast these dual forces are right there slapping you in your face from the moment you begin to breathe. So all my albums have dealt with variations on these themes. For me the point of resolution, on a political and personal level, is the new album *Out There*. The only way we can work it out, politically, is by looking outwards, by re-defining ourselves in the context of Europe, the world. If we just sit, as we have been in Belfast, examining ourselves, we'll get absolutely nowhere.'

*(Andy White, singer)*

# 30    GERRY ADAMS
## 1993

To many people it doesn't matter what Gerry Adams has to say; he is simply 'that bastard who supports the IRA'. To his supporters, on the other hand, he is a man who has given almost thirty years of his life to pursuing his own particular vision of Irish independence and unity. Indeed, apart from Ian Paisley, there are few people in the current political arena who polarise public opinion as effectively as Adams does.

In the wake of the Warrington bombings, however, Gerry Adams's status seems to have sunk to an all-time low – partly because he exhibited what many perceived as base hypocrisy when he expressed a desire to participate in the post-Warrington peace movement while at the same time refusing to withdraw his support for the IRA, which had acknowledged responsibility for the deaths of Tim Parry and Jonathan Ball.

Added to this was the IRA's rejection of Gordon Wilson's plea for peace and the release of the widow which explicitly restated their commitment to the armed struggle. These developments clearly hung a question mark over the 'private' talks Gerry Adams soon afterwards continued with John Hume, and similarly jeopardised the attempts to get inter-party talks moving again in relation to the future of Northern Ireland: an objective which could, arguably, be described as the single most important issue facing this country.

**Joe Jackson:**

Many readers will undoubtedly have a block against even beginning to read this interview, believing the popular perception that, apart from being President of Sinn Féin, you are also on the Army Council of the IRA.

**Gerry Adams:**

I am not, and have not been, a member of the IRA.

J: It has been suggested by authors Bishop and Hallie, in their book on the IRA, and by the British security forces that you joined the organisation in 1969 and have been given permission to deny membership so you can act as President of Sinn Féin.

A: As I said, I am not and have not been a member of the IRA. In fact I was acquitted by a British court of that charge. And you can ask that question any way you want. I'm going to give you the same answer. And we end up just wasting time.

J: Sinn Féin representatives are currently banned from the nation's airwaves. However, it has been claimed that if they were interviewed, Sinn Féin supporters and/or the IRA would 'intimidate' journalists. For example, following my Danny Morrison interview I was told, in a Dublin pub, 'You'll be lucky if you're not taken down a laneway by three fellas and asked what right have you got to ask Danny Morrison about the 'moral rightness of the armed struggle'. What does that tell us about how Sinn Féin may or may not respect freedom of expression among journalists?

A: I don't know. If you print a particular article about a Fianna Fáil politician and some guy comes up to you in a pub and says 'You'll be lucky if you ever get a Morrison visa after that', what does that tell us about the government?

J: So are you condoning that form of intimidation?

A: Not at all. And there are no cases I know of, and no complaints I know of, from the NUJ or any other representative grouping of journalists about any intimidation by republicans. What you encountered may have just been someone taking it upon themselves to respond in that way, and that is not something I support at all.

J: In *The Politics of Freedom*, when you say that 'journalists, imitating the attitudes of their masters' ask you to condemn the IRA, it comes across as either politically loaded or stupid, on their behalf. Surely they ask you because it is assumed you have some kind of influence over the IRA?

A: When was the last time a journalist asked Patrick Mayhew to withdraw the troops from the North? When was the last time somebody doorstepped Mr Major in Dublin and asked him about human rights in the North? I don't hear the questions that are put to myself, and Sinn Féin, being put to those people. A kid gets killed in West Belfast and Mayhew, the next day, can say that the British forces acted within the law and journalists don't push him on that position. That's what I mean when I write about journalists aping establishment positions. And also, journalists have said to me. 'I'm only asking you this because I was told to ask you'. I very often want to get into more in-depth issues, and maybe even journalists do, but editors who send them out just say, 'All we want is to get him to condemn the IRA.' I'm not interested in taking part in that kind of media game.

J: Eoghan Harris recently claimed that the IRA, as he knows it, would be made up of people more like the psychopath in *Patriot Games* than the character riven with moral doubts in *The Crying Game*. What was your response to that?

A: All Harris is doing there is involving himself in propaganda. I certainly wouldn't suggest that British soldiers are psychopaths. I wouldn't even say the RUC, though they are sectarian bigots, are psychopaths. Using phrases like that is demonstration, dehumanisation of a people. If I go, as I did before Easter, to the parents of Pearce Jordan, a 22-year-old from New Barnsley who got killed although he was unarmed, I know the form of propaganda the security forces are going to involve themselves in. The RUC don't even make a statement, they feed a line to the media saying he was armed, that he had gloves, that he had a balaclava, that he tried to run away and that there was bomb-making equipment in his car. It's now a part of public record that none of that was true, but I was there in his house when the coffin came back. That was a heart-rendering scene, yet the state had not yet told that family that their son was dead. These people aren't demons. And when I talk to people in those circumstances I don't see psychopaths. And it is a sociological lie to present them as such. They are people responding to a situation as they find it. And because some of the people take up arms as part of that response, it doesn't automatically follow that they then become psychopaths, a point that was verified by two doctors, Lyons and Harbinson, who studied paramilitaries from both sides of the divide in the mid-1980s. If the conditions that exist in Belfast today existed in Dublin, then maybe Eoghan Harris himself would be in the IRA. And although I enjoyed *The Crying Game*, it was as a movie; I don't think it presented a truthful reflection of the IRA. I know it's more about how Stephen Rea deals with his betrayal of the IRA in the context of the relationship he's having, but where I felt the film went over the top was the other IRA person stubbing the cigarette out on Rea's hand, which is over-the-top behaviour.

**J:** But there have been many suggestions that the IRA would just as quickly snub out a life as let someone leave their ranks, that they certainly would kill someone who betrays them, and that *The Crying Game* is truthful in that sense.

**A:** The IRA have made it quite clear that they are a volunteer organisation and people leave it, or don't, as they wish. I know literally hundreds of former IRA people, even journalists, who were once involved with the IRA and are now just getting on with their lives as far away from it all as possible. That's the truth of the situation.

**J:** You do publicly support the use of violence by the IRA. Can you see why this would lead to accusations of base hypocrisy on your behalf when you declare that you and Sinn Féin want to participate in the peace rally following the IRA's murder of those children in Warrington?

**A:** Sinn Féin is involved in a peace project. Peace is political and we have a peace project ourselves, which we've been running with for some years.

**J:** While publicly supporting the IRA's use of violence?

**A:** If I may finish. What I was warning the people who came out in the wake of the Warrington killings was that their understandable declaration of the desire for peace might be manipulated by the agenda of the organisations I have named. The agenda of those organisations, like New Consensus, was to exploit and manipulate. And I must say that I heard no one defending what happened to the Carraher family, the family that was spat upon and insulted at that particular peace rally. But I myself don't believe that reaction represents the feelings of the vast bulk of the people out there on

O'Connell St that day. And I have argued to Republicans who claim that the same response would not be in evidence at the death of a Catholic child that if a Susan McKay took it upon herself to react that way and could get the backing of the media then a crowd would turn up similar to the crowd that felt compelled to protest against the IRA killing those two children in Warrington. Many Republicans believe that wouldn't be the case; I think it would be.

J: But what about the specific accusation that is the base hypocrisy on your behalf to not condemn the killings, or murder, of those two children, yet want Sinn Féin to join the protest?

A: I have said that Warrington was inexcusable. I have said that Warrington was wrong. And if we continue along these lines then we end up nearly forgetting in the semantics of it all that two kids were killed. And I do want peace; I come from a section of people on this island who have always been denied peace. But I must repeat that I cannot speak out against violence on just one side of the divide when I have witnessed violence on both sides for all of my lifetime.

J: Yet there are suggestions that if the intention of the IRA is to 'sicken British public opinion' to such a degree that the troops will be withdrawn, then the killing of a child, or children is perfect propagandist material in that respect. And likewise, if the intention is to damage British business and the economy, then the 'perfect' place to plant a bomb is in a shopping centre.

A: What I've said, consistently, is that injuries or deaths among civilians – even if it is unintentional – are unacceptable. But, let's face reality here, if the IRA wanted to kill scores of civilians they could. If they thought it was 'good propaganda' it is within their power to do that. But the fact that they don't means they realise it is not good propaganda when civilians are killed unintentionally. I don't want to get into the semantics of it in terms of where the responsibility lies, because I do believe it lies with the IRA. Yet I'd like to knock on the head any logic which even suggests that the IRA might think Warrington was a 'good job'. If that was the case the IRA would be killing hundreds of civilians without warnings.

J: What's your response to the other suggestion – that the IRA, intent on damaging the British economy, would see it as a 'good tactic' to place bombs in shopping centres?

**A:** Whatever the merit, or not, of that strategy, I said the Warrington operation was unacceptable and inexcusable. Not just because the kids were killed – though that, of course, is a major factor – but because it appears to me that kids and civilians are 'good' targets. The onus is upon the IRA to try and avoid hurt, injury or death to con-combatants.

**J:** Yet will you come out today and categorically say to the IRA that they should not place bombs where civilians will obviously be hurt or killed, as in shopping centres in Warrington?

**A:** My attitude and how I articulate it is a matter for me to work out. I will say in response to specific questions that certain things are unacceptable or that this is right, or that is wrong. This is my job. But I'm not a public guardian of the IRA campaign. Sinn Féin has a very specific peace project and I think I can more usefully serve the goal that we set ourselves, which is to seek a lasting settlement within the broad democratic notion, and which sees as one of its clear aims a demilitarisation of the situation. That's where I perceive my role, not in involving myself in a commentary on the last atrocity, or as a Geiger scale of what is acceptable and unacceptable in terms of IRA actions. I want to see an end to all IRA actions. I want to see a situation where we have a complete and total demilitarisation of the situation, no more kids living under threat of death, whether it be in Warrington or in Northern Ireland.

**J:** But surely you could better serve that goal by telling the IRA that you believe they should cease the violence, even in a bilateral context?

**A:** When I argue for demilitarisation of the situation, when I argue for a political settlement, I am arguing for that. I see no point in calling on the IRA to cease or to stop. I don't think that serves any purpose whatsoever. The fact is you have a conflict, and a conflict is usually brought to a resolution in two ways. Obviously this can be achieved by one side beating the other. But I said a decade ago that there was a stalemate and that there can be no military solution, that there's got to be a political situation. Therefore one side cannot militarily beat the other side. So we must look at the methods being used to resolve conflicts in South Africa, with the Palestinians, in what used to be Yugoslavia – and the common factor is that people are sitting down and talking. And I think Sinn Féin can perform a useful role in that context.

J: You once suggested that in a post-settlement scenario there would be 'no public support for an armed struggle'. Do you still believe that to be the case?

A: My view is that when Brooke said he would not rule out talks with Sinn Féin and that the British army could not militarily defeat the IRA that, to me, was the signal that it was time for me, within this party, to start putting together a project that moved along that process sooner rather than later. Whatever logic there is for armed struggle in today's circumstances, in my view it no longer exists once we have reached a situation where we have a national democracy, where the British presence has ceased or it has been signalled that it is going to cease. In that context there is no reason, no logic to armed struggle.

J: Yet despite Brooke once saying he would not rule out talks with Sinn Féin, surely the truth is that no matter what deal is done, people like William McCray and Ian Paisley would rather see you dead than talk with you?

A: If they'd rather see me dead than talk to me, then I am part of the majority. Because Paisley also won't talk to Albert Reynolds, and he won't talk to Dick Spring and countless others. But what he's going to have to face is the fact that Unionism has to give. That's why they won't talk. If there had been slavery in the North, Unionists would not have conceded to ending slavery. Unionism has not brought in even any of the limited reforms of the North. Everything that was brought in they had to be coerced into. Even those who tried to shift, even for their own self-interest, like Brian Faulkner, have been gobbled up by the Orange monster. That's the nature of the beast. And they won't talk now because they don't want to give and they know that if they start to give the whole thing then becomes a domino effect.

J: Two readings given for the failure of the last round of talks were that (1), Unionists wouldn't move on the demand and their status as British citizens be recognised; and (2), that John Hume was afraid the new assembly offered by Loyalists in a power-sharing scenario would be Unionism by another name.

**A:** Those may be the reasons but I'll tell you why they could never have worked and that is because the model on offer was not designed to bring about a solution – it was a British agenda. Because of that the Dublin government did not seek a movement towards a solution. The Dublin government should have been seeking, and should still seek, from London an agreement to end partition. The London government should say they have no self-interest in being in Ireland, and the Dublin government should then say, 'if that is the case could we then draw up an agreement that will end partition', and then work together on how they could do that. As in, set up a policy objective in terms of how to get the Unionists involved, how things would evolve from the current situation.

**J:** But you suggested earlier that Patrick Mayhew seems to be sliding backwards, hinting at an 'internal' solution which would exclude Spring and the Dublin government and lead, perhaps, to the restoration of Stormont. In that context talks surely become a farce?

**A:** I said at the very beginning that these talks would not work and Albert Reynolds said the same thing recently when he said that the British seem to be seeking a 'partial solution'. I said in my Árd Fheis speech that there are no partial solutions. We've moved beyond that. Partition has failed. Partition has failed internationally. And it has certainly failed in this country. But Dublin must now take its share of the blame for this. We can't always keep blaming the British. Mayhew is quite open; he says, 'I am a Unionist, I support the Union, so I'm putting forward a blueprint which is about preserving the Unionists.' Albert Reynolds says, 'I am a Republican', but does he put forward a Republican agenda, does Dick Spring put forward a socialist agenda? They don't. So who is left in the stronger position in terms of negotiations? The Unionists are.

**J:** And have all the models previously put forward as a possible path to peace been invalidated for Sinn Féin because of their 'British origins'?

**A:** All have had acceptable elements, but Sinn Féin's primary objective is for a national democracy. That means self-government for the Irish people, an end to partition, and an end to being ruled by the British. What is needed above all is for the British government to change its policy. For whatever reason, the British policy is to maintain the partition of this country. It should change its policy to one of ending partition. And who has the main responsibility for working that out with them? The Dublin government. And it must pursue such an agreement if it really is committed to the concept of peace on this island. And everyone else must be involved in those talks. Strenuous efforts must be made to bend towards the Unionists, to show them that their civil rights, religious rights, will be respected – even if that means making internal arrangements that will suit Unionists better than they will suit the rest of us.

J: Would you support bilateral calls for a truce among paramilitaries while talks take place?

A: All those issues are matters for negotiation. Republicans have said they will take risks and be flexible, and I think that in the new context we have to put the idea of a truce to them, at that time. If we get a peace process going it has to be inclusive.

J: Do you think the IRA should take the lead, call a ceasefire while talks are resumed, and thus publicly challenge the British government and all loyalist paramilitaries to respond in kind?

A: That's a question you'll have to put directly to the IRA. But the reality is that the IRA have had a number of truces in the past, with the British, which came to nothing. They obviously are very cautions about repeating that. But if the British government really want to pursue peace, Sinn Féin has made it quite clear that we are prepared to provide the vehicle for that and they can talk to us with impunity. It is the British government who have themselves on the hook. And the reason the British aren't talking to Republicans at the moment is because they are trying to defeat us. I've been active for all this phase of the struggle yet the last three years have seen an unprecedented campaign of military containment, of propaganda, of social and economic pressure, censorship – all in an attempt to contain republican resistance. That's why they won't talk. You can't expect them to talk to the people they are trying to defeat, militaristically and politically. When they come to their senses and realise they have failed in those efforts, that's the time they will talk.

J: You've talked a lot about peace in this interview, but that must be seen in the context of the IRA's rejection of Gordon Wilson's initiative and the release of that video reasserting their commitment to the armed struggle. Is there a schism between yourself and the IRA on this issue?

A: Not that I'm aware of. But I don't proceed with that even being a matter for concern. The IRA very clearly has its project and I can see the validity of its position in terms of the politics of what it's at. But I have my project and I can see the validity of its position in terms of the politics of what it's at. But I have my project and part of my project is to go, at some point, to the IRA with a political package. The IRA is a political organisation and I want to see a negotiated settlement and the IRA have said, clearly, that they want to see a negotiated settlement. So the challenge is to marry the two.

J: Does it bother you that no matter what you do or say, on any range of issues, your overall political commitment and career will be reduced by many to where you stand in relation to the North? Indeed, that to many you will still be simply 'that bastard who supports the IRA'.

A: But that's what I have to live with every day. And it is also part of where we are all at, at this moment in time. If people in the twenty-six counties, in particular, have that view of me it is because they rarely see me presented in any other way in the media. Ian Paisley comes on a chat show and people discover he has a sense of humour and accept that. But they haven't seen the bigoted side that Northern Catholics have to live with. Whereas most people only know me in relation to my position on the North. And, yes, they probably will judge me simply on that.

J: Can you accept that, similarly, for many people, your own and Sinn Féin's socialist aspirations will, in the final analysis, be completely negated by the fact that you support the IRA, an organisation that cancels out the key, fundamental democratic right – the right to live?

A: People, in the end, would want to be quite clear on Sinn Féin's position on this issue, because it is so often misrepresented in the media, particularly in the twenty-six counties. Sinn Féin does not advocate violence. Sinn Féin's position is to try and seek a peace process and that project is now a central part of the party's function. The fact that the policy has evolved within the party has been a major achievement in Sinn Féin. Sinn Féin has a vested interest in peace. There must be a political move forward which will bring all of this to an end and usher in a new phase, a new era for Ireland.

# 31 MICHAEL D. HIGGINS
## 1993

Michael D. Higgins is, arguably, the single most influential person in Ireland in relation to the arts – and that includes rock 'n' roll – largely because he is the first government minister with responsibility for the arts, culture and the Gaeltacht. That said, there are many people who believe that the position of the arts is peripheral in the sphere of politics. This view is particularly prominent among those who mistakenly assume that the words 'art' and 'culture' are synonymous and that forms of artistic expression are somehow limited to an educated elite.

Heavily influenced by the Frankfurt School of theoreticians, such as Thomas Adorno and Herbert Marcuse, who integrated mass society critique into the analysis of monopoly capitalism, Michael D. Higgins, on the other hand, sees 'culture' as the set of customs, rituals and products that make up the 'way of life' of every section of the community. As such, art is central to the democratic process and accessible to all.

The difference between both perceptions is hardly just a matter of semantics. Indeed, the more modern view can be seen as part of what Raymond Williams – another of Michael D. Higgins's influences – described as 'The Long Revolution', a reversal of cultural patterns which have been in place since at least the beginning of civilised society. In this sense one could also argue that there is no politician in Ireland better suited to the position of Minister for Arts, Culture and the Gaeltacht.

**Joe Jackson:**
Cocteau's epigram 'Poetry is indispensable – if I only knew what for' is the opening line in a book which you once claimed had a profound effect on you. Why?

**Michael D. Higgins:**

Because Ernst Fischer's *The Necessity of Art* is a book I carried around with me for a very long time after I first read it around 1970. His approach was Marxist and focused partly on Brecht, who I also was very interested in at the time. I also read Raymond Williams, who has heavily influenced my views on broadcasting and, later, Ciaran Benson's writings on the arts. In fact, I was also deeply influenced by being invited by Sandy Fitzgerald, during the 1970s, to chair some meetings of CAFE – Creative Arts For Everyone. And by Ciaran Benson's 1979 report on the arts and even more so by a paper he gave at one CAFE seminar, about whether creativity was to be defined on a totally individual basis or whether it was to be defined socially. Benson had thrown his lot in with the argument that we are symbol-using people sharing symbols, and therefore creativity is social. Linking that to Fischer, if creativity is social it then becomes a right, and that sets up all sorts of questions that are central in the educational system and so on. So, definitely I acknowledge my debt to Ernst Fischer and Ciaran Benson.

**J:** Linking Ernst Fischer to Raymond Williams is the belief that art/culture operates as a site of struggle between ruling and oppressed classes, on a hegemonic level.

**H:** Definitely. And that too is something that was brought into focus for me by studying sociology in the 1960s, out of my reading of Herbert Marcuse and that whole Frankfurt School. What they highlighted was the fact that forms of social forces that were oppressive, regressive, couldn't be confined to exploitation at the point of production. So you had to think of domination within the sphere of culture in relation to class, time, space, gender. That's why, even back then, I never believed that the feminist agenda could simply be disposed of by saying 'When you have a socialist society patriarchy will disappear.' I couldn't see any evidence for that because, obviously, that particular struggle still takes place within the realm of art/culture. Added to this, as part of the legacy of 1968, you also had Foucault and so on, all of whom were sensitive to this reading of art and culture. However, the problem with many of the conceptualists that evolved out of the Frankfurt School is that although they claimed to be committed to communication, these insights were not communicated very clearly. To me, to see and feel and work as an intellectual, you must have a commitment to communication in the clearest form.

J: How much of what you do is fired by the fact that you were, you claim, 'culturally deprived' as a child. How deeply did that effect your desire to make sure that Irish people in the future are not similarly disadvantaged?

H: It's a powerful impulse. I know that, from the earlier part of my life, the function of an education, and high performance, was structured towards escaping my economic conditions. So, yes, I definitely feel that no child should have the exclusion from cultural opportunity and participation that I had. People who work with me here in the Department say, 'Minister, I'm interested in this kind of music' – or whatever – 'but I wouldn't be good on arts in general.' And I reply, 'That's your advantage. Work with me to ensure this never happens again, that all the children of the state have access to all the arts, to whatever form of cultural expression they choose.' And I firmly believe we must put structures in place to open up this area for everybody.

J: Was cultural deprivation during your childhood largely a result of poverty?

H: Yes, but at the same time my mother loved reading, though people nowadays might regard what she read as trivial. She probably read all of Annie M.P. Smithson, who was a district nurse and published about twenty books. I read most of them myself! So, despite the poverty we still had access to books, and to reading, which is the important thing.

J: Do you agree with those who argue that there shouldn't be a hierarchical value system placed on the process of reading itself, that people making the choice to read pulp paperbacks is just as legitimate as people choosing to read Foucault, or whoever?

H: Absolutely. Because, irrespective of the choice, people are making their own way through their own literary curiosity and will arrive at different points. That's their right. And, to me, it's better than swallowing wholesale society's idea that 'we have defined what is great in literature and the great will be rammed down the public's throat and if there are casualties, so be it.' I don't believe in that. It's wrong. There is, of course, such a thing as 'great' literature, music, poetry, et cetera, but the key question is how we define 'great'.

**J:** Some argue that the 'purity' of art will be 'polluted' if greatness is equated solely with how well a poem reflects cultural realities, for example. Eilis O'Hanlon certainly expressed this view recently, in the *Sunday Independent*. Referring to Anthony Burgess's belief in the 'sanctity of art', she suggested that, basically, not everybody has a story to tell and that the 'peasants' should be kept out of the temple, as it were.

**H:** Although her attack on community arts was very much linked to Burgess's comment, it was presented out of context. What he is talking about is how such things would interfere with the fire of inspiration in the realm of the private and the personal. There is a big difference between the private and the personal and crass individualism. So hers was an unfair use of Burgess's quotation for a start. But, on the issue of community arts, what she says is nonsense because what is missing is the fundamental debate about creativity. Creativity, to me, is the ability to use imagination and intellect together. And if she wants to suggest that some social classes have no imagination because they have been despised, let it be clear that this is close to a fascist opinion.

**J:** Ernst Fischer argued that capitalism has always doubted the 'worth' of art because 'art doesn't sell'. Is that the basic problem you encounter in terms of trying to get the business community to invest in the arts?

**H:** Fortunately, that attitude has become outdated in many areas. Indeed, I'd suggest that the attitude you describe, in that old Marxist sense, is more malignant in the music industry than it is in other areas of the arts – specifically in relation to the power of the big international organisations. Recording artists have said to me that their work is mediated through structures which are so heavy in terms of deals and companies and so on that it's only when they become very successful and powerful themselves that they can fight being screwed up by corporate exploitation – particularly in terms of not allowing their art to become debased and homogenised. In that sense it is extremely important to retain control over your mode of artistic expression.

**J:** When we read about U2 apparently chasing Michael Jackson and Prince in relation to the biggest advance in rock history, couldn't they be said to be sending out a questionable signal to would-be musicians? Namely, that chasing the buck is more important than making music?

**H:** That is true. And if that the message people get from those stories then it's a great pity and potentially damaging in terms of the art. But if I can believe the interviews I read about how musicians write music and lyrics, then I also see in the kind of thing Bono, and others, say, an attempt to retain the integrity of the form.

**J:** Some would argue that the rock music business, as part of the entertainment industry, has always been used as a palliative, a means by which endless dreams of romance and materialism are sold, usually in the service of the state.

**H:** There is a lot of evidence to support such a dissertion. Obviously, there are exceptions but, quite frankly, that view strikes me as true. And now that we're in a time of such high unemployment all over Europe the desired political purpose would also be to individualise that experience – as with the use of drugs – to distract people from those realities. And rock has to take responsibility for being used that way. People must ask themselves that fundamental question: what has it made passive and what has it released? Yes, it has released some very positive energies and some vital images, but it has equally been an anodyne for generations of people.

**J:** Radio plays a major factor in this process, obviously. Is it true you favour the model used by Canadian radio in relation to the amount of indigenous Irish music (by law 40 per cent) you believe should be played on the nation's airwaves?

**H:** Yes. What I'm interested in is devising strategies for impeding cultural domination. I see the Irish music industry as being very much part of this site of struggle. The real choice is to decide whether the people who make up the community are to be divided into passive consumers broken down into advertising segments. That was certainly the thrust of policy under Mrs Thatcher. But my view is of citizens within a communicative order and the only way you can establish that order is by retaining concepts of public service broadcasting, with accountability and transparency. As to whether this can prevail we have to fight for it.

**J:** It has taken nearly a hundred years for film to be accepted as an art form in Ireland and forty years for the same status to be accorded to rock, partly because educational institutions are rooted in classical traditions, favouring 'high' art rather than popular culture. Do you think, for example, that Neil Jordan's movies and U2's music should be integrated into studies at universities like TCD and within the educational system in the broadest sense?

**H:** Definitely. What is absolutely urgent is that we accept that, in a democracy, the ability to critique is a necessary tool for participation. That's why I fully support those kind of media studies that help people to translate their own environment in a way that empowers them and enables them to participate, whether it be in the art of film-making or rock.

**J:** Do you agree that it is particularly important for working-class people to see their own cultural choices, and environment reflected in education?

**H:** They are entitled to it. And this too is an absolute imperative. It's no different than when the printing press was introduced and the powers-that-be thought it would be a nice thing if people learned to read, yet confined them to the Bible. But they read Tom Paine's revolutionary pamphlets instead. And in the same way that the drive to literacy was driven by the democratic tendency, the drive towards democracy now requires that you bring the same arguments to bear on the new forms of technology to ensure that, as I say, this process empowers the broadest possible range of people – particularly those who have previously been marginalised within the educational system. So yes, what you're saying is undoubtedly true. And certainly these realities should be taken on board by those institutions that offer teacher-training courses, and who need to bring this awareness into the classroom at the most basic level. I certainly would like to see the language of rock videos studied in schools, because I am worried that too many turn their audiences into passive recipients of a very questionable and influential set of images, in terms of sexism and violence.

**J:** You also want film to be fully explored as both an indigenous art form and in terms of the country being used as a place of location for foreign filmmakers.

**H:** I do. What I have been doing in relation to film is drawing on lessons that have been learned elsewhere. The principal lesson I learned after I became Minister is that there is a pattern to the way other countries approach the film industry, which is that they usually went for a dedicated agency, such as the Film Board in our case, and if that didn't bring results quick enough they then lost their nerve and went for post-production tax breaks. So it is very clear to me that if you are going to do something serious in terms of the film industry you must do a combination of a dedicated agency, which will bring the generic industry into being, and gear your tax incentives to the point of production rather than post-production. The purpose of my giving a certificate under the existing arrangement in Section 35 is that it is used to negotiate investment money, which is an area of key importance. So in this sense I will, finally, be developing in this country a climate in which films can be made. Irish and otherwise.

**J:** Apart from cultural goals and considerations, is job creation in the area of the arts your main aim?

**H:** Absolutely. And what I am eager to prove to people is that this whole area is not simply a matter of vague, abstract concepts. For far too long that reductive view of the cultural space has held us back from developing its full potential in terms of job creation. This is an area that is job-rich and has the added benefit of being personally enriching. And I have similar strategies in terms of turning round the industrial potential of the Gaeltacht. I will be putting a lot more money into, for example, preparations for Teilifís na Gaeilge.

**J:** Is it fair to say that you would be viewed as Republican, broadly speaking?

**H:** It is true to say that I remember taking part in debates with people who say that 1916 was a waste of time and I don't accept that because this is to impose a set of motivations and rational requirements on people who participated in what they felt to be something very important, which led to the foundation of this state and led to the institutions of which I now am a part. It's also true that my father was involved in the War of Independence, as were my uncles. And my uncles were on one side in the Civil War and my father was on the Republican side. I'm very aware of all that being part of my family history. But, on the other hand I've always felt that a republic that was defined simply in terms of territorial integrity betrayed the social and inherent rights content of a republic. I see this as a betrayed republic. I equally draw on what my whole life has been dedicated to – the humanist agenda, which raises the question that the life is always more important than the territory. And, in visiting Northern Ireland quite often I see that what people have to live with is not simply two cultures and two divisions but different remembered versions of history that we'll have to accommodate – even if they are objectively contradicting each other. So that humanist agenda is what is important to me. And there was always a strain within Republicanism that accepted that. It did not become the dominant strain and because it wasn't the dominant strain, after independence those that had concentrated initially on the territorial Constitutional argument took over the field and after that others could define themselves as vaguely associated with this and the word 'Republican' began to mean anything that one wanted it to mean. I see it in its finest, strongest sense – that of the citizens operating in terms of equality and freedom and outside of repression and in a socially just society.

**J:** If the human life is more important than the territory does that mean you can't support the IRA?

**H:** I do not support the IRA. And I do not accept that the IRA is in a direct line from the independence struggle. You cannot, at this stage, with so many civilian casualties, so many people maimed and injured, so many scarred, say that this is the path towards the resolution of the problems on this island.

**J:** So to you the IRA, is definitely not the Irish Republican army.

**H:** Their use of the word 'Republican' is not my use of the word.

**J:** What do you say to Gerry Adams who, in my recent interview with him, accused you of weeping for people in the Third World yet ignoring the suffering of people a couple of hundred miles from your doorstep?

**H:** That's nonsense. And it's cheap too and I'm disappointed that he used that analogy. When I think back to my interests in El Salvador and human rights, et cetera, I similarly recall writing in *Hot Press* about the Kirkpatrick trial. That's because I see these issues as indivisible. I always have done so. I'm interested in the holistic view of things. Let me put it like this: I wish those who make these accusations were as committed as I am to the indivisibility of human rights. And, equally, that they were not quite so capable of running for cover in relation to the most appalling and horrendous civilian deaths. I also think it is obscene when I read, at different times, including from the converts, that they want to apologise for having 'killed the wrong person'. What an abuse of language that is! What are their credentials for questioning my work?

**J:** The Northern/Southern Ireland question is, arguably the single most important problem facing this country as we head for the twenty-first century. Do any other politicians ever suggest to you that being Minister for Arts, Culture and the Gaeltacht is really a peripheral role in relation to Northern Ireland?

**H:** Most realise that I'm working in this area too – from a cultural perspective. For example, the relations between the Northern Irish Arts Council and the Dublin Arts Council are very good. There are a number of joint projects, particularly in the community arts area, where, for example, women from the North are coming down South and vice versa. And this, in particular is a vindication of my belief that the exclusion of the women's experience from politics has been part of our inability to come up with those lateral, sensitive strategies which can bind communities together. In community arts you see this everywhere. And the point is that arts, culture, the Gaeltacht and the Irish language are in the north as well and it would be my hope that Teilifís na Gaeilge will be an all-Ireland station. Likewise, if you look at other areas of culture and the arts you will see that the leading people – the poets, musicians, visual artists and so on – are already committed to a set of transcendent values that are beyond the immediate conflict. And these people are powerful agents of the new discourse that's necessary.

# 32    BONO
## 1993

It's like a scene from ZOO TV or, more specifically, Zooropa 93 – two days before U2's current European tour begins. The setting is a hospitality room in Dublin's Factory on an early Tuesday afternoon where U2 are piecing together what will eventually be the as yet untitled follow-up album to *Achtung Baby*! Bono, 'totally wasted' – having been working in the studio until 3 a.m. on a track titled 'Daddy's Gonna Pay for Your Crashed Car' – suddenly hauls out his Macintosh Powerbook and, to the sound of the DAT tape playing a drum beat sampled from Leni Riefensthahl's 1936 movie *Triumph of the Will*, begins to read a lyric which may be recited to the same music on the forthcoming tour.

Fifteen minutes later he's strapped on an acoustic guitar and is singing a classic U2 blues which turns out to be another track from the album in its raw and unprocessed state. The juxtaposition of this image of Bono as the quintessential troubadour set against the still-lingering sound of his words speaking of how he hopes to layer lines from his personal computer onto a stage cityscape which will also contain audio-visual samples from the work of Leni Riefenstahl is the history of rock music in a snapshot – its past, and maybe even more importantly, its future.

Indeed, one track on the new album highlights perfectly the ways in which U2, probably more so than any band in the world, are intent on kicking rock into the 21st century while refusing to relinquish its equally important links to the past. That track features Johnny Cash, who was originally discovered by one of rock's founding fathers, Sam Phillips, and who first recorded for Sun Records in Memphis in 1955. Back then his base was country-pop heavily influenced by the r'n'b and gospel rhythms he heard in new songs like 'Mystery Train' by his close friend Elvis Presley. In his trio, Luther Perkins played lead guitar, Marshall Grant played double bass and Cash himself played rhythm guitar. Nearly forty years later Johnny Cash is still playing rhythm guitar, but on this recording Bono plays lead while Adam Clayton, Edge and Larry Mullen Jr become the new Tennessee Trio. Likewise, Sam Phillips and 'Cowboy' Jack Clement have been replaced by Eno and Flood.

'Johnny Cash is a very smart man and he's definitely someone who had no problem coming along with us for the ride, for the trip,' says Bono, laughing as he changes the tape. 'He came in from day one and started singing over what we described as this "Holiday Inn band from hell"! And yet, seriously, this song is definitely the antidote to the Zooropa manifesto of uncertainty. If it begins with "I don't have a compass/I don't have a map/in other words, I don't know, I don't know" but I accept, even like, this state of uncertainty then this track gives one possible solution. But overall on the album the key is learning to live with uncertainty, even allowing uncertainty to be your guide.'

Pausing, rolling the cassette tap around in his palm, Bono looks out the Factory window at the sunlight masking all the shit and slime beneath the surface of the water in a Dublin canal. Smiling, he says, 'Because this song is an antidote to all those other demented voices on the album I'd really like to call it "The Preacher". Mostly because Cash also comes from that gospel tradition of songs. At the moment it's called "Johnny Cash on the Moon"! But you tell me what you think.'

Having met Johnny Cash within hours of his finishing the recording session that produced this track on a recent visit to Dublin and heard him 'sing to high heavens', as his manager said, 'a wonderful song he recorded with U2, called "The Wanderer"', wouldn't Bono consider keeping that as its title? It clearly is true to John Cash's lifelong spiritual quest and, evidently, contains enough echoes of the similar, seemingly endless odyssey begun by a man, and the band who once sang 'I Still Haven't Found What I'm Looking For'.

'I guess it does,' laughs Bono. 'But I didn't want to cut across Dion's vibe, who also has his own song called "The Wanderer". So maybe I'll call it "The Wanderer 2". Yet whatever about the title, and the context, Johnny Cash is so right for what we wanted to do with this song. We originally put him in the centre of the album-sleeve picture on *Rattle and Hum* because he is that link between the past and the present. And though he reckons he's Scottish we were having none of that. As far as we're concerned Johnny Cash comes from good travelling people stock, and is Irish, one of us.'

Cue music. Rising at about the same slow, steady pace a camera would zoom in on Monument Valley during the opening scene of a John Ford movie, Cash glides into the frame as if striding along the bass lines provided by Adam. Adam Clayton, that is, not Eve's apple-juice-tempted lover – though it could be.

'I went out walking/Through streets paved with gold/Lifted some stones for the skin and bones/Of a city without a soul/I Went out walkin'/Under an atomic sky/Where the ground won't turn/And the rain it burns/ Like the tears when I said goodbye/Yeah I went with nothin'/ Nothing but the thought of you/I went wandering...'

'There used to be a "wa-wa-wandering" I sang at that point, behind Cash's voice, but we cut that out,' says Bono.

'I went wandering/Through the capitals of tin/Where men can't walk/or dream they talk/where sons turn their fathers in/ I stopped outside a churchhouse/Where the citizens like to sit/They say they want the kingdom/But they don't want God in it/ I went out with nothing/ Nothing but the thought of you/I went wandering.'

Clearly moved by Johnny Cash's earth-shuddering singing, Bono shivers and says, 'That's his voice! It's not a subload! I don't know how he lives, carrying that voice around with him, it's so heavy.'

'I went out walking/Down that winding road/Where no one's trusting no one/And conscience's a too heavy load/I went out riding/Down that old eight lane/I passed by a thousand signs/Looking for my own name/I went with nothing/But the thought you'd be there too/I went looking/ Looking for you.'

Half-jokingly Bono says, 'Have you read Ecclesiastes yourself?' Smiling at the sound of a country guitar lick in the song he points his thumb at his own chest, nods his head and in a boy-like manner says, 'That's me!' As Cash begins to recite the next verse Bono echoes the words – in the room, not on the record.

'I went out there/Looking for experience/To taste and touch/And to feel as much/As a man can before he repents.'

Cash and Bono sing: 'I went out walking/With a Bible and a gun/ The word of God lay heavy on my heart/ I was sure I was the one/ Now Jesus don't you wait up/Jesus I'll be home soon/ Yeah I went out for the papers/Told her I'd be back by noon/Yeah I left with nothing/But the thought you'd be there to/I went looking/Looking for you/ Yeah I left with nothing/Nothing but the thought of you/I went wandering.'

As this quite perfect and undeniably historic song fades Bono improvises a gospel cry as a counterpoint to the muted choir of voices disappearing into the distance. Southern blues and gospel have indeed become 'Liffey soul and gospel', the phrase Bono once used to describe 'The Fly'. And this writer knows precisely what Bono means when, cryptically referring to my own passion for Presley and Sun and maybe even my scepticism about the deification of U2, he says of their new album and the tour: 'It may be a long way from Memphis but it's the same mud.' He's right. And only a fool would deny that if Memphis was the spiritual birthplace of rock 'n' roll during the early 1950s, then forty years later its spiritual home has to be Dublin or, more specifically, wherever U2 choose to record.

Reflecting on the fact that Sam Phillips recently suggested to me that the rhythms of prayer, rather than the rhythms of sex, sit at the heart of rock 'n' roll as he helped create it, Bono concedes that maybe the song with Johnny Cash should finally be called "The Wanderer", thus effectively subverting the codes of cock-rock evident in Dion's original song and in rock 'n' roll in general. However, erotic love also, is obviously, something Bono wanted to celebrate in all its fleshy glory in *Achtung Baby*! Nevertheless some of U2's Christian fans may have sensed the absence of the spirit of the force they call 'The Lord' in the same album, despite the presence of the song 'Until the End of the World', which Bono once described as 'a conversation between Jesus and Judas in the Garden of Gethssemene'. Likewise in relation to ZOO TV, which probably presented a new set of questions from U2 rather than proscribing God as the answer.

'We deliberately kept that record for the most erotic form of love, so as to almost exhaust it as a possibility, and I think that makes it a kind of prayer, in a strange sort of way,' says Bono, pausing and choosing his words even more carefully than is characteristic of the man. 'And, whatever about 'Until the End of the World', in 'Love Is Blindness', the last song, Edge's guitar solo is more eloquent a prayer than anything I could write.'

Does Bono agree with the strand of post-modernism which suggests that art in the twentieth century must reflect a world which has abandoned the concept of a unifying force such as God? What is his response to those who would argue that the concept of God has been atomised for most people and that, as with Picasso post-Guernica, the only truthful way to view mankind is in an irretrievably fragmented fashion?

'No. Because, to me the state of flux which dominates modern times is a good place to be,' he says. 'The status quo is the enemy of God, the enemy of a spiritual life, as it is the enemy of a cultural life, as it is the enemy of a political life. Status is the enemy. And although the concept of God, for me personally, hasn't been atomised and I have a faith, I am not attempting to clearly define it at this point.'

Yet didn't Bono previously define his faith in Christian terms in a very specific sense?

'You go through phases in your attempt to work out what it is you believe. And there was a period back in the early 1980s where we lived a much more ascetic life *[laughs self-consciously]* and got a great grounding in the fundamentals of what Christianity could be. It wasn't the kind of Christianity that I loosely grew up around. It wasn't particularly Catholic or Protestant, it was more the cutting edge of Christianity. And I'm really glad I have that base. At the time we probably were extreme because you are extreme in that honeymoon period. And you're always extreme when you're defensive. So I suppose we did build a wall around us and just get on with what saw then as our faith. But I do remember McGuinness saying to me, even back then, 'Look, I'm not sure I share your faith but I know one thing, I know it's the most important question to you. And that an artist, a writer is going to have to address that in whatever way you see fit. And if you want to do so you'll get a lot of stick, but go for it.' And we did so. And we did get a lot of stick.'

Falling into silence for a few moments, Bono reflects on the problems U2's Christian base created for many of their critics and their fans – particularly those who see rock 'n' roll as having more to do with 'the devil's music' and want, maybe, every band to be a Holiday Inn band, from hell.

'But that's like people who reduce everything to its smallest constituent part, like judging a song only on its words, which we talked about earlier,' he says. 'It's like the way some people view sexuality. They want it dressed up and "legitimised" in the nicest possible clothes. It's the same with religion – people want what they believe in to be very

obviously dressed like religion. I find all that reducing things to an and/
or equation tedious and all that unnecessary paraphernalia very funny.'

And yet, fundamentally, only a person who has a core faith in God
can laugh at such things? Does he still have that core Christian faith?

'Yes. I have. But there's also a line in, I think, the New Testament,
which says that "the spirit moves and no one knows where it comes from
or where it's going. It's like a wind". I've always felt that way about my
faith. That's why on the new album I say "I've got no religion". Because I
believe that religion is the enemy of God. Because it denies the
spontaneity of the spirit and the almost anarchistic nature of the spirit. If
you attempt to follow that spirit you will be taken down roads to
unexpected places. And it's not going to be a journey you can negotiate
because of what somebody has written down in a catechism. I appreciate
that people can have a handbook on how to live, if they want it, but in
fact, when pushed and asked for his greatest hits, though Christ may say
"I'm in a corner so I'll list 'Love God', 'Love Your Neighbour' and 'Love
Yourself', definitely the top three", to me these codes should rise out of
how you live rather than be imposed from the outside. Any attempt to
lead "a religious life" or to "dress up" for God is a mistake.'

Hooking the original question that related specifically to "the devil's
music", Bono returns to a parallel he previously has drawn between the
blues and, not the devil's but God's music.

'I've talked about the Psalms before but to me they really are a
predecessor of the blues. Because there you had an honest dialogue with
God, David shouting at God. And he was this character who was a real
fuck-up. And he wailed at God: "Where are you when I need you? My
enemies are all around me and you call yourself God? What the fuck is
going on here?" That's the tone of the Psalms and that's where I come
into the music.'

Surely Bono himself, when he sees news reports about atrocities in
Bosnia, for example, must feel like standing up and wailing, "You call
yourself God, what the fuck is going on here?" At points like that, how
can he even be certain that there is a God?

'I'm sure of one thing,' he replies. 'Like we say on Europa and as I said
to you earlier, "There's nothing certain/That's for certain". But if I was
certain of anything I'm certain that you can't pin our actions, the actions
of man in places like Bosnia, on God. That is our final arrogance, that we
blame God for our own state. Most people think we got kicked out of

the Garden of Eden. I'm not so sure. I think we kicked God out of it. And what I don't see is evidence of God in man. There is enough food, for example, but we just won't share it out. We always see this planet as belonging to God, I think it belongs to us. We probably stole it from God. But you can try and give bits of it back in any way you can.'

Bono suggests that, from his earliest songs – such as 'Street Missions' – up to the as yet untitled Johnny Cash/U2 song from the latest album, his way of 'giving back' has been through taking his imagery from the Bible and his concepts from his religious base in general. In this way U2 are fundamentally gospel singers, in spirit, if not form.

'I also love the language of the blues, the poetic spirit of the blues and its connection with the Bible,' he explains. 'But, yeah, all the language I draw on is from the Bible and I love that language very much, its poetry. And another thing about the Psalms which is very interesting to me is that in the Hebrew verse you don't rhyme words, you rhyme ideas. That's why it translates so well. And you see that particularly in the songs of someone like Leonard Cohen, who also rhymes concepts and ideas and not necessarily, or always, words. This whole end-of-line rhyming shit is vastly overrated!'

It has been claimed that Bono originally turned to religion seeking solace after his mother died. Did he?

'That's too fairytale a reading of what happened,' he says, dismissively. 'I don't think that complex mechanisms like human beings work in that kind of cause-and-effect way. And one thing I definitely am learning in life is that words can reduce complex emotions and ideas, again to their smallest part – as we were saying earlier in relation to songs and religion itself. It's very hard to use words to talk about things like the death of my mother and such. That's why I'm a musician. Using just words can often be just too glib in terms of trying to explain such things away, trying to explore the core of such emotions.'

But hasn't the need to express such feelings been of pivotal importance in terms of shaping the sound, colour and textures of the music created by Bono?

'Yes, but your use of the word "express" is exactly right. I don't try to explain. The need in me is to express rather than reduce everything by trying to explain. That's why I shy away from that kind of glib analysis of my response to my mother's death. More and more where I am at as a musician is saying, even, privately, to myself: "Don't explain, just express."

How come so much of what Bono has expressed in music over the years is rooted in rage? Couldn't it be said that if the Edge's guitar work defines the sound of U2's music to a great degree, it is Bono's own anger and anguish that often defines the psychology behind the music?

'Love and anger are closely related,' he argues. 'Somebody said that hate is not the opposite to love, apathy is, and I agree with that. Rage can be an assertion of the life-force, a wailing out against everything, as in the Psalms. But people really do not understand why some of the love songs we do are so savage, for example. But that, to me is evidence of the well of emotion within the band, more than some superficial paean to love in a more obvious sense. It's just that we take the back door to saying the same thing.'

But would Bono agree that his own rage has been pivotal to the music of U2, a music he once described as 'very aggressive rock 'n' roll'? Isn't the tone of the even the new album filled with anger, torment, feelings that rise from some subterranean level?

'Yes,' he says. 'But to me rock 'n' roll is taking some kind of revenge on the world. I'm very aware of that. I always say that to my mate Gavin Friday. Because he is a guy who got a hard time for being the way he was and dressing as he did, coming from the area we grew up in. I still believe that the Virgin Prunes were his revenge against the lack of understanding he experienced in those days. And there is also some kind of violence in me. I don't know if that is a reaction to growing up in and around it at home, or just being conscious of it on a broader level. But like everything else about me, I put a suit on my violence and send it out to work for me.'

However, there also are claims that this suit is frequently shredded, that Bono's rage knows no boundaries when certain people cross his path. Allowing for the fact that 'growing up in and around violence' at home was half a lifetime ago, how does he account for this? Would he even agree that, whatever violent impulse sits at the centre of his psyche, it doesn't appear to have loosened its hold down through the years?

'I don't know how to answer that. Hell, I'm really a peace-loving guy,' he says in mock humble rock-star tones before pausing. 'I honestly don't know what to say to say to that. But it certainly is a question that I would be interested in an answer to, myself. And so would a lot of people who work for me!' [laughs]

What about the argument that artists seem to need to hold on to that kind of fire in order to remain creative?

'I don't know the answer to that question either,' says Bono. 'I don't know which I'd choose, if pushed to take one or the other. It's like when people ask me, "Are you exorcising or exercising your demons through your music?" I can only say: "I hope I'm exorcising my demons." That's what I'm banking on. Maybe the word "demon" isn't the best choice, though. It's more a matter of tapping into your own darkness. And maybe that has to be a part of creating any form of substantial art. That certainly is something I've come to believe. Van Morrison said to me, "More light, less darkness in the work", and I said in our defence, "Sometimes you must use darkness to show up the light." And that is something I believe to be true. But this is a problem I have with many religious people today. They refuse to stare into the face of the world they're living in. And they refuse to describe it in anything other than the most bland way. They're not attempting to understand the darkness and the world, or to get into it and describe it from the inside so people can really get a sense of what you're talking about. But more and more I realise that everything tells us who, and what, we are. That, too is why we draw on so much in the ZOO TV tour, from pornography to images of the Gulf War. That's our way of describing the world.'

As Bono speaks fervently on this subject one gets the sense that he is almost a Christian born-again to darkness, suddenly liberated from the Judeo-Christian belief that all that should be celebrated in life is light and living echoes of the Christ, and that Satan must be denied. And yet there have been rumours that Bono is now so interested in exploring darkness that he has begun to examine Satanism. Is that true?

Laughing loudly Bono leans forward in his chair and says, 'Can I say yes, please? Can you imagine the stories that would spin out of that? Like people coming back to me and saying, "So what is One really about?" That would be something else!'

He pauses and waves his head in disbelief before answering more seriously. 'You are attracted to the darkness, attracted, in some strange way, to the things you are afraid of. But I never really had that shit of "deny the darkness in your nature" as a child. It was very much like it would be for young people now. I was just given a few clues and directives and told to get out there and find the answers for myself. But what's really important is that I wasn't spiritually abused. And just as you can be mentally and physically abused as a child, you can be spiritually abused. I wasn't. But a lot of people have enough religion to innoculate them against it. And then they're left with no outlet, no form of expression for their spiritual life. And I really do feel bad for people who are like that. In terms of myself, I'm lucky because that never really happened to me. And although I may not have worked the whole thing out, my faith does provide a lot of light for me.'

Part of the ever-evolving nature of Bono's attempt to define God is dictated by his experiences encountering other countries, other continents, other ways of perceiving deities. 'I go to Central America, Nicaragua, for example and those people have a very different kind of Catholicism,' he explains. 'It's like I became very interested in carnivals. I went to a lot because they are celebrations of the flesh, as in "carn" – before Lent. And the Latin Americans are a sexy people. They have what the blacks have in the US, which is this ability to bring God with them wherever they go, even into that celebration of the flesh – which is not Catholicism as we know it here in Ireland. They don't compartmentalise their lives, saying "That's sex, it goes way over there, and that's religion, it goes on the other side of my life" and so on. All the lines are blurred and they access these sides of themselves in a much more fluid way than Anglo-Saxons or Northern European Catholicism allows.'

Describing black Americans in that way, isn't Bono also describing the true metaphysical rather than merely musical roots of rock 'n' roll? Would he agree with Sam Phillips who claimed that Elvis brought a core celebration of sex and the body to popular music because his base as a Pentacostalist allowed him to dance before the light and the darkness in life, the flesh and the spirit, in the name of Christ?

'To a great degree, yes. And I do have some experience of the Pentecostal base Elvis had, but although it is an acknowledgement of the spiritual realm being a lot closer than you think and you do see more devils, I don't think Presley danced in front of these devils to celebrate their darkness. I think he danced on them. But whatever the impulse it is a core factor in the birth of rock 'n' roll, a factor that isn't always acknowledged.'

And yet blues musicians, through Robert Johnson back to his ancestors in Africa, have also yielded to the desire to duel with, or dance before the devil – if only to call forth his music. Has Bono ever even been tempted to explore Satanism in that sense?

'Again, why do I even have to say no?' he says, laughing. 'This could end up being the missing scene from *Spinal Tap*. *[adopts mock British rocker's voice]* "Yeah, well, man, it's just one of those things, like y'know." Or I could say it's like that Jamaican dub record "Chris Blackwell is a Vampire". *[pauses]* But I will say that I am beginning to see things in a more mythic way in that sense and I see that people do deals with the devil. But I don't buy that Robert Johnson-selling-his-soul-to-the-devil-for-the-blues idea. I know that what you're asking me about is very real for some people and it's going on. And I know that in the vacuum created by the Church people are being sucked into expressions of other kinds. But I see explorations of darkness to that degree as very dodgy. And the truth is that I've too much respect for the devil to fuck with him.'

Some would argue that by hauling onto the screens during the ZOO TV Special the work of William Burroughs Bono is, to an extent, fucking with the devil. Isn't Burroughs perceived as a man whose goal, through art, is a celebration of evil?

'Perhaps, but his work is also oddly prophetic,' counters Bono. 'He's describing the human condition and, to me, his diagnosis is accurate. And as an antidote to the denial of those forces, which we talked about earlier, what he does is a healthy in that sense. I know people talk about William Burroughs and his "relationship" with the devil but I met Burroughs in Kansas and all I'll say is that he looked better than I did! And he's ninety! He arrived in with the leather coat, black hat and a bag full of guns! But I have a lot of respect for people who don't believe and – particularly aggressively – don't believe. That, in itself, is some kind of act of faith. In fact I probably have more sympathy for a person like that than I would for a person who says, "I just don't know". And I always believe that the most interesting music, to me, is made by people running towards or away from God. It's part of the same thing when you hear of Robert Johnson running from a "Hellhound on my Trail".'

When U2 do a set of five or six dark-hearted songs during their concerts, does Bono ever feel there is a hellhound on his trail, or that he, and the band, are falling deeper into shadows from which they may not easily escape? Does he ever get scared, encounter forces he didn't want to draw forth?

'Yes I do,' he says solemnly. 'And you get bullied by a song in that very sense sometimes. There was a song on *The Joshua Tree* called "Exit" and I just want to take a bath after we do that. I just want to wash it off my skin. And I broke my shoulder and did unearth a lot of shit – from within myself- doing the song on stage. It also was a song somebody used in a murder. It came out later that the guy claimed the song had made him do it. That's what I mean about not wanting to fuck with the devil.'

Does Bono feel in any way responsible for the fact that a work of his, and U2's, ended up allegedly making someone commit a murder?

'Not at all. That sounded to me like a good lawyer at work for his client. But I still feel that you have to go down those streets in your music. If that's where the subject is taking you, you have to follow. At least in the imagination. I'm not sure if I want to get down there to live. I'll take a walk occasionally, and have a drink with the devil, but I'm not moving in with him – in any way!'

Yet couldn't one legitimately claim that U2's work has now become, by and large, the musical equivalent of exploring Joseph Conrad's *Heart of Darkness*?

'Yes. A lot of the time it is,' says Bono. 'There was a section on *The Joshua Tree* set which we called The Heart of Darkness. It was part of the "Bullet the Blue Sky" into "Running to Stand Still" then "Exit". But, as part of my answer to your question, let me backtrack a little. This whole question about the nature of the devil is very important to me. But I don't necessarily see the devil in the kind of darkness most people associate with the devil. Like in those dens of iniquity or illegal drinking houses, or wherever. For me you see it more in corporate life. That's what I mean when I talk about having a drink with the devil. There are probably countless guys in suits who have given up their soul to succeed in what they do. Because there is a great power people have if nothing will get in their way, if they have no morality, no uncertainty, no doubt. All those things that trouble the spirit. This, to me, is where darkness lies – though, at the same time these people can be incredibly interesting to talk with.'

So does Bono ultimately believe that the devil sits where there has been complete negation of the spirit and the soul?

'Yes, definitely. But I'm also saying, "Don't look for the devil in obvious places." And I really do believe that the territory I might be exploring, as a writer, is not as dark as if I were, for example, working on Wall Street. But in terms of U2 exploring only the heart of darkness, I think there also is a lot of contrast in our work, a lot of, as I described it to Van Morrison, going through the darkness to finally fully appreciate the light. And no matter what route you take to explore these things, what's really important about music, and art in general, is that it does, at least, attempt to counteract those forces that conspire to negate and kill the spirit.'

# 33 CELEBRATION CONCERT PROGRAMME NOTE

## 1993

Earlier this year I wrote, in both *Hot Press* and *The Irish Times*, articles in praise of The Chieftains double-victory at the Grammy Awards in Los Angeles. Some time afterwards I received a letter in which I was rapped over the wrist by a reader for being 'too eager to celebrate so-called "success" in Irish art'. Needless to say, when I later heard U2's *Zooropa* album, I remembered this wrist-rap and had to restrain myself, for about three seconds, before rushing into print to praise, yeah, you've guessed it, another success in Irish art. And why shouldn't I?

1993 has, after all, been a year which saw Ireland thunder through the world of arts and popular culture, sweeping up awards wherever awards were waiting to be won. From the Grammies to the Oscars, the Eurovision Song Contest and the Booker Prize, this country has surely proved itself to be not just a wellspring of creative energy but a centre for excellence in terms of all forms of artistic endeavour.

What's even more exciting is that this breathtaking burst of seismic energy is evident at every level. You can see it surge to the surface in writing seminars organised by RTE, through numberless community projects in theatre and the visual arts, right across to football, television, journalism, film, novels, fashion and music. Suddenly all those centuries of cultural oppression seem to have given way to the kind of defiant cry of self-assertion that would make James himself re-Joyce. 'I told you this would happen, shite and onions, you can't keep the Irish down!' And he'd be right.

Likewise, James Joyce would not need to be reminded that all art aspires to the condition of music. That's what makes this celebration tonight so appropriate, because it focuses on some of the singers and songwriters who have, arguably, led the charge in relation to the process of cultural rejuvenation that is helping this country redefine itself, at home and abroad, as we near the end of the twentieth century.

All we need now is for our forms of cultural expression to fully realise their aspirations towards the conditions that shape the market place, without, of course, compromising our vision in any way. Jaded arguments such as 'Is rock music art?' or 'Is traditional music more true to the Irish psyche than pop?' really are less relevant now than the core question of 'How does music serve the nation's need for self-identification and how can this be translated into a means by which to fight unemployment?' One immediate answer is that Irish radio must play more music by Irish artists, and more corporate concerns, such as Church and General, should explore ways in which the business community can invest in the music industry.

Two years ago I interviewed Canada's representative at the New Music Seminar in New York, Stuart Raven-Hill. Asked to evaluate the overall performance of Irish artists during the seminar his reply was succinct and to the point.

'I'd use one word to describe Irish music and that is "integrity",' he said. 'There is an integrity about Irish songwriters which is almost the polar opposite of what you find in the rest of the world. That probably has a lot to do with a knowledge of, and a love for, literature. And with your country's history. And when you've got that kind of integrity and quality at the soul of your product then your entry into the world market is assured once the music gets the proper funding and encouragement. I see a limitless potential for the Irish music industry.'

The fact that Mick Hanly's 'Past The Point of Rescue' was recently revealed to be the song most often played on American country radio last year, just might suggest that Stuart Raven-Hill was right. May the celebrations never end.

# 34 SOUND BITES
## 1993

'Let's face it, pop culture has taken over from so-called 'high art' in terms of telling us about the times we live in. And rock 'n' roll itself is an intrinsic part of our culture, an experience shared by everyone from the people out there on the streets to our leaders, like Bill Clinton, who had Bob Dylan sing for him at his inauguration! It's the same in relation to our poets and philosophers, and the way we think, these days. So, to me, there can be no more accurate a barometer of the time, since maybe just after the Second World War, than pop culture. But that's exactly why it has been reappropriated by the establishment, and made to serve the state. This is the most crucial point to remember about the role played by groups like U2. They claim to be "subverting" rock 'n' roll with *Zooropa* but that's a load of bollocks! They have a lot of very clever people working for them, like Brian Eno. And maybe the Edge is quite intelligent. But Bono isn't. He's incredibly naïve when he makes some of those claims for their music. It really struck me as so predictable that the whole *Achtung Baby!* and *Zooropa* concept would draw them into the so-called position of being anti-establishment. They may also be reaching into rock's past but there's nothing "subversive" about their music at all. For example, on our CD cover we include chord changes for each song which, obviously, helps return pop music to its base among the people. U2 could do something similar. It really would be more "subversive" of them to encourage people to sing their songs, or write songs that people could sing in a communal setting. That's how music empowers people, whereas U2 seem to be just baffling audiences with psychobabble. I know the idea of the community has changed and they might argue that they now speak to, and for, a global community. But my argument, in terms of our music, has always been that we should battle to hold on to our own identity in the face of the kind of global homogenisation that I see groups like U2 adding to, rather than fighting. For example, when I listen to *Zooropa*, I don't hear anything specifically Irish. And one thing that really fills me with bile is this feeling that everything is becoming the same, that corporations all over the world have decided that high streets, clothes, films, music, all should be identical so as to accommodate the world market. And I really believe that groups like U2 contribute to this, at a core level, for whatever motives. So they are mostly just a global commodity now, something that can be sold in any city in the world. What's "subversive" about that?

'Maybe that's why I don't hear anything coming out of Irish rock that is particularly Irish. And I hate this whole idea of "Celtic rock", people like Fat Lady Sings, who try to gain this cosmopolitan currency out of being "Celtic rockers" when all they're producing is American soft rock. It's the same with Scottish bands. They all sound American and I just find that loss of national identity terribly sad, and, as I say, disappointing.'

*(Damon Albarn, Blur)*

'I saw them in the Phoenix Park at a point when I was sick to the teeth of my "sensitive-singer-songwriter" thing, and my angst and the sense of self-apology that was written into my songs, my performance and almost everything I did. And I really was looking for a way out of my addiction to drink and maybe even out of my addiction to a negative image of myself. But I'd never really listened to U2, I was more into the Bothy Band. Then that day in Phoenix Park I just stood there in front of the stage, totally transfixed. What really got to me was the music, the power and the fact that these four guys on stage were overflowing with a sense of self-confidence and conviction. I'd spent ten years hiding behind a guitar and a microphone stand yet here was Bono standing in front of 25,000 people, as if saying, "We are the greatest band in the world and it's great to be here with you, and you are privileged to be here with us!"

And at that moment I realised: I desperately need some of that. That's what I set out to build up in myself. Before that I really felt I was nothing.'

*(Luka Bloom, on how his 'epiphany' came about as a result of U2)*

'People kept coming up to me after we won that National Music Award last week, saying, "Dolores, U2 had that Best Band award for ages and now The Cranberries got it, you beat U2!" That really sickened me, because U2 have always been a source of inspiration to a band like us. They came from Ireland and went off and broke internationally and showed us that an Irish band can do that, which is probably one of their greatest achievements. And what was really important to me was that they were just four normal lads from ordinary backgrounds, like the rest of us. And they took on the world and won! But what I've found is that Irish people, in the first place, don't realise what talent there is here in Ireland until it breaks internationally, and then there is a lot of begrudging and bitching. But maybe that will all stop now, with the success of U2 and people like Jim Sheridan, Roddy Doyle and The Cranberries. People should realise we're all in this together, we're not in competition with one another. Certainly, The Cranberries aren't in competition with the likes of Sinead O'Connor and U2. But, definitely, The Cranberries have shown there is more to Ireland than just U2 and Sinead. To tell you the truth, I really love U2. Like when we're on tour in America and sitting, say, at a party where all these guys are into Black Sabbath or whatever, and haven't a clue about Ireland. Then, the next minute, U2 comes on TV and suddenly I'm saying, "There's U2, they're from Ireland, they're brilliant!" And I get really happy, shouting, "Aboy lads, aboy Bono! Fair play t'youse!" And then someone usually says, "Any more Black Sabbath?" and I'm going, "Leave U2 alone, leave their song on." But metallers really don't understand why I get so patriotic and blissful when U2 come on.'

*(Dolores O'Riordan, of* The Cranberries*)*

'There has been a series of sea-changes in Irish society over the past ten years which are only coming to fruition now. There's a feeling, particularly among young people, that the political structures that have been in place for at least the last twenty-five years have not served us well. And all people saw, in the election of Mary Robinson, and in her performance in office, the possibilities for politicians to behave in a way that is both uplifting to the community and effective. Women, in particular, must play as full and active a role in Irish society as is possible, involve themselves more in the political process if they really want to bring about the necessary changes. But taking that on board, even the concept of running for constituencies that are winnable is a difficult process for most women because women have been culturally attuned to not putting themselves forward. Women, by nature and as a result of education, tend to be co-operative and non-aggressive, with women's organisations working on the basis of mutual respect. Political activity means going out there and saying to the electorate: "Put me at number one." A lot of women have not been brought up to say that even to other women, not to mention the electorate at large. And the single greatest event which helped women overcame this core psychological barrier was the election of Mary Robinson. It also was the catalyst for many voters, who realised from her subsequent performance as president of Ireland that they had made a right choice in choosing a woman. That meant that in this election voters were looking at women candidates in the same way they were looking at men candidates and making their choice on the core issue of: who is the right person for this job? That's why I do think we are witnessing what you called earlier a sea-change in Irish politics.'

*(Newly-elected Labour minister Joan Burton, responding to suggestion that she epitomises the 'new face' of Irish politics as a woman who set out consciously to break the male monopoly in the Labour Party and, by extension, in Irish politics as a whole)*

'What I get, in return, from my audiences in Ireland, has always amazed me. It's like Dylan said last night – the amount of love, and good humour and inspiration can't be compared with any other audience in the world. There's also so much appreciation there for the act of singing, for the story in songs. It really is as though Irish audiences have this intrinsic need to sing out, to soar with the angels. And when you're on stage leading that chorus it really is like the moment that makes everything else worthwhile. That's how Dylan felt, that's how I feel.'

*(Nanci Griffiths, American singer-songwriter)*

232

'I used to think that country music originated in America but the more I explored its roots the more I saw that much of it came from places like Ireland. So when I say I really feel at home here I'm speaking in musical terms and I mean it!'

*(Vince Gill, country singer)*

'If we do retain the integrity of the music and seek out its roots, we'll obviously find, as you did with that anecdote about "Heartbreak Hotel" that all music interlocks at some core level. I love the idea that one of the initiating songs in rock history, and one of the primary catalysts for rock culture in general, may originally have come from an Irish jig that later became a bluegrass mountain song. That's great!'

*(Country singer Dwight Yoakam, responding to Joe Jackson's assertion that the melodic structure of Elvis Presley's 'Heartbreak Hotel' was based on an Appalachian tune, of Irish origin, called, 'Sugar Foot Rag')*

'Everything I've done, and certainly everything I've written, is rooted in my Irish psyche and I'm very proud of that. People say, "You were Irish Catholic, raised in the shadow of the Church, look at what anguish that brought you", but they forget that this base also gave me wonder, imagination, pageantry, and an essential understanding of the spiritual side of life, as well as the physical."

*(Dory Previn, Academy Award-winning composer)*

'In Irish literature the father was always a bully. The historical reason for this is that the father had no real power, the true figures of authority were outside of Ireland. *The Playboy of the Western World* is a primary example of the early Irish oedipal story. You kill your father three times and he comes back! And few would deny that the oedipal story is still central to the Irish psychology, because, in ways, the figure of authority remains outside this country. That, to me, is another part of the relevance of *In The Name of The Father*.'

*(Jim Sheridan, film director)*

'People on our side who grew up over the past twenty years have had to endure one set of betrayals after another by English politicians. They see Northern Ireland as an issue that is outside their immediate area of concern. But then, right at the beginning of the Troubles you had the attitude of a secretary of state who spoke about "an acceptable level of violence". I bet it wouldn't have been "acceptable" in his own constituency. That kind of thing confirms the view that British politicians have no time for us and that we're just an appendage to the United Kingdom, about which they don't care at all.

'It's the same in relation to the Official Unionist Party, who, I've always believed, failed working-class people like myself. Many people seem to think that all Unionists are born with a silver spoon in their mouths. I certainly wasn't. I was brought up in a Belfast slum and my parents weren't even able to afford to rent a house of their own till I was eight, nine. So, I'm definitely not part of the Unionist Ascendancy, the power that was in government for fifty years and was disdainful of all working-class people. Indeed, that Unionist establishment probably still despises me, see me as an intruder because I'm not part of the Unionist power structures which were based on wealth, privilege and aristocracy and so on.

'The best thing about the breakdown of the homogeneous Unionist party is that it did give opportunities to people like myself who came from a working-class background. But the difference is that working-class people on the Unionist side did not feel they had to rise up, ruin their own areas and destroy jobs and homes et cetera, as in the case in terms of someone who came from West Belfast. I can't understand how people who talk of the deprivation of their community can then engage in activities that cause greater deprivation. What is it that drives international investment away? The bombing campaign, the breakdown of law and order, the terrorist campaign. I feel justified in making the complaints I make and working to try change things. I don't think there is any justification for the claim that because of the situation we will create more deprivation for the people we represent. So, no, I don't accept Sinn Féin's description of their party as Socialist. I see them as fascists. They like to wear the cloak of socialism because it's trendy on the international stage. But their record on the rights of ordinary people proves to me that they are nothing but fascists. And even if Sinn Féin repudiate IRA violence Unionists will never accept Northern Ireland office plans to include Sinn Féin in talks. We've had twenty years of people being maimed, killed, with their homes destroyed and everything else, as a result of the activities of these people. You don't easily dispense with all of that. And there is very, very deep bitterness towards the IRA, and their political masters, among Unionists.'

*(Sammy Wilson, of the Democratic Unionist Party in Northern Ireland)*

'The DUP and Paisley and some of the hard-liners in the Official Unionist Party are definitely major obstacles to progress. But they won't be there forever. And I believe that when the younger Unionists come more into positions of authority within their parties, they will want to advance these talks at that level. It's something that is achievable within a ten–fifteen year span, but not within six months.'

*(Bobby Molloy)*

# 35 IAN PAISLEY JUNIOR
## 1994

While escorting me out of his offices in East Belfast at the conclusion of this interview, Ian Paisley Jnr suddenly smiled, opened a bullet-proof glass door, and said, 'Here's to the day when there is real peace and we can all get rid of this stuff and live normal lives.'

It was an-off-the-cuff comment which probably sums up precisely how the majority of Unionists feel in the wake of the IRA ceasefire. And yet, the person making this particular comment is obviously not just any Unionist. He is the son of Dr Ian Paisley Senior, his father's personal assistant and Justice spokesperson for the DUP. That said, there also obviously are generational differences between the two Paisleys and in this space one could conceivably place the future of the Democratic Unionist Party, irrespective of who its leader may be in five or ten years, as part of a post-Paisley Snr political landscape.

Nowhere are these differences better highlighted than by the choice of art each Paisley has chosen to decorate his office. In Ian Paisley Snr's office there is a clearly out-of-date caricature of 'Haughey, after getting kicked in the nuts by my dad!' as his son says, laughing. In Paisley's own office there is a post-modern painting depicting shipbuilders coming home from work, painted by George Fleming.

In the programme that accompanied recent exhibitions by George Fleming, Paisley Jnr also addressed the key question of cultural identity, as it relates to Protestants, particularly in terms of the 'jeering criticisms' that are frequently aimed in its direction.

'The most persistent accusations run: Protestants in Northern Ireland are cultureless, they know who and what they are not, but have no idea what they are; their ideas, politics and expressions are overpowered with a siege mentality. [They] are dour, boot-faced sojourners in a chrysalis of identity crisis awaiting the day of emancipation to apologise for their stubbornness and intolerance and embrace an Irish identity they have eschewed so long,' he wrote.

Elaborating on this theme, in the same programme, Ian Paisley Jnr also paraphrased a conversation with a 'young, moderately educated Protestant in Northern Ireland' who tellingly claimed that she didn't 'really feel British' and was not 'truly Irish either', concluding that she was 'part of both, I suppose'. This question of dual identity is of central importance to Ian Paisley Jnr. His recognition of the dualistic nature of Irish identity in Northern Ireland also sets him apart from many Unionists, including, it could be argued, his father.

### Joe Jackson:

Why do you see the arts as so important in terms of expressing, and re-defining cultural identity in Northern Ireland?

### Ian Paisley Junior:

Because we all are shaped by cultural as well as sociological and political influences. For example, I help George Fleming to exhibit his work and so far we've had about twenty-five exhibitions and his art is often criticised for being 'Protestant' in the sense that he portrays the Orange Order. And yet George is not a Protestant, he is a Baha'i in faith. But his paintings obviously were informed by his past, because he was originally a Protestant. And artists must be honest with themselves in that way in order to express, and explain to others who they are. George, for example, was able to start a debate on the subject of Protestant identity, as a result of the polemic in his paintings.

**J:** One would have expected more of a cultural outpouring along these lines over the past twenty-five years – in all the arts – yet that hasn't happened. Why do you think that is?

**P:** It's a result of the sectarianism of the politics here. People are frightened to express that they are from the Protestant community lest their work be dismissed as looking at just one side of the equation.

**J:** On the other hand, one commentator recently claimed that 'the Protestant tradition has never been associated with the arts. They built ships and aircraft and kept the country going and left the art to the Catholics'.

**P:** That's absolute nonsense. One feature of the identity of the Protestant community is the so-called 'Protestant work ethic'. But when you're unemployed and living in the Shankhill Road the Protestant work ethic isn't exactly amenable to you, is it? It was when the shipyard employed thirty-three thousand people, but it isn't now, when it employs only three thousand. Yet this doesn't mean all Protestants have been enslaved by this work ethic and that there haven't been Protestant painters, poets and songsters. But they don't project themselves as Protestants. For example, Van Morrison does not say 'I'm Van the Prod, from East Belfast'. But then another side to this argument is why should he? That would be too narrow for Van Morrison, for his identity. He says, 'I'm Van the Man, I've got a song to sing and it's for everyone.' Mary Black, on the other hand, is perceived as being an 'Irish folk singer', therefore her cultural experience is perceived by others to be something that is Irish and Catholic, which is much more limiting. And we do have Tom Paulin, John Hewitt, all those writers. But many of them feel let down by their own community because they believe that Protestants are not exposed to art, or rather cultural self-expression in the broadest sense, in terms of education, which goes back to your earlier question. We're not taught, in our state schools, how to be creative in that sense. Instead, we're exposed to the sciences, history and so on. And, in his work, John Hewitt certainly has suggested that because we're not exposed to thinking deeply about who and what we are; we just accept it without question. Whereas the 'Irish' community, on the other hand, feel that it is so important to project who they are culturally, maybe because they too don't fully understand who they are. But at last they use art to question such things. That's where cultural expression is obviously of central significance to any people.

**J:** One reading of the 'Irish' community's need for self expression at this level – and one explanation for the current so-called cultural explosion in terms of literature, film, rock and so on – is that the Irish, after centuries of oppression, have finally found their voice. Put very graphically, someone said: 'After eight hundred years of having a British boot in your face, when it's moved even slightly you shout.'

**P:** That's bunkum. It's chip-on-the-shoulder mentality. And let's be realistic here. What is the Protestant inheritance on this island? Is it simply just six counties Irishness? No. Before this island was partitioned, who were the Unionists? They were liberal and conservative Irish Unionists. What is the Presbyterian Church? It is the Irish Presbyterian Church. So the Protestant community quite rightly have a sense that Irishness is ours too. But it's ours in a different way than it is to the Catholic community. It's part of our psyche, which we have the right to accept, or reject. The real problem is that 'Irishness' has been hijacked and become a political weapon. So, to be 'Irish' you can't be Protestant, you can't be a Unionist. To be Irish you have to be everything which isn't British – but the Protestant community would have the goal, the vision to see Irishness as something which says you can be an Irish Protestant, you can be an Irish Unionist, and you can be Irish and British at the same time. And that is something that is very important to us and should be promoted in a more positive way. Unfortunately, the past twenty-five years have really kicked that notion in the teeth.

**J:** You speak of 'culture' in a very modern sense, as encompassing the 'lived experience' of people and how they choose to express themselves, rather than culture as high art. Do you think that distinction is of key importance in this debate? Do you think most politicians miss this distinction?

**P:** Yes and yes in answer to both parts of that question. Definitely. Too many politicians relegate the question of culture to the periphery of the political debate, whereas, to me, it is central. For example, what is your real culture if you're a working-class Prod? It's listening to the blues, it's soccer. People express themselves through soccer, and the teams they support. They express themselves through rap, and even what some people dismiss as 'trash' culture, such as the films and the television programmes they are exposed to. To define Irishness simply as things that happen within this island is very inverted. And, if people don't adopt this broader definition of culture they will just continue to dismiss a great many things which form the Protestant community's identity.

**J:** Do you, therefore, support Co-Operation North, which is a body that promotes links between artists from the north and south of Ireland? Do you agree that in this context Nationalists must be allowed to express themselves?

**P:** I've no problem with any form of real and genuine cooperation along these lines, provided there isn't some political agenda to create a monstrosity. For example, the belief among the Protestant community is that the agenda often is 'we must soften the rough edges of Protestant identity'. Protestant culture attacks and it invokes strong, robust language. And organisations like Co-Operation North want to brush away those rough edges. Likewise, Michael D. Higgins he talks about the importance of culture in the political sphere, in relation to an understanding of Protestants. The aim seems to be 'We want to eradicate those views that are not palatable to everyone, we want some kind of homogenised cross-culture'. That, to me, is mad. Let's accept our diversities and co-exist. Let's not try and create some kind of hybrid monstrosity. Whether that applies to painting, theatre, poetry, novels, films, whatever.

**J:** In terms of film, do you agree with one commentator's suggestion that the psychotic character played by Sean Bean in *Patriot Games* was an accurate depiction of an IRA hitman?

**P:** I think it was, yes.

**J:** But if it's true of the IRA, surely the 'psychotic' tag also applies to loyalist paramilitaries?

**P:** Of course it does. By and large, terrorists are driven by same form of psychotic inner self. There are people, among terrorists who have a genuine love for what they are doing and that doesn't mean killing, it just means their cause. They're not psychotic but, at the end of the day terrorists, no matter what side they are coming from, are driven by the same form of desires. I've interviewed convicted loyalists, and I'm not talking about the UDR Four. And a lot of them are naïve and stupid people, even if they are streetwise. And they can actually remove themselves from the role they play, and see themselves operating as terrorists after they've put on the garb and involved themselves in terrorist activities. If you're able to do that, it does make you psychotic. Because it's calculated, there is malice aforethought, and these people are ruthless.

**J:** Do you feel morally torn when asked to defend the actions of terrorists?

**P:** I would not defend the action of a terrorist. But if a person's rights are being infringed, as in a prisoner's rights to see his relatives, I will speak on their behalf. And although, right now, there is this growing tendency to look forward, not back, I would say that the victims of the past have every right to express their sorrow, anger and sense of betrayal.

**J:** Can you, therefore, empathise with Nationalists who describe themselves as 'victims of history' in Northern Ireland.

**P:** I don't know if I empathise with them but I wouldn't deny them their right to articulate their past, or how they interpret their past.

**J:** Why do you almost instinctively say 'I don't know if I could empathise'? Like so many Unionists, can you not make the leap across that chasm?

**P:** *[pause]* Okay, I understand why they're doing it.

**J:** Why, then, have you suddenly become so afraid to articulate your understanding of the Nationalist need for self-expression along these lines when, earlier, you were so articulate in relation to Protestant self-expression?

**P:** I've given you my answer.

**J:** Are you afraid that if you, as Ian Paisley's son, are seen to be saying something that is sympathetic, empathetic in relation to Nationalists, it may be misused?

**P:** There is always that problem. And, yes, I am just being cautious here. That's one part of the problem. And I've nothing else to say on this question.

**J:** You graduated in history. How do you respond when historians suggest that the current phase of the Troubles in Northern Ireland can be traced back to your father's anti-Nationalist gestures in the late 1960s, such as demanding that the tricolour be removed from a premises on the Shankhill Road. That, surely, is a denial of a people's right to express themselves on a cultural level.

**P:** If people want to hate Ian Paisley, or blame him and interpret history that way, then fair enough, blame him. But the facts of the matter suggest differently. They do not suggest that he was the cause of the Troubles, the instigator, the match which lit the flames. That is an attempt by many politicians and some historians to blame one person. No conflict, at the end of the day, can be blamed on one person.

**J:** But even in terms of your own family, there probably is the perception that, from an early age, your father sat you on his knee and said, 'Repeat after me, I hate Catholics, I hate the Pope, I hate the Republic of Ireland'.

**P:** He is actually a Christian man. But I did, recently, meet a guy from Lisburn who said he was brought up by his mother and father to hate Roman Catholics, and he did say, 'They sat me on their knee and instructed me to hate them.' He automatically assumed my upbringing was the same. But if anyone had sat me down and told me to hate, I would have gone right out and done the opposite. I was given free rein in terms of this, told to go and make up my own mind.

**J:** But surely you must have absorbed some of the attitudinal tendencies in your father's so-called anti-Catholic rants, almost by osmosis, just by being his son.

**P:** There was none of this, what people describe as 'ranting and raving', in the house.

**J:** That said, according to historian Joe Lee, your father 'developed religio-political paranoia beyond the wildest dreams of his Unionist contemporaries', and one can easily imagine him practising those rants at home in front of the children.

**P:** That is crap with a capital C. Firstly, my father is an off-the-cuff man and doesn't write his own speeches, so he certainly isn't going to practise them at home in front of his children. And that view of history just discredits those who write such things. But in answer to your broader question, my own theological background is that yes, I did go to a fundamentalist church and fundamentalist Sunday school. Yet, although my religious views are identical to my father's, because I attend his church, the point is that my political views were influenced more so by my generation than by that religious base. And I see them as separate identities within myself.

**J:** So you agree with those who suggest that your father's political identity is very much shaped by his theological base.

**P:** Definitely. Whereas I am different in that a lot of my views, and my generation's, are shaped not so much by religious baggage, but by political, economic and social baggage. And this, probably in a less emotional way, makes us stronger believers in the Union because it's good socially, good economically and so on. We have that base, instead of just having a political notion based upon emotion.

**J:** So are your father's politics based mostly on emotion?

**P:** Part of it can be explained as that, definitely. He's an orator and oratory only works if you play on people's emotions.

**J:** One could say then that your father has thrived on just engendering fear and hatred in the hearts of Unionists and that he has played to their lowest common denominator, even terrorised them emotionally.

**P:** I ain't scared. And I think the average loyalist in Northern Ireland is fearful of what the British government is up to, and has been up to, behind their backs. My father reflects that. But I do not agree that we perpetuate the ideology of fear, or fear-identity.

**J:** Surely your father does, and always has.

**P:** No. Because that approach would only hold water for so long before people being to think that there's nothing to be scared of. I think he genuinely highlights for the Loyalist community things they ought to be wary of, but his whole political ideology is not based on engendering fear.

**J:** But obviously he does just that, for example, when he compares John Major to Hitler and Jim Molyneaux to Judas. Indeed, it has been suggested that such comments have alienated the Loyalist community at large and risk leaving your father, and the DUP out in the political wilderness talking to themselves.

**P:** Let's face facts here. John Major is the most unpopular prime minister this century in the UK. Let's not pretend for one moment that in Northern Ireland he is even liked. He's not a man of substance. He's not a man who would create much esteem, certainly from among my community. We've no sense of kinship with Major. He's an Englishman, and we're Ulstermen. And the community would hate the fact that he was going to dictate to a major political leader, from Northern Ireland, the terms of reference, for a conversation.

**J:** But are those not just loaded emotional terms, or do you and your father honestly believe them to be politically accurate?

**P:** They are accurate. And if you can't write your ideology on a gable wall, and your average punter can't understand it in those terms, then your ideology sucks. The is fact that Ian Paisley is able to articulate those views and the average punter can understand what's being said.

**J:** But isn't such sloganising a ridiculously reductive view of a very complex political landscape?

**P:** Slogans get to the heart of the matter. They don't tell the whole truth, but they tell most of it. And slogans like that are representative of how the average Unionist and Loyalist is feeling right now.

**J:** Some Loyalists are bound to say rubbish to that and argue that they'd rather see the current political crisis dealt with in a more constructive way, maybe even through talks with John Major, rather than accusing him of probably lying when he says there was no secret deal done with the IRA in relation to the recent cease-fire.

**P:** That's their right to say that but they didn't get 166,000 votes in the last election. Ian Paisley did.

**J:** Yet isn't it fundamentally true that the reason your father and the DUP won't get involved in talks is because they can't face the fact that this will, inevitably, lead to them having to relinquish the position of power they've held in Northern Ireland? Particularly your father, who, as you implied earlier, has built his political career on selling himself as an oppositional politician, against the South, against the Pope and so on?

**P:** But what power has Ian Paisley got? The only power he has are the votes from his community. Ian Paisley can't introduce an Act of Parliament, he can't rule Northern Ireland, any government department. He's powerless. But look at John Hume. People say it was a 'great act of statesmanship' when Hume talked with Adams. That it was 'real leadership'. It wasn't. It was inverted. It was going back on one's self, back to Republicanism from nationalism. Talking to people who share your ideology isn't 'leadership'. But talking to people who have a different ideology is. If he'd gotten on the phone to Ian Paisley Snr or Jim Molyneaux and said right, we've to sort out our differences, that would have been a statesman-like role.

**J:** Surely your father would, in effect, have said to Hume to go to hell – as he has – because Hume had talks with Gerry Adams.

**P:** *[cuts across]* No, he wouldn't. We made an offer to John Hume, between 1991 and 1992, which his party agreed to and John Hume dismissed. It was about governing Northern Ireland in a particular way. Yet Hume walked away because he has never wanted to face the consequences of dealing with Unionists on the terms of who, and what they are – a majority community. All he wants is to have the Irish government on side. But at the end of the day what determines everything is how the people of Northern Ireland – Catholic and Protestant, Unionist and Nationalist – are going to co-exist in Northern Ireland. Let the people of Northern Ireland alone determine their own future. That will clear up all the questions and doubts about who we are and what we want to do. But the British government have got to learn that they can't treat the people of Northern Ireland like dirt on the heel of their shoe. And all we're asking for is a level playing field. We want to see a Northern Ireland that is as peace with itself, where Roman Catholics and Protestants can co-exist and where we can have respect for one another. We want to see a political framework which recognises the real social and political needs of the entire community, a new relationship between the two states who share this island. We want to see the Irish Republic coming into the twentieth century by removing its illegal claim over us and then saying, 'Let's be good neighbours, let's cooperate in the EC, let's build new structures where we can have agreement on, like agriculture, tourism, economic regeneration of border areas. But let's build that future relationship on trust, and mutual recognition of each other's right to do our own thing.'

**J:** What is your response to the concept of a joint authority forming the basis of this future relationship?

**P:** Joint authorities have never worked. You can't have a dual sovereign position. The concept hasn't worked anywhere and I don't think Northern Ireland should be a laboratory for men like Albert Reynolds and Gerry Adams. Let's be honest about what is happening right now. Let's stop pretending we're living in some kind of Alice-in-Wonderland world. And now they're talking about Adams receiving a Nobel Peace Prize. And it disgusts me to see him being packaged as a credible politician. Seeing him on television this way will alienate people, frustrate people and play right into the hands of Loyalist paramilitaries. And this is all part of the reason there is deep anger, and despondency in the hearts of the Loyalist community. But our message is that we have got to keep our heads and listen to the person who speaks as the authentic voice of the Loyalist community and that is Ian Paisley. None of these other

Loyalist or Unionist politicians have the trust of the Loyalist community, my father has.

**J:** If he has, why does the DUP get only 13 per cent of the vote in general elections, compared with the OUP's 34 per cent?

**P:** I believe we have to reorganise and campaign to make our party stronger.

**J:** What's your response to the suggestion that the DUP will only be strengthened when your father retires, or is replaced?

**P:** In that context it will either strengthen or disintegrate. And in ten, fifteen years time, we are going to be in a post-Paisley Snr situation, and we'll see what happens then.

# 36

## SOUND BITES
## 1994

'My objections to the Downing Street Declaration go much further than its parentage being the Hume–Adams talks, though I accept that its parentage was the Hume–Adams talks and that the government ended up producing a modification of the Hume–Adams talks in the Downing Street Declaration. But my objections to that declaration is that the most fundamental issue in Northern Ireland is the issue of self-determination. As far as I'm concerned, the people of Northern Ireland have the sole and separate right to self-determination. That's the principle that is enshrined in my political beliefs. The Downing Street Declaration gives away the right of self-determination, then qualifies the means by which that self-determination is to be exercised. I don't accept that. And I believe that those Unionists who have acquiesced in this have made a fundamental error and weakened, very considerably, the Unionist position. And I maintain that any agreement signed between Dublin and London is not binding to me. I am only bound by agreements that are signed by me, and the Unionist community in Northern Ireland. And until the people of Northern Ireland consent to give away their self-determination then we will maintain our position that we ourselves are entitled to determine what our future will be. And nobody else. On a number of occasions in the declaration reference is made to consent. Happily, Mr Reynolds has defined that for us and indicated that it only refers to the final act of severance, so that you can live in quasi-united Ireland but until the final legal act of hand-over is to be signed your consent is neither asked for, nor is it to be granted. So much for "consent". Our consent wasn't asked for the Anglo-Irish Agreement, our consent wasn't asked for the Downing Street Declaration, and now we're told our consent isn't required for the new North/South structures.

'I can see all of the ingredients that make up civil war being played out by the setting aside of the democratic process in Northern Ireland, the elevation of men of terror, the refusal to accept that the majority have rights. All of these elements are ingredients which necessarily force people to set aside democracy as a way of making change.'

*(Peter Robinson, Democratic Unionist Party)*

'There are still two sets of private armies in this island and neither of them has any intention of disarming. They have opposing intentions. When the Loyalist paramilitaries agreed to a ceasefire it was based on their conviction that the Union is safe and that nothing would be done to disturb the United Kingdom of Great Britain and Northern Ireland. We also know from the statements by a spokesman for Sinn Féin that the Sinn Féin/IRA assumption is that rapid progress must be made towards what they call "demilitarisation", by which they mean Brits Out, and they have specified that is not just to the barracks in Belfast but, as Martin McGuinness put it "to mainland Britain". McGuinness, Gerry Adams and Mitchell McLoughlan have all indicated that if the IRA don't get what they want they could be back in business. This will be a prolonged ceasefire, but I don't see it as durable. And when Albert Reynolds says we must build on the two ceasefires the question remains: what can you build on a contradiction? One side of the ceasefire says Northern Ireland must stay for ever, and the other side says Northern Ireland must go soon. You can't build on that.

'One could talk about all sorts of things if the private armies weren't there. But with their arsenals there, and their incompatible objectives there, that overshadows everything else. Particularly, for example, if one talks about when Sinn Féin meets the Brits. Sinn Féin have just one card, which is "if you don't do what we want you to do at the pace we want you to do it, you will find the IRA back in business". They have nothing else to say. And a united Ireland, finally, is what will be forced on Unionists through these cross-border institutions with executive powers, despite their legitimate wish to remain part of the United Kingdom, which I accept without reservation. Albert Reynolds accepts it and tries to shove the Nationalist agenda in by the back door. Therefore, if we do make "progress" along these lines the Loyalists will be looking to that ceasefire of theirs because their basic assumption that the Union is safe will turn out to be false. And if we don't make progress the IRA will say, "What did we get? We made this big gesture of a ceasefire and the bloody Brits just behaved as if they own the place, as they did before." The Sinn Féin/IRA position will get tougher when they've got those things they can get, such as meeting officially with the British. That's important for them and they'll keep quiet-ish till they get that. But when they've got that and find that the British answer is no to their maximal position of Brits out and a united Ireland, then we will be back to what Morrison describes as "the unarmed struggle", which, I fear, will finally lead back to the guns.'

*(Conor Cruise O'Brien)*


'I still wouldn't go to war for a country. People are too ready to pick up a gun or even to kill through speech in this country. All because of something that happened three hundred years ago. Even something that happened thirty years ago wouldn't be enough to make me want to go to war and that's a general feeling among people my age, that I know. The way I see Northern Ireland is that there are minorities keeping the whole thing going and everyone else is just plain fed up, and sick of it all.'

*(Pat Gallagher, Goats Don't Shave)*


'The national question is still the question facing Ireland and we all should do what we can to face it. And, going back to my play *The Dogs*... after I did it I will admit I felt defensive, maybe even paranoiac, because I'd taken the title from that *Daily Mirror* headline after the Gibraltar killings: "Why the Dogs Had to Die". And I did feel I was putting my neck on the line, though six months later I wouldn't have felt that way because we started to read about the

Hume/Adams talks and then got the Declaration, so now it is all like suddenly breathing fresh air and knowing you have the right to address these things, whether it is in plays or journalism, and not be branded. So that's one thing I'd like to pass on to lots of other people reading this, who may be feeling nervous about tackling this subject. And it is equally important that plays such as *The Dogs* be presented from a purely Unionist point of view and staged extensively in the twenty-six counties. But I think that will be a part of the whole healing process we'll see taking place over the next few years. And the arts are going to have a critical part to play in this process. We need to know what makes the Loyalist mind tick, we need much more interaction in this area. In terms of theatre, *Charabanc*, has been our way into that landscape but we need so many more of these plays. I'm certainly going to have to make the effort by kicking myself in the arse and going up to Belfast and start exploring things from that perspective.'

*(Donal O'Kelly, playwright)*

'To throw all that history onto the shoulders of Gerry Adams is ridiculous. Maybe part of it is that, as Catholics, we're raised to demonise evil but the powers that be tapped into this and manipulated our emotions, in that sense. But I, myself, met Adams years ago and was amazed how much he knew about my songs, Mary Black, Christy Moore and all Irish music. In fact, on that day somebody gave me a green, white and gold T-shirt, with a green root coming out of the concrete and above that a white dove. And I said to Adams, "Is this what it looks like?" and he said, "Yeah," and from that day on, I was convinced that peace was in the air. I still am. But even though certain tracks on my latest album were written since the unveiling of the Downing Street Declaration last December, none of them refer specifically to this, although I hope they capture the general optimism around, at the moment. Yet in terms of my views on Ireland I'd point out something like 'Mystic Lipstick'. The song doesn't point a finger, saying who's right or who's wrong, it just states things like 'she wears mystic lipstick' which is the voice of a country, the way we speak, as a poetic nation rooted as much in the realm of the imagination as we are in the sod. Another line – "she wears stones and bones" – refers to the people we once were and the stones we prayed at. And "she tells myth and legend, she sings rock 'n' roll" is the same thing, taking in our history from the past right up to now. Ireland is all those things, a country wearing "chains of bondage" but also "wings of hope" which will, one day, take us beyond oppression. And, whatever you may think about Adams he says the same things about Irish freedom that were said by Pearse, Connolly. "Mystic Lipstick" says all that for me.'

*(Jimmy McCarthy, songwriter)*

'I now live in Newcastle and really get galled to the gills when English people think they can take the piss out of you, say fairly extreme racist things, which assume that because I'm Irish I must be intellectually subnormal. Apart from irritating the hell out of me, this also deepens a sense which never decreases in intensity inside me, that feeling of not having a place which I would ever remotely think of calling home. And, in terms of my songs, my approach is artifice-centred. It's natural for me to obfuscate, delinearise, fictionalise, to make things more interesting. Maybe I've got an inferiority complex about my own life as a source of interest, which is very Irish. But also, absolutely Irish, is the stubborn streak that makes me go ahead and make my statement anyway, secretly believing that the Irish always do it better anyway!'

*(Cathal Coughlan, songwriter)*

# 37 PATRICK CASSIDY
## 1995

This obviously is Patrick's Day in more ways than one. Patrick Cassidy, that is, who clearly has every reason to celebrate events of the past week. Last Tuesday his cantata *The Children of Lir* received its American debut in Boston, and was followed by a second concert in the JFK Centre in Washington last night. Allied to this was the inclusion of his cantata as part of the *Celtic Heartbeat* seven-CD marketing package launched in America by, among others, Paul McGuinness, manager of U2. Another cultural success story for Ireland? Of course it is.

And yet former British prime minister Margaret Thatcher almost spoiled the party last week. When it was announced that the same college which was sponsoring Patrick Cassidy's debut was also about to bestow an award on Maggie, many Bostonian Irish-Americans threatened to boycott the gig.

'And that was a response I totally understood, though the whole thing deeply disappointed me at first,' says Cassidy, taking a break from working on his next cantata, *Deirdre*. 'Maybe the people who invited her thought that because of the peace process we've buried the hatchet, but Maggie Thatcher is a warmonger. It's not as though she is John Major and all this was happening ten years down the line. It's also ludicrous that this award was to be given to her on the anniversary of Bobby Sands's death. But, happily, the college has decided not to give her the award.'

So, from this can one surmise that Cassidy is not about to compose a cantata for Margaret Thatcher? And what would he say to those who might cheekily suggest he should take as his musical inspiration a contemporary up-yours-Maggie figure like Sands and stop all this reaching back for Ireland's long-distant, already over-mythologised and maybe even politically irrelevant past?

'I definitely will not be writing in praise of Thatcher, but then neither would I write about Bobby Sands because his story doesn't have the lingering resonance of, say, the myth of *Deirdre*, which goes back over a thousand years and relates to Ulster and its people in a timeless sense rather than just in terms of the past twenty-five years,' he says. 'And I think *Deirdre* could provoke more thought than a Sands thing because it is all about what it means to be an Ulster person – a subject that is particularly appropriate in the context of the peace process. I also don't go along with that 1960s 'let's-shake-off-our-past' ethos. Too often it's a just a denial of our past, part of the post-colonial syndrome, reflecting a time when we didn't have any cultural confidence and were afraid to assert where we come from, in a core sense. Instead we just aped other people's art and forms of expression. There's no point in us marching into the twenty-first century with a sham identity. We are who we are and should be proud of it.'

Patrick Cassidy also believes that part of this process of self-definition for Irish people is 'accepting, rather than rejecting our religious past' and claims that the 'real cultural significance' of *The Children of Lir* is its theological base. 'The story is a microcosm of the way Irish people were converted to Christianity. We Irish love symbolism, as in the shamrock signifying the Trinity, and on that level I think there is an awful lot of our history in *The Children of Lir*, particularly in terms of St Patrick's role as a missionary,' he suggests.

Conversely, couldn't one argue that St Patrick colonialised this country in the name of Christianity, leaving it locked inside a crippling Rome–Britain double bind from which it has yet to escape?

'This may be unfashionable in our secular age but I just don't buy the line that Ireland was a better place before St Patrick came,' counters Cassidy. 'It's obvious the early Christian period was our golden period in art and culture. Look at the Book of Kells. Besides, St Patrick originally came here as a slave, not as a colonialist. But when I said earlier that we must be proud of what we are, that directly relates to the positive aspects of Christianity. I love Ireland and its people, but we do moan too much. Maybe part of that post-colonial syndrome is our tendency to see ourselves as victims – of Rome, Britain, whoever. But it's too easy to blame someone else for our own failures. That's the real form of oppression we've got to rise above now: self-oppression.'

Is this particular Patrick a missionary for God? Does Cassidy create his work in the name of the Almighty?

'Let me answer that by saying that Eisigh Re Clog An Chlerigh, the last movement in *The Children of Lir*, really moved me, as a poem,' is his response. 'Its second last verse is "Eisigh le clog an Chlerigh/ Togbaidh bhur n-eith agus eirghidh/Beiridh a bhuidhe re Dia a theacht/ agus attaighidh a eisteacht" which translates into "Listen to the Cleric's bells/ Elevate your wings and rise/ Give thanks to God for his coming/ And be grateful for having heard him." And obviously part of the reason it moved me is because I believe in some of this. Again, it may be unfashionable, but I am religious. And I love that wonderful tradition in classical music that goes back to composers like Bach and Mozart who did obviously believe that art was a reflection of God's majesty. I certainly don't think that atheist composers reached the same heights.'

Patrick Cassidy also rejects the 'politically divisive' claim that Irish classical composers haven't exactly scaled the same heights as, for example, their counterparts in Britain. This prejudicial view is particularly apparent among those who 'think we should be just aping the European tradition' rather than blending those influences with our own indigenous music, he suggests. And with our language.

'The boundaries between different types of music in Ireland isn't as clearly defined as it is in other countries and that's actually a good thing,' he explains. 'And although British historians, in particular, say we have no classical tradition here, that's because they've claimed our composers as their own, such as Stanford, who taught a whole generation of English composers. In classical music we also had people like John Field, as well as having dance music, and somewhere in between, Carolan's music, which was kind of neither and both!'

Cassidy laughingly agrees that 'we Irish are neither and both in a lot of respects!' but also argues that we should, as a race, uniformly recognise Sean Ó Riada as 'our most important musical figure this century'. His own epiphany as a music-lover, and composer, came as a result of originally hearing Ó Riada. 'I've really been influenced by Ó Riada, especially a really thrilling live album, *Ó Riada sa Gaiety*, which I heard when I was about ten,' he recalls. 'And our whole concept of traditional ensemble playing came from Ó Riada; before that we only had ceilí bands. His music also was beautifully arranged, particularly the music he did for films like *Mise Eire*. But the most important thing he did was build up our self-confidence because here was a composer with a

European reputation, who told us we had a great tradition that we should tap into. People talk about groups like U2 giving us cultural confidence, but Ó Riada did the same thing, in music, long before U2.'

Looking to his own future, Cassidy claims he'd like eventually to work in the field of film music, citing contemporary composers like Ennio Morricone as being 'just as important as people like Vivaldi'. Cassidy has already composed the score for the Irish movie *Broken Harvest*.

'I also am a composer who needs to eat and to do that I have to make money! And composing for films is quite lucrative. Yet, apart from that, working on *Broken Harvest* was a great experience because it involved the challenge of setting images to music and that's something I'd love to learn even more about,' he explains.

'But I really do think we've over-hyped ourselves in terms of Ireland being, supposedly, a new cultural centre of the universe. We have some very talented people here but don't yet have a film industry or music industry in the sense that would cancel out the need for a composer such as myself going to America to get the breaks. Me and Frank, my manager, certainly wouldn't have gone to Los Angeles to do our publishing deal if things had been going well over here. But I'd been two and a half years on the dole after quitting my job as a statistician and never, for example, got a commission from RTE. They have a closed-door policy out there and it's only once you're in that they start helping you, when you no longer need it. So the government needs to look at these areas and put in place structures that will help these industries grow in the broadest sense.'

Patrick Cassidy also obviously isn't besotted by the Riverdance culture of self-celebration currently sweeping Ireland. 'It could lead to complacency. And, worse, we could become culturally arrogant,' he concludes sagely. 'It's too easy to tip over from self-celebration into the kind of Nationalistic fervour that defined the British for so long and has, ultimately, led to their downfall. The English certainly haven't much to be proud of theses days. And I'd hate to see the same thing happen to us. The Irish have always been loved because we are not arrogant, or truculent, but we're in danger of losing that. Fine, we're on the world stage now, but let's not screw things up. In a sense we're acting like a band who gets a record deal and start celebrating but forgets they've yet to make the album! So maybe it's time to stop all these celebrations of being Irish and get back to work.'

# INDEX